A SHORT HISTORY OF
MODERN GREECE

A SHORT HISTORY OF
MODERN GREECE

RICHARD CLOGG

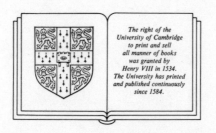

The right of the
University of Cambridge
to print and sell
all manner of books
was granted by
Henry VIII in 1534.
The University has printed
and published continuously
since 1584.

CAMBRIDGE UNIVERSITY PRESS

CAMBRIDGE

LONDON   NEW YORK   NEW ROCHELLE
MELBOURNE   SYDNEY

Published by the Press Syndicate of the University of Cambridge
The Pitt Building, Trumpington Street, Cambridge CB2 IRP
32 East 57th Street, New York, NY 10022, USA
10 Stamford Road, Oakleigh, Melbourne 3166, Australia

First published 1979
Reprinted 1980, 1983, 1984
Second edition 1986

Printed in Great Britain at the University Press, Cambridge

Library of Congress cataloguing in publication data
Clogg, Richard, 1939–
A short history of modern Greece.
Bibliography: p. 229
Includes index.
1. Greece, Modern – History. I. Title.
DF757.C56   949.5   78–72083

ISBN 0 521 32837 3 hard covers
ISBN 0 521 33804 2 paperback

(First edition ISBN 0 521 22479 9 hard covers
ISBN 0 521 29517 3 paperback)

Contents

Preface

Every afternoon there is a broadcast on Greek radio on behalf of the missing persons bureau of the Greek Red Cross. Inquirers seek news of relatives who disappeared without trace in southern Russia in the troubled aftermath of the Russian revolution, after the chaotic defeat of the Greek army in Asia Minor in 1922, during the hard years of the German occupation and during the bitterly fought civil war that racked Greece between 1946 and 1949. These pathetic appeals for information afford a graphic insight into the history of Greece in the twentieth century. Few countries in Europe have had such a harrowing and strife-torn recent history. To attempt to sketch the troubled modern history of Greece within the short compass of this book has inevitably posed problems of selection, and in providing the essential narrative framework I am conscious of having devoted less attention than I would have wished to social, economic and cultural developments.

As this book was being completed negotiations were well advanced for Greece's entry into the European Economic Community. Greece's historical experience has been very different from that of the existing nine member countries. Her heritage of Orthodox Christianity and several centuries of Ottoman rule have left their distinctive impress on the development of Greek history and society. I hope that I have been able to give some insight into the way in which these different historical forces and traditions have helped to shape the Greek state.

It is a pleasant duty to record my gratitude to a number of friends and colleagues who have read part or all of the book in draft form: Nikiforos Diamandouros, John Iatrides, John

Koliopoulos, Donald Nicol, Thanos Veremis, George and Yannis Yannoulopoulos. I know that not all of them agree with all my views but they have saved me from many errors of fact and interpretation. Those that remain are of course my responsibility alone. Some of the earlier works of which I have made use are recorded in the bibliography. I am very grateful to Kate Blade for her cheerful and efficient typing of the manuscript. But my greatest obligation is, as always, to Mary Jo Clogg whose editorial scrutiny has been invaluable. It has proved impossible to avoid a number of inconsistencies in the transliteration of Greek names, the use of English first names, etc., without resorting to an unwarranted pedantry.

Some five years after Greece's entry into the EEC as its tenth member in January 1981 and the election of the first socialist government in the country's history in October of the same year, the opportunity has been taken to rewrite the final chapter so as to incorporate developments down to the re-election of Andreas Papandreou's PASOK government for a second term in June 1985.

1 November 1985
King's College, London

RICHARD CLOGG

For J.A.E.C.

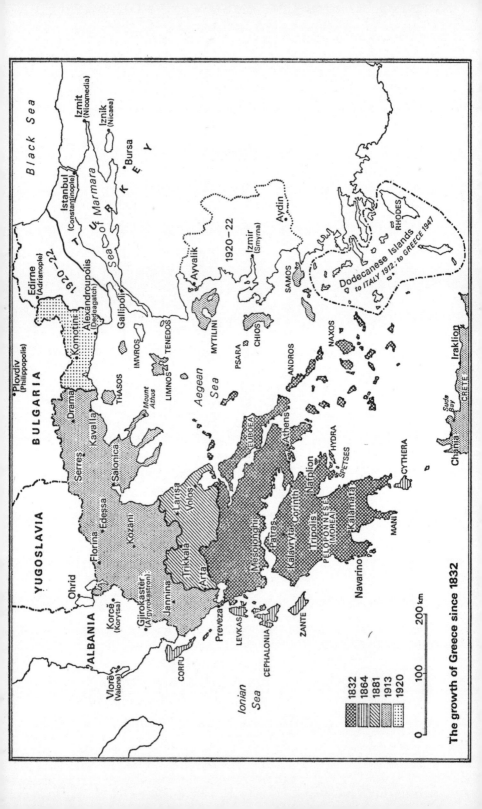

The growth of Greece since 1832

1

'Waiting for the barbarians': the downfall of Byzantium, 1204–1453

Ever since Edward Gibbon almost two centuries ago chronicled in *The Decline and Fall of the Roman Empire* 'the extinction of a degenerate race of princes' and the 'triumph of barbarism and religion' historians have debated the reasons for the downfall of Byzantium. In the long centuries of decline one date stands out above all others, 1204, the year of the sack of Constantinople that followed the diversion of the Fourth Crusade. For the first time since its foundation by Constantine the Great in AD 330 'The City', as it was known to the manifold peoples that constituted the Byzantine Empire, and as it is still referred to in the Greek world, had been overrun. The notional solidarity of Christendom in the face of the infidel Muslim had been shattered and Frankish marauders had run amok in the streets of the once proud and mighty capital of the *Romaioi*, or Romans, as the Byzantines called themselves. Yet although the sack of Constantinople was to inflict a trauma on the Byzantine Empire from which it was never to recover, it was but one stage in the gradual transition of the Byzantines from a haughty independence, via a precarious tutelage to the Ottoman Sultans, to their total subjection to the infidel in the great siege of 1453. Long before 1204 the integrity of the Byzantine Empire had been threatened by internal crises and external enemies.

The Bull excommunicating the Patriarch Michael Cerularius, which the papal delegate Cardinal Humbert had laid in 1054 in the Great Church of the Holy Wisdom (Aghia Sophia) in Constantinople, was the outcome of a long period of growing antagonism between the papacy in Rome and the patriarchate in Constantinople. Although it was not fully realised at the time,

I

the excommunication marked a crucial stage in the process by which many Orthodox/Christians came to look upon the Latin Catholics with greater fear and hostility than they did the Muslim Turks. From the mid-eleventh century until the very last years of the empire the question of the relationship of the Churches was to constitute a permanent source of bitterness and conflict between western and eastern Christendom, at a time when the latter was facing a growing challenge from the Seljuk and later the Ottoman Turks. The seriousness of this threat was strikingly brought home by the crushing defeat inflicted by the Seljuk Turks under Alp Arslan on the imperial armies at the battle of Mantzikert in eastern Asia Minor in April 1071, during which the Emperor Romanos IV Diogenes was himself taken prisoner. Disaster at the eastern extremities of the empire was matched by disaster in the west, for in the same year, 1071, the Normans under Robert Guiscard overran Bari, the last of the empire's Italian possessions.

The Italian losses, even if they struck at the ecumenical pretensions of the emperor, could be borne, but the massive incursions of the Seljuks, who were able to exploit civil strife within the empire in the years after Mantzikert, were far more serious. By the early thirteenth century the Seljuks controlled most of Asia Minor either directly or through their Turcoman vassals. This was a body blow, for Asia Minor constituted the empire's principal source of food, of manpower and of tax revenue. Moreover, the power and authority of the emperor were further diminished during the eleventh and twelfth centuries by the increasing independence of the members of the military and landowning aristocracies who manifested a growing disregard for imperial authority. The civil strife that resulted from the emergence of these overmighty subjects was matched by serious economic crisis, with the empire being forced to rely more and more on the exactions of tax farmers for its income and with the free peasantry being reduced to vassal status by the powerful provincial aristocracy. In the course of the twelfth century the Serbs and the Bulgarians, both Orthodox by religion, broke away from the authority of Constantinople and were to remain a thorn in the flesh of the empire until they too were finally subdued

2

by the Ottoman Turks in the course of the fourteenth century. Almost as calamitous from the point of view of the long-term survival of the empire as the inroads of the Turks was the development by the Christian powers in the West of an interest in the fate of the eastern Mediterranean. The battle of Mantzikert had been followed by the Seljuk conquest of Jerusalem in 1077, an attack on the holy places of Christendom that happened to coincide with a period of religious revival in the West. The news that the Holy Land had fallen to the infidel added impetus to a mounting religious fervour and resulted in the proclamation by Pope Urban II of the First Crusade in 1095. Urban's call for the liberation of the holy places, to which were added the appeals of Peter the Hermit, met with a powerful response. The Byzantine Emperor Alexios I (1081–1118) had sought to recruit mercenaries in the West but could scarcely have bargained for the motley army of idealists and freebooters that began to make its way to the Levant. The fact that many of the crusaders were Normans can have done little to reassure Alexios, for the Normans, from their base in southern Italy, had already begun to raid the imperial territories across the Adriatic, capturing Durazzo in 1081.

Alexios' fears were confirmed by the predatory behaviour of the crusading armies during their successful sieges of Antioch in 1089 and Jerusalem in 1099. Although they had now achieved their ostensible purpose in securing the holy places for Christendom the crusaders showed little interest in helping to restore the fortunes of the Byzantine Empire. Instead they created a number of independent principalities, including the Kingdom of Jerusalem and the Principality of Antioch. The fall of Edessa to the Turks in 1145 prompted the Second Crusade, led by Louis VII of France and the Emperor Conrad III. This set out in 1147 and ended in disaster a year later at the battle of Antalya. In the wake of the crusaders came merchants, and as the price of continued Western support, the empire was obliged to grant advantageous commercial concessions to the Italian city states, Naples, Florence and Amalfi but above all to Genoa and Venice, whose inhabitants had already been granted important trading privileges in 1082. In this way much of the seaborne commerce of the empire came to be dominated by Frankish merchants just as, under the Ottomans, it came to be dominated by Greeks. The privileged position of these merchants combined with the anti-Latin religious prejudices of the Byzantines resulted in first the confiscation of Venetian property in 1171 and then a wholesale massacre of foreigners in 1182. The Venetians, who were the principal victims of this violent outburst, increasingly inclined to the view that the only guarantee of Latin interests in the Levant was to bring the empire itself under Western domination.

Crusading zeal in the West was re-awakened a few years later with the capture of Jerusalem by Saladin, the Sultan of Egypt, in 1187. This prompted the proclamation of the Third Crusade by Pope Gregory VIII, who enlisted the support of the Holy Roman Emperor, Frederick I Barbarossa, and of King Richard I (Cœur de Lion) of England. Isaac II Angelos' anxieties as to the crusaders' intentions were reflected in his conclusion of an alliance with Saladin. Fearing an outright attack on Constantinople, which Frederick Barbarossa had long coveted, Isaac was forced to treat with the Emperor Frederick but his apprehensions were further increased by Richard I's capture of Cyprus in 1191 and its subsequent cession to the House of Lusignan. Although he was able to capture Acre, Richard failed to retake Jerusalem.

Once again the arrival of the crusaders had served to weaken rather than to strengthen an empire whose condition by the end of the twelfth century was parlous The deposition of Isaac II Angelos led to disputes over the succession, the Bulgars successfully resisted a Byzantine invasion in 1196-7, the Serbs showed a scant respect for imperial power, and the authority of the central government was everywhere challenged. When Pope Innocent III proclaimed the Fourth Crusade in 1198 the empire presented an inviting target to its Latin enemies, now led by the Venetians, still smarting under their earlier humiliations at the hands of the Byzantines. The avowed object of the crusade was to strike at the root of Saracen power in Egypt, before laying siege to Jerusalem. Such a strategy played into the hands of the Venetians who alone were capable of supplying the requisite ships to transport the crusading forces. They drove a hard bargain with the French,

Italian and German crusaders and succeeded in diverting them to capture Zara on the Dalmatian coast in 1202 and then to Constantinople itself in 1203. Their ostensible purpose was to restore to the imperial throne Alexios, the son of Isaac II, for he was prepared to agree to union with Rome. But Alexios' Latinophile sympathies alienated him from almost all his new subjects. Moreover he proved manifestly incapable of fulfilling his various promises to his Latin patrons. Whereupon in 1204 the crusaders decided on an outright partition of the empire and indulged in an orgy of destruction and plunder in the capital. The Saracens, one Byzantine chronicler bitterly complained, were merciful in comparison to the Christian crusaders.

Count Baldwin of Flanders was crowned Emperor of Constantinople, ruling over territories straddling both sides of the Bosphorus and Sea of Marmara, together with the islands off the west coast of Asia Minor. His principal rival for the imperial throne, Boniface of Montferrat, was compensated with the Kingdom of Salonica. The Venetians, the prime movers in the sack of Constantinople, appointed a Venetian as patriarch and secured control over Euboea, Crete and several other islands in the Aegean, together with a number of fortresses in the Peloponnese. Other Frankish principalities also came into existence, including the Duchy of Athens, the Principality of Achaia and the Duchy of the Archipelago. Although the crusaders had had little difficulty in overrunning Constantinople, it was not long before a focus of Byzantine opposition to the Latin intruders appeared in the form of the Empire of Nicaea. This covered the north west of Asia Minor between the territories of the Latin Empire and the lands that constituted the Seljuk Empire of Rum. Its first Emperor was Theodore Laskaris, son-in-law of the Emperor Alexios III. A further Greek principality was created in Epirus, which was ruled by another relative of Alexios III, Michael Doukas. Even before the Latin conquest yet another Greek principality had come into existence in Pontos, in the north east of Asia Minor, where Alexios Komninos laid claim at Trebizond to the title of Emperor.

It was not long before the Byzantines were in a position to counterattack. The Emperor of Nicaea was able to extend his frontiers in Asia Minor and in the Aegean at the expense of the Latin Empire, while as early as 1224 the Kingdom of Salonica fell to the ruler of Epirus. Salonica in turn was recovered for the Nicaean Empire by John III Vatatzes in 1246. Under Michael VIII Palaiologos (1259–82) Constantinople itself was recaptured in 1261 and the Latin Empire collapsed. But the re-establishment of an Orthodox emperor on the imperial throne in Constantinople by no means signified an end to a Latin presence in former Byzantine territories. Large areas remained under Latin control. Some, such as the Duchies of Athens and the Archipelago and the County Palatine of Cephalonia, were to remain under Latin rule until after the fall of Constantinople to Mehmet the Conqueror in 1453. Moreover, in the late thirteenth and early fourteenth centuries, the Genoese and the Knights of St John secured control of a number of Aegean islands, many of which were already under Venetian control. The rich island of Chios was governed by a Genoese commercial company known as the Maona, and the Knights of St John established themselves in Rhodes in 1308 following the fall of the Holy Land in 1291. The Genoese were granted concessions by Michael VIII in an effort to boost commerce after the recapture of Constantinople. Established in Galata, across the Golden Horn from Constantinople, they soon came to dominate the commerce of the Black Sea. The separatist state of Epirus was not brought under imperial control until 1338, while the pocket Empire of Trebizond was to remain independent until it fell to the Turks in 1461.

The Byzantines, then, had been able to check but by no means to eliminate the Latin threat to the territorial integrity of the empire and many Greek communities in the eastern Mediterranean were to remain under alien rule until the Ottoman conquest. The Fourth Crusade, besides irreparably undermining the territorial cohesion of the empire, had also effectively destroyed the crusading ideal, although subsequent crusades were to be launched, as in 1396 and 1443. Even though the increasingly dire situation of the empire from time to time necessitated efforts at rapprochement with the Frankish powers, nonetheless the tragic events surrounding the Fourth Crusade left a lasting legacy of bitterness and distrust of 'Frangia', or the West. However much the rulers of the empire may have perceived the need for Western support or sought compromises in order to prevent further Latin depredations, the mass of the population remained steeped in anti-Latin prejudice and firmly convinced that Orthodoxy was indeed the true faith. These profound convictions manifested themselves, for instance, when the Emperor Michael VIII, in an effort to avert a threatened invasion by Charles of Anjou, the ruler of Sicily, pursued a pro-Western policy which culminated in his submission to Rome by the Union of Lyons of 1274. In the event, Charles of Anjou's Eastern pretensions were only finally extinguished in the bloody killings of 1282 known as the Sicilian Vespers. But Michael's submission provoked a profound upheaval at home. His patriarch had to be removed and replaced by the unionist John Bekkos, and Michael instituted a brutal reign of terror against the many opponents of the union. This was subsequently repudiated by his son, Andronikos II, who even agreed to the demands of Orthodox zealots that his father be denied a Christian burial. Subsequent emperors were, however, again to submit to the papacy in a desperate, and largely fruitless, effort to buy Western support. The bitter and at times bloody conflict between unionists and anti-unionists was to rack Orthodoxy until the very last days of the empire.

The prolonged struggle to wrest the empire from the Latins had placed a heavy strain on Byzantine resources and the empire was by now irreversibly set on a course of decline. The power of the Byzantine aristocracy continued to grow as the authority of the central government diminished. More and more properties held in *pronoia* became heritable instead of being granted for a fixed term at the discretion of the emperor, and their possessors increasingly ignored their obligation of military service. Powerful landowners evaded their tax obligations at a time when the empire's growing dependence on mercenaries increased the central government's need for taxation. The position of the peasantry worsened. The empire's growing economic crisis was reflected in the declining value of its coinage. Debasement of the coinage led to increased food prices, which, added to measures to increase tax revenue, served to increase the general discontent. The situation was further aggravated by the flood of refugees into the capital seeking to escape from endemic disorder and war.

Moreover, the increasingly apparent economic weakness of the empire was compounded during the course of the fourteenth century by the rise of the Ottoman Turks, who constituted a new and even more formidable threat to the continued existence of the empire than the predatory Latins. Indeed the Ottomans were able to exploit the empire's preoccupation during the thirteenth century with the Latin threat to consolidate their position. Under the leadership of the founder of their dynasty, Osman I (1288–1326), they eclipsed the Seljuk Turks of Iconium and by the early fourteenth century had, with the exception of the Pontic Empire of Trebizond, effectively ousted the Byzantines from the traditional heartland of their empire, Asia Minor, although Smyrna was briefly to be recaptured in 1343 as the result of a crusade. Bursa, which became the first capital of the Ottoman Sultans was captured in 1326, and by 1337 the Ottomans had secured the important Byzantine cities of Nicaea (Iznik) and Nicomedia (Izmit), within a hundred miles of the capital. In 1303 Andronikos II had hired the Catalan company against the Turks but they had turned against their Byzantine masters and in 1311 established the Catalan Duchy of Athens and Thebes. It was a measure of the increasingly desperate situation of the empire that during the civil war of 1321 to 1328 neither side scrupled to enlist the aid of Turkish mercenaries. By 1354 the Ottomans had secured their first foothold on European soil at Gallipoli, at the invitation of the energetic John VI Kantakouzinos who had married his daughter to the Emir Orhan, and by 1362 they had secured Adrianople (Edirne) as their first European capital. Soon the important towns of Didymoteichos and Philippopolis (Plovdiv) were in Ottoman hands. During the first half of the fourteenth century the Serbs were also able to overrun substantial areas of Thessaly and Epirus, and in 1346 Stephen Dushan had himself crowned Emperor of the Serbs and Greeks.

On the death of Andronikos III in 1341, civil war, even more destructive and divisive than that of 1321-8, once again broke out. The immediate cause was, as before, a disputed succession, but on this occasion the empire's underlying social and political tensions were more apparent. The increasingly glaring gap between rich and poor was reflected in the antagonism shown towards one of the claimants, John Kantakouzinos, a prominent and enormously wealthy representative of the provincial landowning aristocracy. Alexios Apokaukos, who acted as regent for Kantakouzinos' chief rival John Palaiologos, adroitly exploited the resentment of the Constantinopolitan mob, but it was in the towns of Macedonia, where Kantakouzinos possessed vast estates, and of Thrace that social discontent manifested itself most openly. When early in 1342 Kantakouzinos made for Salonica, the second city of the empire and the key to Macedonia, there was a large-scale uprising against his aristocratic supporters in the city. After several days of looting the popular party, known as Zealots, seized power and ruled the city as a virtually independent commune until 1350. Estates belonging to the landed magnates and the Church were expropriated and the Zealots were known for the harshness of their rule. To add to the empire's troubles the Black Death decimated many of its cities in 1347.

Moreover, despite the brave attempts of the Emperor John VI Kantakouzinos in the mid-fourteenth century to restore the empire's waning fortunes, the Ottoman penetration of the Orthodox world continued. In 1373 the emperor was obliged to accept, as the rulers of Serbia and Bulgaria already had accepted, the formal overlordship of Sultan Murad I. In recognition of his vassal status the emperor was henceforth required to pay the Sultan a money tribute and afford him military assistance. In 1389 the last pretensions of the Serbs to an independent political existence were crushed in the great battle of the Kossovo plain. A few years later, in 1393, Sultan Beyazit overran the remaining Bulgarian lands and besieged the imperial capital itself. These developments prompted King Sigismund of Hungary to summon a crusade, and in 1395 a large crusading army marched towards Constantinople, obliging Beyazit to lift his siege. The predominantly Hungarian and Burgundian invading armies, however, met with a crushing defeat at Nicopolis on the Danube in 1396.

Although it was by now clear that the final eclipse of the

thousand-year-old Empire of Byzantium was only a matter of time, nonetheless the intellectual and artistic life of the Palaiologoi displayed a remarkable intensity and vigour. In the field of art, the mosaics and frescoes dating from the early fourteenth century in the Church of St Saviour in Chora (Kariye Camii) in Constantinople are the outstanding products of the 'Palaiologan Renaissance', and work of high quality was also carried out in such provincial centres of culture as Trebizond in the Pontos and Mistra in the Peloponnese. Under the patronage of the Emperor Andronikos II there was a considerable revival of interest in the culture of ancient Greece, despite its pagan connotations. Nor were intellectual developments in the West ignored. The *Summa Contra Gentiles* of St Thomas Aquinas was translated into Greek by Dimitrios Kydones, whose admiration for Aquinas' theology led to his conversion to Rome. Greek scholars helped to disseminate the teaching of Greek in the West. The Latin penetration of the Levant, moreover, had the somewhat paradoxical effect of stimulating the emergence and development of vernacular Greek literature. By cutting off large areas of the Greek world from contact with the archaic and formalistic Greek of the capital, the Latin conquests boosted the vernacular trends first reflected in the mid-twelfth-century poems of Theodore Prodromos. A flourishing vernacular literature came into existence, much influenced by Western models, and consisting of romances such as *Kallimachos and Chrysorrhoe* and chronicles such as the thirteenth-century *Chronicle of the Morea* (Peloponnese) and the fifteenth-century *Tale of the Sweet Land of Cyprus* of Leontios Machairas.

The intellectual and artistic revival that characterised the empire in the fourteenth century was paralleled by religious ferment. The fourteenth century saw a revival of mystical doctrine in the form known as *hesychasm*, a revival that found its most determined apologist in Gregory Palamas, a monk of Mount Athos who was subsequently to become metropolitan of Salonica. The hesychasts were attacked by some Byzantine theologians, but particularly by the Greco-Italian monk Barlaam of Calabria who essentially represented the Latinisers. Inevitably, perhaps, the hesychast controversy that shook the Orthodox Church in the fourteenth century came to have distinct political overtones. During the great civil war of 1341–7 the anti-hesychasts controlled the patriarchate in Constantinople but when John Kantakouzinos finally wrested control of the empire, the hesychasts captured the patriarchate and the higher reaches of the hierarchy and the orthodoxy of their beliefs was established at a council in 1351. As always throughout their long history the Greeks found comfort in times of distress in a variety of oracular and prophetic beliefs. Since the earthly kingdom of Byzantium was the paradigm of the heavenly kingdom of God then, as surely as night followed day, the downfall of the empire, they believed, would be followed by the end of the world.

Perhaps the most significant development during the last centuries of Byzantium was the emergence of a specifically Greek, as opposed to merely Orthodox, consciousness. As the Ottoman Turks advanced on the very heart of the empire and as the territories over which the emperor reigned shrank almost to the point of extinction some, at least, of the inhabitants of this rump came to look upon themselves as the descendants of the ancient Hellenes. This theory was propounded particularly in the Despotate of the Morea where, during the early fifteenth century, George Gemistos Plethon stressed the physical continuity of the inhabitants of the Peloponnese with their Greek ancestors and even changed his name so that it would more nearly resemble that of the Plato he so admired. In contrast to the resigned acquiescence of the theologians who interpreted the empire's plight as a sign of divine displeasure at the sins of the Orthodox people, Gemistos Plethon adumbrated a comprehensive scheme of social, even socialistic, reform to reverse the catastrophic decline in the empire's fortunes. Towards the end of his life, to the scandal of the Church hierarchy, he argued for the substitution of an 'Hellenic' religion, heavily influenced by Platonic ideas, for Orthodox Christianity.

But the time was long past when schemes for reform could do much to stem the irresistible course of decline. After Sultan Beyazit's defeat of the crusaders at Nicopolis in 1396 he resumed his siege of Constantinople. It was a measure of the Emperor Manuel II Palaiologos' desperation that he followed the advice of the commander of a small relief army despatched in 1399 by King Charles VI of France and decided to visit Western Europe to put his case for Western support in person. Manuel travelled to Venice and the courts of France and England, where he met with considerable sympathy but little in the way of concrete help. But relief was to come from an unexpected quarter. Sultan Beyazit lifted his six-year siege of the Byzantine capital in order to confront the threat posed to his forces by the Mongol leader Timurlenk (Tamerlane or Timur the Lame). The Ottomans were defeated at the battle of Ankara in 1402 and Beyazit was himself captured. The Byzantines profited from the temporary discomfiture of their enemies. Salonica and other places were restored to them by a treaty with the son of Beyazit in 1403, and the tribute which the Emperor Manuel II had been obliged to pay to the Ottomans was annulled.

But the respite afforded by the Mongol invasion was brief. Sultan Mehmet I (1413-21) was able partially to restore the fortunes of the Ottomans. His son Murad II renewed the siege of Constantinople in 1422 and annulled the privileges accorded by his father to Manuel II. Salonica, which had been ceded by the Byzantines to the Venetians in 1423 was recaptured by the Turks in 1430, the same year in which they captured Jannina. Manuel's son John VIII Palaiologos, who succeeded to the throne in 1425, once again decided to appeal for Western support to meet this new challenge. To achieve this he was prepared to submit to the papacy. After almost a decade of negotiation the union of the Western and Eastern branches of the Church was sealed at the Council of Ferrara and Florence (1438-9) which was attended by the emperor himself, his patriarch Joseph, and a large retinue of Orthodox bishops. After months of wrangling the Byzantines accepted the Latin version of the creed, which had for centuries been a major bone of contention between Catholics and Orthodox, and acknowledged the supremacy of the papacy. Although the Orthodox had been obliged to capitulate on the basic doctrinal issues little pressure was placed to bring Orthodox ritual into line with Latin practice. Only one Orthodox bishop, Mark Eugenikos, refused to sign the formal act of union, a refusal which turned him into a popular hero in Byzantium, where news of the submission to Rome was met with widespread revulsion, so much so that John VIII himself never dared formally to proclaim the union in Constantinople itself. One of the signatories of the act of union in Florence, George Gennadios Scholarios, who was to be the first patriarch after the Ottoman conquest of the empire, subsequently repudiated his signature.

John VIII's submission to Rome had been calculated to win Western military support and this was soon forthcoming. The new crusade announced by Pope Eugenius was led by Ladislas, King of Hungary and Poland, John Corvinus Hunyadi, the *voyvoda* of Transylvania, and George Brancovich of Serbia, who set out with an army of Hungarians, Serbs, Wallachians and Bulgarians in 1443. The moment was a propitious one. For the Albanian George Kastriotis, or Skanderbey, who had reverted to Christianity after apostasising to Islam, in the same year launched a successful defiance of the Ottomans from the mountain fastnesses of Kruja which was to last until his death in 1468. Sultan Murad II, however, after the crusaders had broken a negotiated truce, was able to amass an army of almost 100,000. This was approximately three times as large as the crusading army he confronted at Varna on the Black Sea coast. The crusaders were overwhelmed and King Ladislas was killed in a fierce battle. Thus the last crusade of Christian Europe against the infidel collapsed.

John VIII died in 1448 and was succeeded on the imperial throne by his brother, the Despot of the Morea, who took the title of Constantine XI Palaiologos. He was crowned in Mistra in 1449 and his pathetic inheritance consisted of Constantinople and the Peloponnese, over which his two brothers, Thomas and Dimitrios, continued to rule. Two years later, Mehmet II (Fatih Mehmet or Mehmet the Conqueror) succeeded his more conciliatory father, Murad II, and immediately began preparations for the siege of Constantinople. Constantine realised that the only hope of Western help rested on the formal promulgation of the union of the Churches in Constantinople itself, but opposition to the union, led now by George Gennadios Scholarios, was widespread and the emperor himself was jeered in the streets of the city as a unionist. Increasingly the mood of the inhabitants of the city became one of fatalistic resignation, suffused with bitterness against the Latins for seeking until the bitter end to impose papal supremacy on the Orthodox. Their inevitable fate, conquest at the hand of the Muslim Turks, was seen as part of the divine dispensation. The prevailing mood was well summed up in the Grand Duke Loukas Notaras' famous declaration that it would be preferable to see the turban of the Turk in the City than the mitre of the Latin. Prophetic and apocalyptic beliefs and rumours circulated with a renewed intensity. It was widely believed, for instance, that the end of the world would coincide with the end of the seventh millennium since Creation, which was calculated as the year 1492.

Although Constantine XI himself was convinced of the need for union, and indeed on Christmas day 1452 there was a celebration of the Orthodox and Catholic liturgies in the Church of the Holy Wisdom, there were few signs of Western help for the besieged City. But when Mehmet began his siege in April 1453, individuals and small groups of Latins hastened to the assistance of the beleaguered inhabitants. The most important of these volunteers was a group of Genoese, led by Giovanni Giustiniani Longi. Altogether the forces available for the defence of the City numbered some 5000 against the 80,000 troops mustered by Mehmet II. Despite the paucity of the troops at its disposal, the massive land walls were in good order while the entrance to the Golden Horn was protected by a floating boom. The Turks, for their part, however, enjoyed the advantage of efficient cannon, which soon began to take their toll of the City's defences. The defenders suffered a severe blow to their morale when on 22 April Mehmet's troops succeeded in dragging ships along a ramp constructed from the Bosphorus to the Golden Horn over the hill behind Galata, thus bypassing the boom at the entrance to the Golden Horn. This compelled Constantine to divert troops from the land walls to the hitherto lightly guarded shores of the Golden Horn. Shortages of food served further to undermine morale and portents of impending disaster were read into a strange glowing of the great dome of the Church of the Holy Wisdom on 24 May.

Sultan Mehmet made a last offer of terms which was proudly refused by Constantine.

The final onslaught was launched on Tuesday 29 May with thousands of troops being hurled at the walls. They were met with fierce resistance but the morale of the defenders was seriously weakened when Giustiniani, who had fought heroically with his Genoese contingent, was struck down at dawn and carried off wounded. Shortly afterwards the sultan's crack troops, the janissaries, made the first breach of the walls. Soon afterwards one of the gates, the Kerkoporta, was forced and Turkish troops poured into the City. The Emperor Constantine threw away his imperial vestments and was last seen fighting alongside his troops. Within a matter of hours the City was overrun, including the Church of the Holy Wisdom where the priests were celebrating a last liturgy before a vast and terror-stricken congregation. According to a widely believed legend, as the Turkish troops stormed into the church, the priests celebrating the liturgy were enfolded with the holy vessels into the marble walls of the sanctuary, to re-emerge when the City once again became Christian. Because the defenders had refused Mehmet's offer of peaceful capitulation in return for the payment of a tribute, no mercy was shown to the defeated and for three days the City was given over to rapine and plunder. The great Empire of Byzantium, which had lasted for over a millennium, was no more.

2

The Greeks under Ottoman rule, 1453-1800

'The City' of Constantinople fell to the Ottoman Turks on 29 May 1453, a Tuesday, a day of the week still regarded as ill-omened in the Greek world. The fall of the Byzantine capital may have occasioned shock waves in the West but the plans that continued to be made to expel the infidel from the Christian East were ineffectual. Its significance for the Greek world was more symbolic than real. For most of the Greek lands had passed under Ottoman rule many years previously, and, in the years following the fall of Constantinople, the Ottomans merely consolidated their grip on the lands that had constituted the Orthodox Christian *oikumene*. The pocket Empire of Trebizond on the south-eastern shores of the Black Sea was overrun in 1461, by which year the Ottomans had established their authority over the Duchy of Athens and the Peloponnese with the exception of a few isolated Venetian strongholds. Euboea was captured in 1470, and by the 1450s and 1460s the Ottomans had extended their sway over many of the Aegean islands, although Rhodes did not fall until 1522, Chios and Naxos until 1566, Cyprus until 1571, Samos until 1577, Crete, after a twenty-year siege, until 1669, and Tinos until 1715. Of the seven Ionian Islands, Corfu (Kerkyra) was to remain a Venetian dependency until 1797. The others, Zante (Zakynthos), Cephalonia, Kythera (Cerigo), Paxos and Ithaca, were to revert to Venetian control after short periods of Ottoman occupation, with Levkas (Santa Maura) coming under Venetian sovereignty in 1684.

Although there is evidence that many Orthodox Greeks actually preferred Ottoman to Venetian rule, for the Muslim Ottomans offended the religious susceptibilities of their Orthodox subjects to a lesser extent than did the Catholic Venetians, nonetheless Venetian rule proved relatively benign and tolerant. A flourishing vernacular Greek literature, much influenced by Italian models, for instance, flowered in seventeenth-century Crete, on the eve of the capture of the island by the Ottomans. The fact that the Ionian Islands remained under Venetian rule until the end of the eighteenth century gave the Greeks a window to the West, and they proved an important channel for Western influences in an Orthodox world that was otherwise largely insulated from the rest of Europe. The University of Padua, for instance, numbered among its graduates many Greeks, not only from Venetian but from Ottoman Greece, while Venice was to be a major centre of Greek printing until well into the nineteenth century.

With the exception of the scattered Venetian possessions in the Levant, the Ottoman conquest united within the jurisdiction of a single political authority, the Ottoman Porte, and of a single ecclesiastical authority, the ecumenical patriarchate, Greek populations which had, in the declining years of the Byzantine Empire, fallen under various forms of alien rule, Venetian, Genoese, Norman, Angevin, Catalan as well as Ottoman. The most compact areas of Greek population were in the regions that now compose the Greek state, namely the islands of the Archipelago, the Peloponnese, mainland Greece, or Rumeli, which included Thessaly, Epirus, Macedonia and Thrace. There were also substantial Greek populations on the western littoral of Asia Minor, around the shores of the Sea of Marmara, in the region of Constantinople itself, along the southern shores of the Black Sea and in central Asia Minor. Orthodox Christianity and the Greek language were manifestly the most important factors linking together these scattered populations. A Greek of Epirus would nonetheless have experienced difficulty in comprehending one of the Greek dialects of Cappadocia in central Asia Minor, while the Greek of the isolated Pontos on the southern shores of the Black Sea gradually began to assume some of the characteristics of a distinct language.

Besides extending their authority over the Greek lands, the Ottomans, in the years after the fall of Constantinople, further consolidated their rule in the Balkans, bringing Serbia, Bosnia, Albania, the Danubian principalities of Moldavia and Wallachia, Bessarabia and a large part of Hungary under direct, or in the case of the principalities indirect, Ottoman rule. This massive increase in territory achieved in a short period of time created a problem of the governance of these heteroglot and largely Christian populations. For the Ottoman Empire was essentially theocratic, a society well geared to expansion by military conquest but less well adapted to the administration of conquered territories. Islam had traditionally prescribed tolerance for People of the Book, Christians, Jews and Zoroastrians, and in keeping with this tradition the Ottomans maintained their authority over their non-Muslim subjects through the *millet* system. The subject peoples of the empire were organised into *millets* not on the basis of ethnic origin but of religious belief. In addition to the dominant Muslim *millet*, there was the Orthodox *millet*, the Gregorian Armenian *millet*, the Jewish *millet*, a Catholic *millet* and even, in the nineteenth century, a Protestant *millet*, created for the handful of Armenian and Greek Christians who were converted by American Protestant missionaries.

Uncertainty surrounds the origins of the *millets* and the classic form of the *millet* as it emerged in the eighteenth and first half of the nineteenth centuries took some time to develop. In the case of the Greeks it is clear that Mehmet the Conqueror afforded important privileges to George Gennadios Scholarios, a noted adversary of the Catholics, when he summoned him from captivity in Adrianople (Edirne) to become Patriarch of the Great Church of Constantinople in January 1454. Mehmet engaged in discourses with Gennadios on the respective merits of Islam and of Christianity and, as a token of his respect, restored to the new patriarch the powers and privileges which the Church had enjoyed in Byzantium, together with a large part of its properties. Some confusion exists as to the exact nature of the privileges accorded to Gennadios and his successors by Mehmet II. These were presumably recorded in a *berat*, or imperial warrant, but when the Patriarch Theoleptos I in 1521 protested to the Sultan Süleyman I against his persecution of Christians, he was unable to produce any written document of Mehmet the Conqueror confirming the Church's privileges. The earliest surviving imperial *berat* confirming a patriarch in office is in fact that of Dionysios III Vardalis, dating from 1662.

Despite this uncertainty it soon became accepted that the patriarch as *ethnarchis*, or *millet bashi*, of the Orthodox *millet* had a wide jurisdiction over his flock, not only in purely ecclesiastical matters but in many aspects of the administration of civil justice and the provision of education. The patriarch also had the right to raise ecclesiastical taxes. Moreover, this delegated authority was shared at provincial level by the metropolitans and bishops of the Orthodox Church. As Bishop Theophilos of Kampania put it in his *Nomikon* of 1788: 'In the days of the Christian [Byzantine] Empire (alas) . . . prelates administered only the priesthood and ecclesiastical matters and did not intervene in civil matters . . . Now, however, . . . provincial prelates undertake secular lawsuits and trials, in connection with inheritance, with debts and with almost any aspect of the Christian civil law'.* As Theophilos rightly noted, the jurisdiction of the Orthodox ecclesiastical authorities under the rule of the Ottoman sultans was in fact greater than under the Byzantine emperors. In many parts of the empire, Orthodox Christians had more dealings with their own ecclesiastical authorities than they ever did with the Ottoman civil power. Moreover this extensive jurisdiction was exercised by the patriarch not only over the Greeks but over all the subject peoples of the Ottoman Empire who were Orthodox Christians by religion. For the *Millet-i Rum*, or 'Greek' *millet*, of which the ecumenical patriarch was the head, embraced Serbs, Romanians, Bulgarians, Vlachs, Orthodox Albanians and Orthodox Arabs besides the strictly Greek element. Nonetheless, Greeks retained a firm grip on the ecumenical patriarchate, the Holy Synod and the higher reaches of the Orthodox ecclesiastical hierarchy.

In the early centuries after the conquest, this Greek ecclesiastical hegemony was accepted by the non-Greek Orthodox as constituting part of the natural order of things, but from the eighteenth

---

* Quoted in N. J. Pantazopoulos, *Church and Law in the Balkan Peninsula during the Ottoman Rule* (Salonica 1967) 44–5.

century onwards it came to be increasingly resented. In many respects the Balkan national movements of the nineteenth century were as much a reaction against Greek ecclesiastical and cultural domination as against Ottoman rule. The predominance within the Orthodox *millet* exercised by the Greek element was paralleled by the precedence which the 'Greek' *millet* enjoyed over the other non-Muslim *millets*. The ecumenical patriarch, who enjoyed the exalted rank of a pasha of three horse tails, took precedence over the leaders of the other religious communities at official functions. But the grant of these privileges by the sultans was by no means wholly disinterested. The essential *quid pro quo* which the sultans expected in return was that the patriarch should act as the guarantor of the fidelity of the Orthodox populations of the empire.

Although the Christians of the empire enjoyed a substantial degree of communal autonomy they were also subject to a number of disabilities *vis-à-vis* the Muslim populations. A Christian's evidence was not accepted against that of a Muslim in the Muslim *cadi's* court; he could not marry a Muslim woman; he could not wear certain types of clothing; and he was barred from bearing arms and riding horses, although these particular prohibitions were frequently ignored. A Christian was required to pay special taxes, notably the *haradj*, a tax levied on men in lieu of military service. The *haradj* was undoubtedly resented but on the other hand it is clear that many Christians were glad to be able to purchase exemption from long and arduous periods of service in the Ottoman armies. Probably the most onerous imposition to which the Christians of the Balkans were liable was the janissary levy (*devshirme* or *paidomazoma*). This was the obligation, imposed at irregular intervals, for Christian families to deliver a certain proportion of the most intelligent and best-looking of their children to the officers in charge of the janissary levy. They would then be raised as Muslims and educated for the imperial service in either a civilian or military capacity. Those who served in a civilian capacity, as *ich oghlan*, frequently rose to assume the highest offices of the state, while the janissary corps constituted the élite fighting formation of the empire.

Not surprisingly the practice of removing Christian children from their families at a tender age and raising them in an alien faith was bitterly resented. Christian parents resorted to numerous subterfuges, including early marriage of their children and lavish bribery, to protect their children from the levy, and the activities of the recruiting officers from time to time met with violent resistance. On the other hand, for the children of poor families, the levy formed a unique channel of advancement to some of the highest offices of state and there is evidence of Christian, and indeed Muslim, parents actually volunteering their children for the levy. Some of those recruited in the janissary levy seem to have retained strong memories of their Christian origins and were able to intercede on behalf of friends and relatives at the imperial court. The levy began to fall into abeyance in the seventeenth century and had completely disappeared by the early eighteenth century.

In certain areas of the empire, particularly in remote mountainous regions of the Balkans, imperial authority was never able fully to establish itself. Such were the *Agrapha* villages in the Pindus mountains, so called because they were 'unwritten' in the tax registers. Other areas of the Greek world enjoyed a high degree of self-government and virtual autonomy, frequently combined with special tax privileges. Among these areas were the *Dervenochoria* (seven villages in the plain of Megara), the *Eleftherochoria* (three confederations of villages in the Chalcidice peninsula near Salonica), the *Zagorochoria* in Epirus, Ambelakia and Pelion in Thessaly, Sphakia in Crete, Melnik, Ayvalik (Kydonies) in Asia Minor, Chios, which traditionally formed part of the patrimony of the sultan's mother, and the whole of the Peloponnese. In the eighteenth century the Peloponnese enjoyed a high degree of self-government, with three levels of local representation. The Peloponnesians also had the right to maintain their own representatives, known as *vekils*, in Constantinople. Communal government tended to be oligarchical in character and the elders of the community had wide ranging powers in matters such as the allocation and collection of taxes.

Although Ottoman rule was relatively tolerant and the Greek populations of the empire were afforded a considerable degree of control over their own communal affairs, nonetheless in the years after the conquest there were many examples of Greek conversion to the ruling religion of Islam. Such conversions were particularly pronounced in Asia Minor and the extent of the decline in the Greek population in this region is indicated by the fact that by the fifteenth century there were only seventeen metropolitanates, one archbishopric and three bishoprics whereas as recently as 1204 there had been forty-eight metropolitanates and 421 bishoprics. Moreover, a sizeable proportion of those Greek Christians of Asia Minor who did not change their faith nonetheless adopted the language of their rulers. These Karamanli Christians, as they are known, were Orthodox by religion but Turkish in speech, employing the Greek alphabet to write the Turkish language. A whole literature was printed in Turkish with Greek characters from the eighteenth century onwards for this group, who were mainly concentrated in the interior of Asia Minor but who were also to be found in sizeable numbers in the Ottoman capital.

Some Greeks, particularly the wealthy, apostasised so as to be able to retain their estates, others as a result of duress. Still others changed their faith to better themselves or their children for, despite the tolerance of their Ottoman overlords, Christians nonetheless remained essentially second-class citizens. But no obstacles were placed in the way of Christian (or Jewish) converts to Islam achieving high office. As in the Byzantine Empire what mattered was not a man's ethnic origin but his religion. In some parts of the empire mass conversions to Islam occurred. Such mass apostasies took place in Crete in the seventeenth century and the apostates assumed the religion but not the language of their rulers. This explains the presence of a sizeable body of Greek-speaking Muslims in Crete right up until modern times. Others hedged their bets by outwardly subscribing to Islam but secretly adhering to the tenets and practices of Orthodox Christianity. Such a Crypto-Christian would openly have a Muslim name but within the closed family circle would use his baptismal name and would take care only to marry a fellow Christian. Substantial numbers of these Crypto-Christians were to be found in southern Albania, in Crete, in Cyprus, where they were known as *linovamvakoi* or 'linen-cottons', and above all in Pontos on the southern shores of the Black Sea, where they numbered many thousands.

The Greek population of the empire, then, was much depleted in the years after the conquest by full or partial conversion to Islam, and by the wastage that was a natural consequence of military conquest. The ruling élites of Byzantium had been decimated by war, exile or conversion, although some members of the old ruling houses lingered on in Constantinople in much reduced circumstances. Some managed to restore their fortunes by placing their talents at the service of their new masters. One such was a scion of the great Byzantine family of the Kantakouzinoi, Shaytanoghlou, the Son of the Devil, as the Turks called him. Through his control of the fur trade and of the salt monopoly he amassed a fortune large enough to enable him to equip sixty fighting galleys for the sultan's navy and to build up a famous library. The privileged position he enjoyed within Ottoman society enabled him to interfere in the affairs of the patriarchate. But inevitably the wealth and power of this over-mighty subject made him many enemies and Shaytanoghlou was executed in 1578.

One result of the Ottoman conquest was that it put an end to the domination of the trade of the Levant and the Black Sea by Venetian and Genoese traders. Some Greeks, such as Shaytanoghlou, were able to fill the vacuum left by the Italians but in the early centuries after the conquest Jews and Armenians, to whom the stigma of a defeated enemy did not attach, played a more important role in commerce than did the Greeks. It was only in the eighteenth century that the Greeks became the predominant force in the commerce of the empire. During the first centuries following the conquest, during which the Ottoman Empire was at the zenith of its power and military might, the shattered remnants of the Greek population of the Byzantine Empire concentrated their energies more on physical survival than on harking back to past glories or plotting future emancipation.

The ecumenical patriarchate, which in 1601 had moved to the small Church of St George in the Phanar quarter on the Golden Horn, proved the natural focus of Greek life during this period. In the course of the seventeenth century the school attached to the patriarchate, under the directorship of Theophilos Korydalefs, a graduate of the University of Padua, became the leading centre of Greek culture within the Ottoman domains, and important Greek academies were established in Jassy, the capital of Moldavia, and in Bucharest, the capital of Wallachia, during the seventeenth century. But although the Orthodox Church during this period acted as a patron of Greek learning and, through the use of Greek in the liturgy, helped to preserve a sense of Greek identity, it fell victim in the sixteenth and seventeenth centuries to the institutionalised corruption of the Ottoman governmental system. The office of patriarch could only be purchased through the payment of a massive *peshkesh* or bribe to the Grand Vizier. By the second half of the seventeenth century the going rate for the office was fifty purses of five hundred dollars each, an enormous sum. An English traveller, Sir George Wheler, pinpointed in the late seventeenth century the deleterious effects of this system at all levels of the Church hierarchy. The patriarchs, he wrote 'buy their Dignity dear, and possess it with great hazard'.

Yet so ambitious are the Greek Clergy of it, that the Bishops are always buying it over one another's Heads, from the Grand Vizier; . . . as soon as they are promoted, they send to all their Bishops, to contribute to the Sum they have disbursed for their Preferment . . . Again, the Bishops send to their inferiour Clergy; who are forced to do the same to the poor People.*

One of the consequences of this deeply rooted corruption was that, despite the fact that a patriarch, once elected, theoretically enjoyed life tenure, the office of ecumenical patriarch during the seventeenth century changed hands fifty-eight times, the average tenure in office being some twenty months. It was by no means unknown for a patriarch to hold office on more than one occasion. Dionysios IV Mouselimis, for instance, was five times patriarch between 1671 and 1694. The situation was much the same in the eighteenth century and the jibe of an Armenian banker that 'you Greeks change your patriarch more often than your shirt' was sufficiently

* *A Journey into Greece . . . in Company of Dr Spon of Lyons . . .* (London 1682) 195.

near the mark to make its recipient, the chronicler Athanasios Komninos Ypsilantis, feel uncomfortable. One patriarch, Kallinikos III, is reputed to have died from joy on hearing the news of his election in 1757.

Yet if the condition of the Orthodox Church and more particularly of the patriarchate during the sixteenth, seventeenth and eighteenth centuries was scarcely edifying, nonetheless a number of simple Orthodox Christians steadfastly maintained their faith in the face of Ottoman pressure or blandishments to apostasise and the example of these 'neo-martyrs' confirmed many more in an attachment to their faith. Many Greeks during the centuries of Ottoman dominion drew comfort, too, from a corpus of ballads and messianic beliefs foretelling their eventual liberation from the yoke of the 'impious Hagarens'. One of these ballads, 'The Taking of the City', painted a moving picture of the last celebration of the liturgy in the Great Church of the Holy Wisdom in Constantinople as the city's defences were crumbling. In the middle of the Cherubic Hymn an archangel bade the priests to gather up the Holy Vessels and to send the Cross, the Gospel and the Holy Altar to safety in 'Frangia', the West, 'Lest the dogs take it from us and foul it' . . .

> The Virgin trembled, the icons wept.
> 'Hush, Virgin Lady, do not weep too many tears,
> Again with the passing of the years, in time,
>   again they will be yours'.

Legends and messianic beliefs about an eventual liberation abounded: that 'The Emperor turned into Marble', the last Emperor of Byzantium, Constantine XI Palaiologos, would on the appointed day rise up to emancipate his people; that the Turks would return to the Red Apple Tree whence they had come; that a *xanthon genos*, or fair-headed race from the north, would one day liberate the Greek people from their Babylonian captivity. This *xanthon genos* was widely taken to be the Russians, on whom the Greeks increasingly placed their reliance for ultimate liberation. As Paul Rycaut, the British consul in Smyrna between 1667 and

1677, noted, 'the *Greeks* have also an inclination to the *Moscovite* beyond any other Christian Prince, as being of their Rites and Religion, terming him their Emperor and Protector, from whom, according to the ancient Prophesies and modern Predictions, they expect delivery and freedom to their Church'.* Some Greeks, such as the Metropolitan of Myra in 1618, sought to warn their fellow countrymen that in placing their faith in oracles and false prophecies, and in expecting liberation from Spain, Venice or Moscow, they were wasting their time 'in vanities'. Nonetheless the overwhelming mass of the Greek people continued to listen to the oracles and prophecies. In short, they believed that their emancipation would not be, and could not be, brought about by their own efforts but rather as a result of divine intervention.

Yet even in the centuries immediately after the conquest when the Ottoman Empire was at the height of its power there were Greeks who did not despair of armed resistance to their foreign overlords. The naval expedition launched by the Holy League of Spain, Venice and the papacy which resulted in the shattering defeat inflicted on the Ottoman navy at Lepanto in 1571 sparked off sympathetic uprisings on the mainland and in the islands of the Archipelago. The great war between Venice and the Ottoman Empire of 1645-69, which resulted in the loss of Crete in 1669 and the Venetian occupation of the Peloponnese between 1684 and 1715 were a further source of encouragement to the Greeks. Sporadic revolts that were not stimulated by hopes of foreign deliverance included those fomented by Dionysios Skylosophos in Epirus in 1611 and by Efthymios Blakhavas in Thessaly in 1808.

Moreover a form of pre-nationalist armed resistance manifested itself within a few decades of the conquest in the form of the klephts, who are mentioned in documents as early as 1480. The klephts were essentially bandits who had taken to the hills for a variety of reasons, usually to avoid the payment of taxes or to escape pursuit by the authorities. They had no hesitation in robbing rich Greeks, but their depredations were also directed against Ottoman tax collectors and other visible symbols of Ottoman authority, and as such their activities came to assume some of the

* Paul Rycaut, *The History of the Present State of the Ottoman Empire* (London 1682) 176.

characteristics of a primitive form of national resistance. The ethos of the klephts, which is best expressed in the magnificent corpus of klephtic ballads, stressed personal honour, bravery, resistance to hunger and torture and unusual physical prowess. One famous klepht, for instance, Nikotsaras, was reputed to be able to leap over seven horses. Klephtic bands were generally small, although bands of fifty or more were not unknown. The sea-going equivalent of the klephts were pirates. Piracy flourished, particularly from the seventeenth century onwards, and the myriad of small islands in the Archipelago afforded excellent cover for their depredations.

To hold in check the activities of the klephts the Ottoman authorities recruited local irregular troops, for the most part Christian, known as *armatoloi*. An important function of these *armatoloi* was the guarding of the mountain passes, much favoured by the klephts for their ambushes, and the protection of officials, merchants and travellers generally. Rumeli, or mainland Greece, at various periods seems to have been divided into between fourteen and eighteen *armatoliks*, each commanded by a *kapetanios*, an office which in some cases passed from father to son. In the Peloponnese the functions of the *armatoloi* in maintaining public order were carried out by *kapoi*, working for the local Greek magnates. The distinction between an *armatolos* and a klepht was often a narrow one. An *armatolos*, for instance, might easily resort to banditry if his pay was not forthcoming from the Ottoman authorities. Equally, a klepht, if the proceeds of banditry were on the decline, and the local *armatoloi* were being regularly paid, might be tempted, at least temporarily, to enlist in the *armatoloi*. As Kapetan Rompheis put it:

> For forty years I was an *armatolos* and a klepht,
> With my hand as a pillow and my sword as a mattress,
> And with a rifle at my side to awaken me.

Through the period of Ottoman rule in Greece, then, there were armed formations of Greeks, engaged in either thwarting or upholding Ottoman authority. Their importance was to increase as the Ottoman Empire went into decline and former klephts and *armatoloi* were to provide the military muscle of the insurgent Greeks when their struggle for independence broke out in the 1820s.

During the sixteenth and seventeenth centuries, however, the sporadic outbreaks of resistance to Ottoman rule that occurred had no chance of achieving any permanent success, especially in view of the inability of the Christian powers to unite in the face of the Ottoman threat. Nor did the economic and social circumstances of the Greeks during this period permit of the development of an articulated national movement. The essential precondition for any moves towards emancipation was a decline in the authority, both at central and at local level, of the Ottoman government. The protracted process of the decline in Ottoman power, then, was of fundamental importance to the development of a Greek national movement. Historians tend to push further and further back the roots of this gradual decline, which certainly began to manifest itself long before the first stirrings of the Greek national movement in the middle of the eighteenth century. But the decline rapidly gained momentum in the eighteenth century, under both internal and external pressures, with the result that, in the decades before 1821, the Ottoman Empire had in a number of important respects ceased to function as a unitary state, a development that was to prove of great benefit to the Greeks in the successful prosecution of their struggle for independence.

By the early years of the seventeenth century Ottoman observers were themselves reflecting on the reasons for the empire's waning fortunes. One memorandum, composed by Kochu Bey, the 'Turkish Montesquieu', drew attention to the consequences of the increasing withdrawal of the sultans from direct involvement in the business of government and to the debasement of the office of Grand Vizir, with a resulting growth in corruption, place-seeking and intrigue. By the beginning of the eighteenth century provincial governorships were often held for as little as a year, as competition for the lucrative spoils of office intensified. Increasing administrative decay and venality at the centre of the empire was accompanied by territorial retreat at the periphery. The halting of the empire's westward expansion had been dramatically high-lighted by the failure in 1683 of the siege of Vienna and the slow but steady retreat of the empire in Europe was marked by the treaties of Karlowitz (1699), Passarowitz (1718) and Belgrade (1739). This withdrawal cut at the very roots of an imperial system based on military expansion and colonisation. Moreover, the loss of territory it entailed seriously depleted the empire's reserves of manpower and narrowed its tax base, a development that further aggravated the already serious economic problems that were plaguing the Porte. These were compounded by infla-tion on a massive scale which repeated debasements of the coinage did little to abate. The Porte's growing shortage of money helped to consolidate bribery, extortion and rapacity as a basic instrument of government.

The empire's military capabilities were further undermined by the decline in the provinces of the system of military fief-holders, the *sipahis*, who had traditionally provided the Ottoman armies with cavalry. Their fiefs (*timars*) increasingly fell into the hands of tax farmers or lapsed into heritable *chiftliks*, or estates, and the obligation to supply troops in times of crisis was increasingly neglected. The tax farmers and *chiftlik* owners were principally concerned with maximising the returns obtainable from their land holdings. As a result the burdens placed on the peasantry in-tensified and the proprietor of a *chiftlik* estate frequently deprived his peasants of as much as half of the produce of their labour. The empire's fighting capacity was further diminished by the degenera-tion, with the fading out of the janissary levy, of the janissary regiments from a *corps d'élite* into a largely hereditary military faction, which, until its bloody suppression by Sultan Mahmud II in 1826, was to constitute an actual or potential threat to imperial authority.

These developments meant that the empire was increasingly less able to confront the external challenges facing it from the Austrians in the west, the Persians in the east, and above all the Russians in the north. Russia's territorial ambitions at the expense of the Ottoman Empire were matched by her increasing political interest in the Orthodox, and at this time particularly the Greek, populations of the empire. It was during the reign of Peter the Great (1682-1725) that these ambitions began seriously to manifest themselves and Peter was certainly aware of the potential afforded by the Greeks as a kind of fifth column within the Ottoman Empire. He despatched propaganda leaflets to the Greeks of the empire, thus exploiting the widespread belief that the Russians would one day act as liberators. More direct Russian attempts to incite the Greeks against their Ottoman overlords were made during the great Russo-Turkish war of 1768-74. In 1770 *armatoloi* in Macedonia, at the instigation of George Papazolis of Siatista, took up arms against the Turks. This uprising met with no greater success than did the insurrection fomented in the same year in the Peloponnese by Catherine the Great's emissaries, the brothers Orloff. The Orloff insurrection ended in total disaster, with the province being subjected to devastating reprisals at the hands of Albanian irregulars called in by the Ottoman authorities.

Greek expectations of imminent liberation during the 1768-74 war were greatly heightened by the widespread belief in the prophecy attributed to the Byzantine Emperor Leo the Wise to the effect that the 'City' would be liberated 320 years after its fall, i.e. in 1773. In fact, of course, no such liberation took place and the Treaty of Kutchuk Kaynardja of 1774, which concluded the hostilities, was regarded by the Greeks as a bitter disappointment, although the Russians were later erroneously to claim that the Ottomans had conceded them a general right of protection over all the Orthodox Christians of the empire. Nonetheless the fact that the Greeks felt themselves to have been abandoned by the Russians in no way diminished their belief in the prophecies. Rather their non-fulfilment was seen as signifying God's wrath at the departure of the Orthodox people from His precepts. However, if the peace settlement had brought little direct amelioration of the Greeks' lot, it did at least demonstrate, once again, that the once mighty Ottoman Empire was no longer invincible. Moreover, the Russian rulers had by no means abandoned their interest in the Greeks. The Empress Catherine now took up her Greek Project, her notion of a revived Byzantine Empire to be reconstituted under Russian aegis and to include the Slav as well as the

Greek populations of Ottoman Europe, under the imperial rule of her own grandson Constantine. The Greeks' faith in Russia as their potential liberator persisted and when war once again occurred between Russia (allied from 1788 with Austria) and the Ottoman Empire between 1787 and 1792, the Greek merchants of Trieste financed a flotilla under Lambros Katsonis to fight alongside the Russians. By the time peace was concluded at the Treaty of Jassy in 1792, however, an entirely new factor had emerged: the French Revolution and the impetus it gave to nationalist movements throughout Europe. The impact of the French Revolution in the Greek world, however, more properly belongs to a consideration of the immediate origins of the Greek revolt in 1821.

During the course of the eighteenth century, then, the Ottoman Empire was increasingly threatened by internal and external crises. Some members of the Ottoman ruling class sought valiantly to check and reverse this seemingly inexorable process of decline, and attempts were made to stem the pattern of military defeat by introducing the superior military technology of the West. French military experts and European renegades were employed to supervise the empire's defences and the re-equipping and re-training of its armies. The most sustained effort to strengthen the state's military power was made by Sultan Selim III (1789–1807) in his *Nizam-i Djedid*, or New Order. His attempt to modernise the empire's army and navy met with fierce opposition from the janissaries and the reactionary *ulema* of theologians and judges who combined in 1807 to overthrow him. Other attempts to introduce reforms during the course of the eighteenth century were to be frustrated by the growth of centrifugal tendencies in the provinces. Of all the phenomena associated with the process of Ottoman decline it was the growth of provincial autonomies in many of the far-flung regions of the empire that was most directly to assist the development of the Greek national movement. This new provincial élite consisted of the Anatolian *derebeys* (valley lords) and the Rumeliot *ayans* (notables) who developed strong local roots in the territories over which they ruled. The *ayans* and *derebeys* formed dynasties which were frequently *de facto*, if not *de jure*, independent of the Ottoman central government. By the end of the eighteenth century these 'overmighty subjects' controlled large areas of the empire. Two who dominated the European provinces of the empire were Ali Pasha of Jannina and Osman Pasvanoghlu of Vidin. Even if their rule was often harsh they did, nonetheless, fulfil a useful function in establishing a basic framework of law and order which was often beyond the capacity of the central government. Some of them, too, went out of their way to assist the Christian populations in their domains. Above all their successful defiance of the authority of the Porte over long periods of time afforded a suggestive example to the Greeks and once again demonstrated the relative impotence of the Porte. This chronic disorder of the Ottoman provinces in the eighteenth century was paralleled by a breakdown of authority in the provincial cities, where the indiscipline of the janissary regiments frequently created a climate of fear and disorder, as in the ferocious anti-Greek and anti-foreign outburst known as the Smyrna 'rebellion' of 1797.

The breakdown of the empire in the eighteenth century into virtual anarchy was accompanied by significant changes in the nature of Greek society. One direct consequence of the increasing external threat to the Porte was the rise to power and influence of a small Greek élite, known as the Phanariots, who were in effect a kind of *noblesse de robe*. For, as the empire was forced into retreat towards the end of the seventeenth century, so it was obliged to negotiate with the Christian powers, rather than simply dictate to them as hitherto. Lacking a knowledge of the requisite languages, the Porte came increasingly to rely on Greek interpreters, whose influence over the conduct of Ottoman foreign policy was much greater than the title implies. The Treaty of Karlowitz of 1699, for instance, was largely negotiated by Alexander Mavrokordatos o ex Aporriton ('of the Secrets'). These Phanariots, drawn from a tightly knit group of eleven families in Constantinople, during the course of the eighteenth century came to monopolise other influential posts in the Ottoman bureaucracy besides that of principal interpreter. They became interpreters to the admiral of the Ottoman fleet, the *kaptan pasha*, and again this entailed responsibilities greater than the title suggests, for they became in effect governors of the islands of the Archipelago, from whose Greek inhabitants the crews of the Ottoman fleet were in large part drawn.

The most influential positions acquired by the Phanariots were the posts of *hospodar*, or Prince, of the Danubian principalities of Moldavia and Wallachia. Although under Ottoman suzerainty since the fourteenth century, the principalities had enjoyed a quasi-autonomous status under the rule of native princes. When these had proved disloyal they were replaced from 1709 (1715 in the case of Wallachia) by Phanariot Greeks. Until 1821, when their rule in the principalities was abruptly terminated, the Phanariots ruled with vice-regal pomp, their courts in Jassy and Bucharest reproducing in miniature the splendour and ceremonial of the imperial court. Many of the *hospodars*, and their hangers-on, grew exceedingly rich on the fruits of office and this led to furious competition for the posts, with all the corruption and intrigue that this entailed under the Ottoman system of government. The office of *hospodar* changed hands thirty-six times in the course of the century in Moldavia, and thirty-eight times in the case of Wallachia, the average tenure in office being under three years. Phanariot rule in the principalities became a byword for rapacity and intrigue. But its positive aspects should not be overlooked for some of the *hospodars* proved to be rulers in the tradition of the Enlightened Despots and introduced a number of important reforms. Moreover their courts and the academies which were attached to them proved to be important centres of Greek culture. The principalities under Phanariot rule were a significant channel for influences from the West and a valuable school of politics for the Greeks.

The Phanariots' rise to power and influence at the highest levels of Ottoman society was certainly a very important development. But of even greater importance for the Greek national movement was the emergence during the course of the eighteenth century of a large Greek mercantile class, both within the Greek lands and, more significantly, without. For Greeks during the seventeenth century had begun to rival the Armenians and Jews as the dominant element in the internal and external trade of the empire. During the seventeenth and eighteenth centuries, they formed a substantial element in the great seaport towns of the empire such as Constantinople itself, Smyrna and Salonica, and large Greek commercial colonies were also to be found in the western Mediterranean, in Venice, Trieste, Leghorn, Naples and Marseilles. These mercantile communities of the diaspora attracted many of the most enterprising and prosperous Greek merchants.

The Ottoman retreat from central Europe was accompanied by increased Greek commercial activity in the newly liberated regions and soon a Greek commercial presence was to be found throughout central Europe. Goethe recalled in his autobiography having been charmed as a young man by the traditional dress worn by Greeks at the Leipzig fair, and one contemporary Greek source estimated that there were, towards the end of the eighteenth century, as many as 80,000 Greek families settled in the Habsburg domains alone. Schools for the children of these Greek merchants were to be found in seventeen towns in Hungary. Russian colonisation of the shores of the sea of Azov and the northern shores of the Black Sea afforded another important outlet for Greek commercial enterprise. Catherine the Great deliberately attracted Greek settlers to such towns as Odessa, Mariupol and Taganrog and they were able to trade in the Black Sea, flying the Russian flag, following the Treaty of Kutchuk Kaynardja of 1774 and the Russo-Turkish commercial convention of 1783. Greek commercial enterprise was not restricted to Europe. For example, a Greek community, with its own church, flourished in Bengal in the late eighteenth century. Extensive networks of commercial contacts were developed, often on a family basis. One British traveller in 1812 came across a family of four brothers, one in Jannina, one in Moscow, one in Constantinople and one in Germany, all engaged in trading with each other and able to exploit the mutual confidence engendered by close family ties. During the last decades of the eighteenth century the Greek merchant marine developed very rapidly, particularly during the French Revolutionary and Napoleonic wars, when Greek freebooters made large fortunes running the blockade. The three

'Nautical Islands' of Hydra, Spetses and Psara built up large merchant fleets. That of Hydra, for instance, almost doubled between 1806 and 1820. By the end of the Napoleonic wars the Greek merchant marine had risen to well over 500 vessels, whose crews were to be an invaluable asset in the prosecution of the War of Independence.

The burgeoning entrepreneurial skills of the Greeks were mostly deployed outside the boundaries of the empire, where profits were safe from the depredations of the Ottoman authorities. The endemic anarchy of the empire in decline inhibited investment of capital and entrepreneurial skills within Ottoman territory, although a few rudimentary industrial enterprises did emerge under Greek control. By far the largest and most successful of these was the manufactory of spun red cotton established at Ambelakia in Thessaly. This developed a flourishing export trade to the markets of central Europe, and in the words of the French consul at Salonica resembled 'by the activity of its inhabitants . . . rather a city of Holland than a Turkish village'. Only in the Peloponnese was there a substantial class of Greek landowning notables or *prokritoi* but even in this region some 40,000 Turks controlled three million *stremmata* (a *stremma* is equal to one thousand square metres), while 360,000 Greeks shared one and a half million. The Peloponnesian primates often combined landownership with trade and tax collection on behalf of the Ottoman authorities.

Undoubtedly, then, there was a major upsurge in Greek commercial activity in the eighteenth century. How did this commercial revival affect the development of a Greek national movement? Historians have frequently argued that this new mercantile bourgeoisie, finding the arbitrariness, inefficiency, hostility towards commercial enterprise, and general lawlessness of the empire increasingly intolerable, were thus persuaded to throw their weight behind the struggle for national liberation, hoping thereby to create an independent state less inimical towards the generation of profit. There is undoubtedly some truth in such an interpretation, but in the final analysis most of these Greek merchants, at least the wealthier among them, showed a marked reluctance to aid or participate in any moves towards the creation of a dynamic opposition to Ottoman rule. One undoubted way in which the merchants did, however, contribute to the national revival was by generating the wealth that underlay the intellectual ferment which was such a notable feature of the decades before independence. Wealthy Greeks, who for the most part had acquired their fortunes abroad, shared to the full the local patriotism so characteristic of the Greeks. This prompted them to provide the funds for schools, libraries and scholarships in their local communities. There was also a more practical motive, for the development of a Greek commercial empire created an increasing demand for numerate and literate Greeks with a knowledge of foreign languages.

Schools of a kind had existed throughout the period of Ottoman rule, although with rare exceptions, such as the Patriarchal Academy in Constantinople, they had concentrated on imparting a basic knowledge of reading and writing to their pupils. In the eighteenth and early nineteenth centuries, however, a number of more advanced academies were either founded or revived. Besides the Princely Academies of Jassy and Bucharest, important schools were founded on the island of Chios, in Smyrna (The Evangelical School, 1733, and Philological Gymnasium, 1808) and Ayvalik. In these more advanced schools there was a heavy emphasis on the Greek classics, together with an attempt to inculcate the rudiments of mathematics and the natural sciences. Many of the teachers had studied at the universities of western Europe, particularly in Italy, and many of their graduates were also to study abroad, thanks to the subventions of the merchants.

Books in Greek for a Greek readership had been printed in substantial quantities, mainly in Venice, in the sixteenth and seventeenth centuries. In the eighteenth century, however, the production of books for a Greek audience increased dramatically. During the first twenty-five years of the century just over a hundred such books were printed. During the last twenty-five years well over 700 were published, while some 1300 titles were published during the first two decades of the nineteenth century. They were generally small editions, though they did sometimes run to several thousand copies. A more significant indicator of the intellectual climate in Greece, perhaps, than this dramatic increase in the numbers of such books published was the change in their content. Whereas at the beginning of the eighteenth century these books were overwhelmingly religious in character, by the years before 1821 their content had become increasingly secular. Numerous translations were published of the works of Western scientists and philosophers, including Locke, Voltaire, Montesquieu, Beccaria and Rousseau. Some Greeks such as Evgenios Voulgaris themselves published learned philosophical treatises, making use of works of philosophers such as Kant. But in essence the 'Neo-Hellenic Enlightenment' was derivative rather than original, its protagonists seeking above all to make the achievements of Western philosophers and scientists known to their fellow countrymen. The works of the Western Enlightenment also began to circulate in the Greek lands in their original languages, often remarkably soon after publication.

The most significant aspect of this increasing secularisation of Greek culture was the rediscovery by the Greeks of a sense of their own past, a realisation that they were the heirs to a glorious heritage that was universally admired by the educated classes of western Europe. During earlier centuries there had been a limited awareness of the ancient world but the nascent Greek intelligentsia embraced the study of Greece's classical past with an intensity approaching fervour during the fifty years or so before the outbreak of the Greek revolt. New emphasis was given in the schools and academies to the study of ancient Greek, new editions of the classics were published and Greeks saw in the wars between the Greeks and the Persians analogies with their present situation. Some Greeks began to baptise their children with the names of ancient worthies rather than the saints of the Orthodox Church. This rediscovery of the past engendered in the Greek intelligentsia a new self-confidence, aptly epitomised by Benjamin of Lesvos' claim in 1820 'that neither the Greeks of old nor the Greeks of today are subject to the laws of nature'.

An unfortunate outcome of this obsession with Greece's classical heritage was the increasingly bitter dispute that developed over the Greek language. Some argued that if the Greeks were truly to become worthy of their great heritage then they should reverse the natural development of the language and restore it to its pristine Attic purity, purging it of its Turkish, Slav and Italian accretions. Others argued that the spoken or demotic language should be made the basis of the written language. Still others advocated an intermediate position, arguing for the 'purification' of the demotic without going to the extremes of the archaisers. The 'language question' was by no means resolved at the time and has continued to bedevil Greece's cultural development right up until modern times.

It must be emphasised that the intellectual ferment that characterised the Greek world in the seventy years or so before the outbreak of the Greek War of Independence was largely confined to a small, predominantly Western-educated intelligentsia, many, perhaps most, members of which actually lived outside the Ottoman Empire. It largely passed over the heads of the great mass of the Greek people, who were mostly illiterate and who remained steeped in a thought world that was essentially Byzantine. The prophecies, folk songs, tales of Alexander the Great and popular romances such as the *Erotokritos* remained the staples of popular culture. The obsession with Greece's classical past was not widely shared. When someone compared the prowess of a klephtic leader to that of Achilles, the former asked 'Who is this Achilles? Did the musket of Achilles kill many?' Moreover the intellectual revival was for the most part resolutely opposed by the hierarchy of the Orthodox Church, which regarded the new emphasis on philosophy, the natural sciences and the culture of the ancient world as likely to lead to moral degeneration and indifference in matters divine. To counter what it regarded as the flood of atheistic and seditious literature circulating among the Greek populations of the empire a printing press was set up in Constantinople by the patriarchate in 1798, where uplifting and improving books were published under strict censorship.

If the mass of the Greek population was largely indifferent to its enthusiasms, and the hierarchy of the Orthodox Church actively opposed to them, nonetheless the new intelligentsia did serve a useful function in articulating the aspirations of the Greek

national movement. A leading role in this was played by Adamantios Korais, whose own career affords some interesting insights
into the intellectual origins of Greek nationalism. Born in 1748,
the son of a merchant in Smyrna, Korais was sent as a young man
to Amsterdam to acquire commercial skills. But he proved a
miserable failure in the highly competitive world of European
commerce. In the Netherlands he gradually shed the austere
mores and traditional attitudes of the Orthodox world in which
he had been raised. Abandoning all thoughts of a mercantile
career, he studied medicine at the University of Montpellier. His
real interests, however, lay not in medicine but in classical philo-
logy and he was able to give full rein to these after he had moved
to Paris in 1788. Korais was tremendously impressed by the
material civilisation and intellectual culture of France which
formed a painful contrast with the pitiable state of his compatriots. Soon after his arrival in the city he wrote to a friend in
Smyrna that, instead of men of the calibre of Miltiades and
Themistocles, the Greeks were governed 'by riff-raff and camel
drivers, or by monkish barbarians'.

Although far from a revolutionary himself Korais lived through
the dramatic events of the French Revolution in Paris and these
were to have a profound effect on his thinking. He never returned
to Greece and until his death in 1833 devoted himself with a
furious energy to his classical studies, of which he was one of the
leading exponents in Europe, and to raising the educational level
and national consciousness of his fellow countrymen. One of his
major undertakings was an edition of the Greek classics, prefaced
with uplifting discourses on the present state of the Greeks, which
were distributed free to Greek schools thanks to the generosity of
the brothers Zosimas, wealthy merchants from Jannina. He also
expended much energy in sending books to the academies of the
Greek world, and particularly that of his beloved Chios, where
just before the outbreak of the revolt in 1821 a printing press was
briefly established.

Korais was never very explicit as to how the Greeks were to
achieve their emancipation from the Ottomans he so detested. He
seems to have believed that if only his compatriots would imitate

the virtues of the French, the people of contemporary Europe who, in his estimation, most nearly resembled the ancient Greeks in virtue, then somehow they would be rewarded with their freedom. Education he saw as a kind of universal panacea. Once the Greeks had attained a sufficiently high level of education then, and only then, could they begin to hope for their freedom. Korais saw the 'monkish barbarians' of the Orthodox Church as constituting a major obstacle to raising the cultural level of his compatriots. As a true man of the Enlightenment Korais despised the Christian civilisation of Byzantium. He once wrote that to read so much as a page of a Byzantine author was enough to bring on his gout, and he was a vigorous critic of the Orthodox Church. He was angered not only by the hierarchy's cultural obscurantism and opposition to the new learning of the West and the revival of interest in Greece's classical heritage but also by its attitude of *ethelodouleia*, or voluntary submission to the powers that be.

For at the time of Bonaparte's invasion of Egypt in 1798 the Patriarch Anthimos of Jerusalem had argued in his *Patriki Didaskalia*, or Paternal Teaching, printed at the newly re-established Patriarchal Press in Constantinople, that the Greeks should remain loyal to their Ottoman masters, for the Ottoman Empire was in itself a creation of the Divine Will, raised up specifically to protect Orthodoxy from contamination by the heresy of Latin Catholicism. Views of this kind were by no means rare among the clergy and the laity but were of course anathema to Greek nationalists such as Korais. Korais, in the same year, penned a vigorous rebuttal which he was careful to buttress with scriptural references, not only because he was anxious to avoid offending the religious sensitivities of his Orthodox fellow countrymen but because he was anxious to steer a course between what he termed the Scylla of superstition and the Charybdis of atheism.

For all the frequently expressed fears of the Orthodox hierarchy that their flock was in danger of being lured into atheism, there were very few Greeks who rejected Orthodox Christianity as such. There were many more, however, who rejected the corruption of the Church as an institution and its attitude of eager submissiveness to the Ottoman authorities. Many of these anti-clericals were members of the small Greek intelligentsia but there was also a deeply rooted current of popular opposition to the pretensions and exactions of the hierarchy. A British traveller in the Peloponnese in the 1820s noted that there was 'a saying common among the Greeks, that the country labours under three curses, the priests, the *cogia bashis* [primates], and the Turks; always placing the plagues in this order'. Numerous other indications exist as to the strength of popular anti-clericalism. In the *Rossanglogallos*, for instance, a popular satire of the early nineteenth century, the metropolitan is made to say:

> I do not know of the yoke [of the Turk] . . .
> I do not feel the tyranny . . .
> Two things I crave, yes indeed, by the Icons
> Lots of money, and nice girls.
> Now as for Hellas, . . .
> It is of little concern to me if she has been tyrannised . . .

The *Rossanglogallos* takes the form of an imaginary dialogue between a Russian, an Englishman and a Frenchman, making the Grand Tour of Greece, and the personification of Hellas. In the satire it is not only the metropolitan who is signalled out as a friend to tyranny but in effect all the ruling élites of pre-independence Greek society, the Phanariots, the merchants and the *kodjabashis*, or primates. The poem ends with an exhortation to the Greeks not to place any faith in foreign powers as potential liberators as they were only interested in furthering their own interests.

The same point is made by the anonymous author of the *Hellenic Nomarchy*, printed in Italy in 1806, and which is perhaps the most original tract of the Greek national movement. He pointed to the successful struggle of the Serbs against the Ottomans which had begun in 1804 and which owed nothing to outside intervention. In an interesting analysis of the reasons for the continued enslavement of the Greeks he emphasised two basic factors. These were, as he put it, 'the ignorant priesthood and the absence of the best fellow citizens'. In familiar but unusually virulent terms he attacked the clergy for their ignorance, greed and sloth and above all for attempting to hold the national aspirations of the Greeks in check. In bemoaning the 'absence of the best fellow citizens' he urged the most educated and dynamic elements in Greek society, the Greeks of the mercantile diaspora, to return to their homeland and enlist in the struggle for national liberation.

There were, then, during the last decades of the eighteenth and the first decades of the nineteenth centuries a considerable and growing number of Greeks with a well-developed national consciousness. Yet the key question remained. How were their aspirations to be given concrete form, given the fact that many of the élites of Greek society, those who had achieved positions of power and influence within Ottoman society such as the Phanariots, the hierarchy of the Orthodox Church, the *kodjabashis* and the merchants, were strongly attached to the existing *status quo*? One acute observer of the state of pre-independence Greece, John Cam Hobhouse, was led to conclude in 1810 that the likelihood of any 'general revolution' of the Greeks without foreign support was 'quite impracticable': 'for although the great mass of the people, as is the case in all insurrections, has feeling and spirit enough to make the attempt, yet most of the higher classes, and all the clergy . . . are apparently willing to acquiesce in their present condition'.* But within ten years of this gloomy prognostication the Greeks had managed to launch a large-scale rebellion which, against all the odds, was to result in the emergence of an independent Greek state. How did this remarkable development come about?

---

* *A Journey through Albania and other provinces of Turkey in Europe* . . . (London 1813) ii, 597.

3

The struggle for emancipation, 1800–1833

If the national aspirations of a growing number of Greeks during the last decades of the eighteenth and first decades of the nineteenth centuries were ever to achieve concrete form then some means had to be found of mobilising the disparate elements in Greek society and of preparing them for an armed struggle against their Ottoman overlords. The ruling élites in Greek society were so wedded to the existing *status quo*, however, that this was clearly going to be no easy task. Moreover, although the decline in the authority of the central government over the provinces and the external pressures on its integrity might favour the Greek cause, nonetheless the Ottoman Empire, weakened though it might be, remained a formidable adversary. The sporadic uprisings which had taken place throughout the centuries of Ottoman rule had been essentially unplanned. Now, however, some Greeks were beginning to work towards a co-ordinated insurrection as the logical outcome of the efforts of the intelligentsia to instill a sense of national consciousness in their fellow countrymen.

These advocates of dynamic action to overthrow Ottoman rule in the Greek lands were much influenced by the revolutionary doctrines of the French Revolution. One stalwart of the War of Independence, the klephtic *kapetanios* Theodore Kolokotronis, wrote that 'the French Revolution and the doings of Napoleon opened the eyes of the world', bringing home to the Greeks that kings were no longer 'Gods upon the earth'. Dictating his memoirs in the 1830s it may be that Kolokotronis' reflections were coloured by hindsight. But one Greek who undoubtedly was directly and explicitly inspired by the ideals of the French Revolution was

Rigas Velestinlis, or Rigas Pheraios as he is also known, the proto-martyr of Greek independence and the first prophet of armed revolution. Born in 1757 in Velestino in Thessaly, Rigas was a man of considerable education and linguistic accomplishment. As a young man he served in the entourage of prominent Phanariots both in the Ottoman capital and in the Danubian principalities. During the 1790s Rigas was much influenced by the events in France and by the spread of revolutionary liberation through Europe, and in 1796, during his second prolonged stay in Vienna, he may have founded a secret revolutionary society. This is un-clear, but what is certain is that he embarked on an ambitious programme of publishing revolutionary literature. These tracts were secretly printed at a Greek press in the city, that of the brothers Markides-Poulios, who produced the first news sheet circulating in the Greek world, the *Ephimeris*. Between 1790 and 1797 this kept the Greeks, both within and without the boundaries of the Ottoman Empire, informed of the dramatic events that were occurring in the West.

Rigas' productions at this time included a large map of the Balkan peninsula and Asia Minor, in which the boundaries of the Greek world were set very wide, together with an engraved portrait of Alexander the Great, the symbolism of which was clear. But his most important endeavour was the printing in 1797 of a revolutionary tract. This contained a stirring proclamation, addressed to 'all who groan under the most unbearable tyranny of the most abominable Ottoman despotism', a declaration of the Rights of Man, the *Thourios* or War Hymn, and, most signifi-cantly, a *New Political Constitution of the Inhabitants of Rumeli, Asia Minor, the Islands of the Aegean and the Principalities of Moldavia and Wallachia*. Just as his declaration of the Rights of Man was ex-plicitly based on the French model, so his *Constitution* was strongly influenced by the French constitutions of 1793 and 1795. He in-tended this *Constitution* to provide the detailed framework of the new political order that he envisaged as arising from the ashes of the Ottoman Empire. The essential articles provided for the equality, without distinction of race or religion, of all the hetero-geneous populations that made up the Ottoman Empire, including

the Turks themselves, whom Rigas regarded as being as op-
pressed by the Ottoman tyranny as were the Christian inhabitants
of the empire. He elaborated a complex hierarchy of representative institutions, advocated the right of citizens to work and of the
poor to receive assistance, and called on women to bear arms. The
defence of the new *Constitution* was placed in the hands of its
citizens who had an obligation to take up arms against tyranny.
Although a number of articles were of a radical nature Rigas
respected property rights and relied upon an independent judiciary to guarantee the rights of the citizen.

It is sometimes suggested that Rigas was an early advocate of
Balkan federation but federalist notions are nowhere apparent in
his writings. Indeed he called his proposed Republic the 'Greek
Republic' and insisted on the mandatory study of Greek in the
schools. This insistence on Greek as a unifying force among the
Balkan peoples has led to charges that Rigas was at heart a Greek
chauvinist. Yet in placing a heavy emphasis on Greek language
and culture he was simply recognising the fact that Greek was the
lingua franca of Balkan commerce and that Greek culture was
during this period widely admired by the other Christian peoples
of the Balkans. In effect Rigas was advocating a revived Byzantine
Empire, with republican in the place of monarchical institutions
and ruled by an élite that was Greek by culture if not necessarily
by race.

Moreover, Rigas did not limit his activities to drawing up
elaborate paper constitutions. After printing several thousand
copies of his manifesto and setting in hand the printing of a
military manual, he set off to revolutionise the Balkans. As a first
stage he secretly shipped three thousand copies of the manifesto
to Trieste, where he himself arrived in December 1797. But he
was betrayed by a Greek merchant and was arrested by the
Habsburg authorities, who rounded up a further seventeen of his
associates. Eight of these were of Ottoman nationality and were
handed over, together with Rigas, to the Ottoman authorities in
Belgrade in May 1798. The following month they were strangled
to death and their bodies thrown into the Danube. If in practical
terms Rigas achieved little, nonetheless his martyrdom made him

a powerful symbol of resistance to subsequent generations of Greeks. Moreover, his activities occasioned a disproportionate degree of alarm in the Ottoman authorities, and indeed in the ecumenical patriarchate, for his death was very shortly to be followed by Bonaparte's successful invasion of Egypt, thus bringing the Ottomans into direct confrontation with the French.

The Ottoman Porte initially adopted an attitude of lofty disdain towards the French Revolution, regarding it as an irrelevant quarrel among infidels. This attitude changed dramatically with Bonaparte's Italian campaign of 1796–7 and above all with the signing of the Treaty of Campo Formio in October 1797, under which the Ionian Islands formally passed from Venetian to French sovereignty, for this brought the perfidious and atheistical doctrines of the Revolution to the very borders of the empire. Bonaparte, dreaming of French conquests in the East, declared that the possession of Corfu, Cephalonia and Zante was more important than the whole of Italy. The French occupation of Corfu in June 1797 had been carried out with all the trappings of revolutionary liberation: the burning of the *Libro d'Oro* of the Ionian nobility, the planting of a Tree of Liberty, the wearing of the tricolor cockade and the emergence of Corfiot 'Jacobins'. It was not long before the French had developed contacts with Ali Pasha, the heartland of whose domains lay in Epirus just across the water from Corfu, and French agents were also reported to be active in the Mani, the southernmost region of the Peloponnese. Then in June 1798 Bonaparte launched his invasion of Egypt, thus challenging the integrity of the empire itself.

Thoroughly alarmed and fearful that the insidious notions of the French might begin to infect its Christian subjects, the Porte ordered the ecumenical patriarch to remind his flock of its obligation of absolute and unquestioning loyalty to the sultan, and hastily concluded an alliance with Russia, the traditional enemy. A joint Russo-Ottoman expedition drove the French from the Ionian Islands, which briefly passed under a joint Russo-Turkish condominium. From 1800 to 1807 the islands were under a Russian protectorate and, following the Peace of Tilsit of that year, reverted to French rule. By 1814 all the islands had been captured by the British and in 1815 they became 'a single, free, and independent state under the exclusive protection of His Britannic Majesty'. Although the independence of the islands was formally recognised, the prerogatives of the British Lord High Commissioner were virtually untrammelled under the terms of the constitution elaborated in 1817 by the first holder of the office, 'King Tom' Maitland. Nonetheless, although the islands' independence was essentially a fiction, even the notional example of an area of free Greek soil proved a suggestive example to the Greeks of the mainland. More concretely, the islands offered a safe refuge for the klephts of Rumeli and the Peloponnese when harassed by the *armatoloi* or during the winter months when they suspended their activities. The British presence in the islands also enabled some of the klephts to acquire useful experience of service in a regular army. Theodore Kolokotronis, for instance, enlisted as a captain in the Duke of York's Greek Light Infantry, whose commander, Major Richard Church, was later, as General Sir Richard Church, to prove one of the most effective volunteers in the cause of insurgent Greece. A further encouraging example to the Greeks was provided by the ultimately successful revolt of the Serbs against Ottoman rule. This broke out in 1804, and resulted in the Ottomans conceding a quasi-autonomous status to Serbia in 1815.

Undoubtedly the most decisive development in preparing the groundwork for a co-ordinated insurrection against Ottoman authority was the foundation of the secret *Philiki Etairia*, or Friendly Society, in Odessa in 1814. Earlier societies had had almost exclusively cultural objectives. These had included the *Ellinoglosson Xenodocheion*, or Greek Hostel, founded in Paris in 1807, and the *Philomousos Etairia*, or Society of Friends of the Muses, founded in Athens in 1813, with a branch being established in Vienna in 1815. The *Philomousos Etairia* sought to support schools, to initiate archaeological excavations (yet another significant pointer to the rediscovery of a 'sense of the past') and to endow scholarships to enable young Greeks to study at the universities of Europe. In the context of the early nineteenth century, of course, the foundation even of ostensibly educational and cultural societies implied a political purpose but the *Philiki Etairia* was the first society founded with an explicitly and purely political objective, namely the 'liberation of the Motherland', an end that was to be achieved through armed revolt. The initiative in founding the *Philiki Etairia* was taken by Emmanuel Xanthos, a freemason and one-time clerk whose merchant company had ceased to trade, Nicholas Skouphas, an artisan, and Athanasios Tsakaloff, a clerk in a shipping company, all, significantly, men who had failed to make the grade in the harshly competitive world of the Greek mercantile diaspora.

Partly under the influence of masonic prototypes they evolved an elaborate ritual of initiation, which required the aspiring member to swear undying hatred towards the tyrants of his country and to accept death as the inevitable punishment for betrayal of the secrets of the *Etairia*. Four grades of membership, in ascending order of importance, were created: the *vlamis* (brother), the *systimenos* (recommended one), the *ierefs* (priest) and the *poimin* (shepherd). To these were subsequently added two military grades, the *aphieromenos* (dedicated one) and the *archigos ton aphieromenon* (leader of the dedicated ones). The *Etairia*'s affairs were controlled by the *Anotati Archi* (Supreme Authority), whose membership was kept secret from the rank and file. Although none of its initiates was left in any doubt that the *Etairia*'s ultimate objective encompassed the violent overthrow of the Ottoman yoke, its leadership never articulated any view as to the kind of society it envisaged once the Greeks had won their freedom. This very lack of any coherent ideology, however, worked to its advantage, for the *Etairia* was able to recruit in all areas of the Greek world and among all elements of a society that was becoming increasingly complex and stratified. Some uncertainty surrounds the total number of those recruited into the *Etairia*, whose membership in the early years grew only very slowly. Until the months immediately before the outbreak of revolt in 1821 the membership seems never to have risen much above a thousand. This figure, however, is somewhat misleading, for the recruitment of a provincial notable such as Petros Bey Mavromichalis of the Mani in effect implied the enrolment of his large and loyal retinue. Recruiting was carried out by apostles who found the greatest response in the Danubian principalities, in southern Russia, the Ionian Islands and the Peloponnese. Few were recruited in Rumeli, the Aegean islands or Asia Minor.

A recent study of the known membership of the *Etairia* has produced some interesting results. Some 54 per cent were merchants, 13 per cent 'professionals' (teachers, students, lawyers, officials, doctors and the like), 12 per cent provincial notables, mostly from the Peloponnese, 10 per cent clergy, few of whom were drawn from the higher ranks of the hierarchy, 9 per cent fighting men, be they klephts or *armatoloi*. Fewer than 2 per cent of known members were either peasants or artisans, on whom the impact of the *Etairia* was minimal. Historians have argued that the preponderance of merchants in the membership of the *Etairia* indicates that the mercantile bourgeoisie, whose emergence in the course of the eighteenth and nineteenth centuries was such a significant development, was moved to throw its economic weight behind the embryonic movement for national liberation. Yet it has been convincingly shown that very few of the established and wealthy merchants either within or without the empire (Panayiotis Sekeris was a notable exception) were prepared to have anything to do with the seemingly madcap conspiratorial schemes of the *Etairia*. The bulk of the 'merchants' who did enrol were merchants' clerks or little more than pedlars, men on the margin of society, who had failed to adapt to *xeniteia*, or exile from their own traditional societies.*

The *Etairia* was not without its internal tensions and a few recruits were liquidated, either because their indiscretions were threatening its very existence or because they had come to realise that its claims to enjoy Russian patronage were false. For such claims had proved a powerful attraction in recruiting new members, most of whom had been nurtured in the traditional belief that the Russians would be the future liberators of Greece. If the myth of Russian support was to prove highly convenient to the conspirators, the fact that it lacked substance was not for want of

---

* George Frangos, 'The *Philiki Etairia*: A Premature National Coalition', in Richard Clogg, ed., *The Struggle for Greek Independence* (London 1973) 87 ff.

endeavour. Two approaches were made to Count John Capo-distrias, a Corfiot Greek who had gained his initial political ex-perience in the government of the Septinsular Republic and, since 1816, had served as a joint foreign minister of Tsar Alexander I of Russia. Neither in 1817 nor in 1820 was Capodistrias prepared to give any encouragement to what he regarded as the fantastic schemes of the Etairists. But, although he informed the Tsar of what was afoot, he made no attempt to expose the *Etairia*, even though he believed that its endeavours were necessarily doomed to failure and could only end in disaster for the Greeks.

He continued to counsel his fellow countrymen to place their hopes for emancipation in moral regeneration and in the Russo-Turkish war which he believed sooner or later to be inevitable, for the Treaty of Bucharest of 1812, which had concluded the Russo-Turkish war of 1807–12, had left unresolved a number of outstanding disputes. Following such a conflict, he believed, the Greeks might hope, if not for full independence, then for an autonomous status such as the Porte had already been obliged to concede to Serbia. Undeterred by this rebuff, the second emissary to Capodistrias, Emmanuel Xanthos, seemingly acting on his own initiative, offered the supreme leadership of the *Etairia* early in 1820 to Prince Alexander Ypsilantis. Ypsilantis, the son of a Phanariot *hospodar*, after service in the Russian army in the course of which he had lost an arm at the battle of Ulm, had risen to the rank of general and was an aide-de-camp to the tsar. He accepted the offer with alacrity and, although he was to prove an uninspir-ing leader, the high office which he held in the Russian service helped to maintain the fiction that the conspirators enjoyed official Russian backing.

As the conspiracy gathered momentum and as the *Etairia*'s membership increased the leadership began to consider various concrete strategies for revolt. It was hoped to mobilise support both from the Serbs under Milosh Obrenovich and the Bulgarians and also to launch an uprising in the Ottoman capital itself which would include the capture of the Ottoman fleet. But increasingly the *Etairia*'s plans revolved around Ali Pasha, the satrap of Jannina,

who, with his sons Veli and Moukhtar, controlled much of mainland Greece. Ali had come to hear of the existence of the *Etairia*,
which was by now something of an open secret in the Greek world,
and began to make overtures to the conspirators, even claiming
that he himself was an initiate. For he was coming under increasing pressure from the Porte which, as part of Sultan Mahmud II's
resolute efforts to restore the authority of the central government,
was determined to crush the warlords that had for so long held
sway in the provinces. The *Etairia*, however, treated these approaches with reserve, for they feared treachery on his part and
were mindful of his ruthless suppression of the Christian Suliots.
Nonetheless they encouraged Ali to think that he might hope for
Russian support in his struggle with the Porte. When the Porte
in the summer of 1820 launched a large-scale campaign to sub-
due Ali Pasha, a campaign tying up large numbers of Ottoman
troops, this clearly afforded a chance to launch the revolt that
might not recur for years. Ypsilantis was determined to exploit
this opportunity to the full, initially planning a co-ordinated
revolt timed to break out in November 1820 both in Constantinople and in the Peloponnese.

This plan was then changed to an invasion of the Danubian
principalities timed for the spring of 1821. Such a move, it was
calculated, might both strengthen the belief in Russian backing
and, by encouraging the Turks to despatch troops to Moldavia
and Wallachia in contravention of the treaties, provoke Russian
intervention. Moreover, Michael Soutsos, the *hospodar* of Moldavia
and a member of the *Etairia*, could be expected to look with
favour on such an enterprise. Ypsilantis thus launched his invasion
in March 1821. In a proclamation issued in Jassy, the Moldavian
capital, he called on the brave and magnanimous Greeks to invite
'Liberty to the classical land of Greece', invoking the shades of
Epameinondas, of Thrasyboulos, of Harmodios and Aristogeiton,
of Timoleon, of Miltiades, of Themistocles and of Leonidas. But
the motley band that crossed the Pruth river was to meet with one
disaster after another. Although individual Serbs, Bulgarians and
Romanians fought with Ypsilantis' troops, the organised help on
which he was counting was not forthcoming from the Serbs or

Bulgarians, nor indeed from the indigenous Romanian inhabitants of the principalities.

Ypsilantis hoped to be able to exploit a revolt that had broken out a few weeks previously under the leadership of Tudor Vladimirescu, who had received some support from the *Etairia*. But Vladimirescu's followers were as much opposed to Greek Phanariot oppression as to the misrule of the native *boyars* and showed little interest in combining with Ypsilantis' forces, the only result of which might have been to consolidate Greek rule in the principalities. Moreover Tsar Alexander I, as soon as he heard of Ypsilantis' incursion, agreed to the despatch of Ottoman troops to the principalities. When Ypsilantis learned that Vladimirescu had been negotiating with the Turks he had him arrested and executed. After a short campaign, Ypsilantis' forces, which seem never to have risen above some four thousand, were crushed in the battle of Dragatsani in June 1821, at which the 'Sacred Battalion', composed of Greek students, fought particularly bravely. After the disaster Ypsilantis fled across the borders into Habsburg territory where he was imprisoned in Mugats castle until his death in 1828, by which time it was clear that some kind of at least autonomous Greece would come into existence. His forces were scattered, and in an heroic act of defiance Georgakis Olympios and some of his followers blew themselves up in the Moldavian monastery of Secu rather than submit to the Turks. Ypsilantis' invasion, then, soon collapsed but it did serve some purpose by diverting Ottoman attention from the almost simultaneous and ultimately far more significant uprisings in the Peloponnese, which was to prove the epicentre of the rebellion and the eventual nucleus of an independent Greek state.

The extent to which the nearly simultaneous uprisings in the Peloponnese were co-ordinated with Ypsilantis' invasion of the principalities is not clear, although Etairists had long been urging Ypsilantis to make a move while the Ottomans were preoccupied with Ali Pasha. It was the fear that Ali might be successful in his endeavours to enlist Greek help that prompted the Ottoman authorities, in an atmosphere brimming with tension, rumour and apocalyptic expectation, to summon the Peloponnesian primates to Tripolis, the provincial capital. Fearing a trap, the primates declined to attend and almost simultaneously a number of uprisings erupted against Turkish authority. Traditionally Germanos, the metropolitan of Old Patras, is credited with having raised the banner of revolt at the monastery of Aghia Lavra near Kalavryta on 25 March, which ever since has been celebrated as independence day In effect, however, the revolt was under way before this date. Once the first killings of Turks had taken place, the revolt spread rapidly through the Peloponnese and had soon taken root in parts of mainland Greece and in the three 'Nautical Islands' of Hydra (where the reluctant shipowners were pressured by their seamen to throw in their lot with the insurgents), Spetses and Psara. The accession of these islands to the insurgent cause was to prove of considerable significance, for it ensured effective control of the sea for the Greeks. Greek sea captains such as Miaoulis, Kanaris and Tombazis were to make a major contribution to the Greek war effort, their use of fire ships proving particularly effective against the cumbersome ships-of-the-line of the Ottoman fleet. Some weeks later there were also uprisings in the region of Salonica, although these were soon suppressed.

In the Peloponnese, however, the insurgents met with considerable success. After bitter fighting, with atrocities being committed by both sides, the Turks, who numbered perhaps some ten per cent of the overall population, largely withdrew to their strongholds and fortresses. One of these, Tripolis was invested in October and its Turkish defenders massacred by guerrilla chieftains anxious to lay their hands on the town's rich booty and oblivious of the effect that such rapacity might have on the Greek cause in the outside world. Those among the insurgents with some experience of the wider world, such as the Phanariots Dimitrios Ypsilantis, who had arrived in the Peloponnese in June as the emissary of his ill-fated brother Alexander, and Alexander Mavrokordatos, who had hastened to Greece from Italy on the outbreak of hostilities, were well aware that the initial successes of the insurgents were somewhat unreal. For the Ottomans until February 1822 were preoccupied with eliminating Ali Pasha, while the Greeks could have little hope of prevailing against the still considerable might of the Ottoman Empire unless they were able to enlist the support of one or more of the Christian powers. And there was no indication that such support would be forthcoming.

The initial response of the Powers, who were meeting at Laibach (Ljubljana), to the news of the outbreak of the revolt was discouraging. This was a predictable reaction in the Europe of the Holy Alliance, which feared any threat to the newly restored and fragile equilibrium of post-Napoleonic Europe. Metternich, the Austrian chancellor, was, of European statesmen, the most hostile to the Greek cause, dismissing Greece as a mere geographical expression with no claim to a separate political existence. He feared that the revolt would provide a pretext for further Russian intervention in the affairs of the Ottoman Empire. But Tsar Alexander I was disinclined to give any encouragement to forces seeking to subvert legitimate authority, despite the Russian claim to exercise a protectorate over the Orthodox Christians of the empire and the high hopes placed in him by the great majority of Russia's co-religionists in the Greek lands. A gesture was made, however, by the withdrawal of the Russian ambassador in the Ottoman capital, Count Stroganoff, in the wake of the execution of the ecumenical patriarch Gregory V. For a time there existed a real threat of a renewed Russo-Turkish war, with the Greek issue being only one of a number of outstanding differences between the two countries. In the event, until mid-1823, all the Powers manifested an attitude of strict neutrality towards the hostilities in Greece.

The execution of Gregory V, together with a number of metropolitans and leading Greeks of the capital, formed part of a series of reprisals taken against the Greek populations not only of the capital but also of cities such as Salonica and Smyrna which remained firmly under Ottoman control. The patriarch and the Holy Synod had anathematised Ypsilantis and his comrades in arms in the most vigorous terms as 'impious leaders, desperate fugitives and destructive traitors' as soon as the news of the crossing of the Pruth had reached the capital. Notwithstanding this forthright denunciation Gregory was hung from the lintel of a gate at the patriarchate, a gate that has remained closed to this day, and his body thrown to a Jewish mob who dragged it to the Golden Horn. This was regarded as a particularly humiliating fate given the traditional antagonism that existed between the Greek and Jewish communities of the empire. The news of Gregory's martyrdom provoked outrage in the Christian West. But in Ottoman eyes Gregory had manifestly failed to fulfil his fundamental duty, that of ensuring the loyalty of the Orthodox *pliroma*, or flock.

If the response of the Powers to the outbreak of the revolt was distinctly discouraging, then the news that the Greeks were struggling to regain their freedom struck a responsive cord with enlightened opinion throughout Christian Europe. The educated classes of Europe for the most part shared a common heritage of classical culture and it was not long before the enthusiasm of liberal opinion manifested itself in concrete form in the establishment of philhellenic committees, in the raising of funds for the embattled Greeks, and, most importantly, in the departure for Greece of philhellenic volunteers from virtually all the countries of Europe and from the United States (one solitary Cuban is recorded). Many of these philhellene volunteers were appalled by what they found, for the former klephts and *armatoloi* who, along with the peasants, made up the bulk of the fighting formations of the Greeks, bore precious little resemblance to the worthies of Periclean Athens. The Russian poet Pushkin was one of those who had early expressed a passionate interest in the cause of Greek emancipation, penning an ode to *Eleftheria*, or freedom, and expressing the hope that the Turks would withdraw from Hellas 'the legal heir of Homer and Themistocles'. But when he actually came across some real Greeks in the shape of the merchants of Odessa and Kishinev he dismissed these 'new Leonidases' as completely worthless, terming the Greeks 'a nasty people of bandits and shopkeepers'. Some of the philhellene volunteers, disillusioned to find that the Turks had no monopoly of brutality and atrocity, forthwith retraced their steps. The majority, however, stayed to offer their services to their sometimes bemused new allies.

As was only to be expected, the Greek cause attracted its share of cranks, do-gooders and out-and-out rogues. But there were in their ranks many genuine idealists, men such as General Sir Richard Church and Captain Frank Abney Hastings, who were able to contribute very considerable military and naval skills, and Lord Byron, whose arrival in Greece was a great boost to morale. Byron's death from a fever at Mesolonghi in 1824 was to focus world-wide attention on the struggle. Moreover the contribution of the non-military philhellenes should not be overlooked. Leicester Stanhope, the 'typographical Colonel', brought with him a printing press and saw in Greece fertile ground for the application of the principles of Benthamite utilitarianism, while the Irishman William Stevenson introduced the potato to Greece, and the American Samuel Gridley Howe established a hospital and refugee colony. The London Greek Committee, on the security of the lands vacated by the fleeing Turks, was able to raise two substantial loans in the City in 1824 and 1825. These, under-standably in the circumstances, were heavily discounted and were surrounded by a number of scandals, but nonetheless constituted an important source of finance for the embattled Greeks, besides giving bondholders a vested interest in the success of the Greek cause. The contribution of the philhellenes should not be over-rated, but their presence did encourage the Greeks to believe that they were not alone in their struggle, while the agitation of the various philhellenic committees in Europe served to keep the Greek issue alive in the face of the indifference or hostility of the governments of Europe. Indeed an exasperated British prime minister, the Duke of Wellington, was prompted to complain that 'there never was such a humbug as the Greek affair altogether'.

After the initial outburst of violence that accompanied the uprising, in which each side was bent on exterminating the other, the war proceeded at a somewhat leisurely pace. Until the spring of 1822, the Ottomans continued to regard the humbling of Ali Pasha as more important than the crushing of the insurgents. In both 1822 and 1823 the basic strategy of the Ottoman armies was to march in the summer campaigning season down the western and eastern coasts of mainland Greece, negotiating the passes of

Makrinoros in the west and Thermopylae in the east. Their intention, after liberating the besieged Turkish strongholds of mainland Greece, was to join forces at the Gulf of Corinth before crossing over into the Peloponnese and freeing the fortresses still in Turkish hands. But the Greek mastery of guerrilla tactics in terrain that was ideally suited to irregular warfare, together with their command of the sea which effectively inhibited sea-borne reinforcement, enabled the insurgents to hold the Ottoman armies in check.

The relatively static nature of the war after the early Greek successes in the Peloponnese soon raised in an acute form the question of who was to fill the power vacuum left by the retreating Turks. There was no shortage of candidates and questions of internal politics began to loom large at a remarkably early stage as the various elements among the Greek insurgents sought to secure an ascendancy in the newly liberated areas Within a matter of months three governmental bodies had come into existence in the liberated or partially liberated areas. The most important of these exercised a loose authority in the Peloponnese and, dominated as it was by the primates, essentially represented a continuation of the Peloponnesian senate of the pre-independence period. But the primates could no longer take for granted their traditional ascendancy. This was strikingly illustrated when in July 1821 at Vervaina a large gathering of 'simple and unknown men of the people' threatened to kill a group of primates and were only dissuaded by Kolokotronis, who, as a former klephtic leader, enjoyed their confidence. Rivalry between the primates and the *kapetanioi* was to be a persistent theme of the complex internal politics of the insurgents, whose intrigues and rivalries at times almost defy analysis. In the newly liberated areas of western mainland Greece power was nominally exercised by a senate headed by the Phanariot Alexander Mavrokordatos, while another Phanariot, Theodore Negris, nominally controlled an assembly known as the *Areios Pagos*, which theoretically exercised power in eastern mainland Greece. In both assemblies, however, it was the *kapetanioi* who exercised real power and the Phanariots, despite their greater political experience and knowledge of the ways of the world were, like the Peloponnesian primates, forced to acknowledge that the military contribution of the *kapetanioi* to the war effort inescapably carried with it political power.

All three regional assemblies were, in theory at least, conscious that circumstances demanded the creation of a centralised political authority. Accordingly, in December 1821, thanks to the initiative of Dimitrios Ypsilantis, a national assembly was convened at Argos, subsequently moving to Piada, near the ancient Epidauras. On the instructions of the assembly a provisional constitution was drafted by Mavrokordatos and Negris, with the assistance of the Italian philhellene Vincenzo Gallina. This document, like Rigas' constitution of 1797, reflected the influence of the French constitutions of 1793 and 1795 and its highly democratic forms, with guarantees of freedom of religion, and of the press, were undoubtedly calculated to appeal to enlightened opinion in Europe. The preamble declared that the Greek nation, 'under the monstrous Ottoman dynasty, unable to bear the crushing and unexampled yoke of tyranny' proclaimed before God and man 'its political existence and independence'. Legislative and executive powers were not separated, for each branch of government was entitled to revise the actions or enactments of the other. But whatever high-sounding principles the constitution may have proclaimed on paper, Greece was no nearer to having a central government authority, for the three existing assemblies were left intact and the Peloponnesian senate, dominated as it was by the primates, was determined to exercise its prerogatives in the only area in which the new government might have hoped to exercise its supposed authority, namely the Peloponnese. It was not until the second national assembly was convened at Astros in March 1823 that these regional bodies were suppressed, but this did not lead to any diminution of the internal antagonisms and tensions that characterised the Greek side. Indeed during much of 1823 and 1824 factional strife verged on civil war.

The main purpose of the assembly at Astros was to revise the constitution of 1822 which had proved unsatisfactory in a number of respects. The most significant changes were to transform the executive's absolute veto over enactments of the legislature into a suspensive one and, in an effort to curb the power of the former klephtic leader Theodore Kolokotronis, to substitute a three-man committee, representing regional interests, in place of a single minister of war. Kolokotronis, however, managed to manoeuvre himself into the position of vice-president of the executive, of which Mavrokordatos was secretary-general and Petros Bey Mavromichalis president. Kolokotronis showed scant respect for his colleagues on the executive and forcibly removed them to Nafplion, whereupon Petros Bey Mavromichalis aligned himself with Kolokotronis, thus bringing about a temporary alliance between the Peloponnesian primates and the military interest represented by Koloktronis and the *kapetanioi*. After Kolokotronis had tried to pressure the legislature, many of its members fled to Kranidi on the mainland, just opposite the island of Spetses, where they could enjoy the protection of the Spetsiot and Hydriot fleets. In recognition of the dependence of the Kranidi assembly on the islanders, George Koundouriotis, a prominent Hydriot of Albanian descent, was appointed president of a rival executive. There thus came into existence in 1823 two rival governments, each claiming to be the legitimate representative of the insurgent Greeks. It was not long before open warfare had broken out between the rival authorities. Not until October 1824 was the Koundouriotis government able to establish its authority in the Peloponnese, thanks to the influence exercised over the chieftains of mainland Greece by John Kolettis, a Vlach doctor who had gained his political experience in the intrigue-ridden court of Ali Pasha. Kolokotronis, who at one stage was in danger of being executed, was imprisoned, although his indispensable military prowess was to ensure that the imprisonment was of short duration.

Thus the political situation in liberated Greece during 1823 and 1824 was one of bewildering complexity. Some historians have sought to explain this propensity to internecine strife in class terms, but these bitter antagonisms owed more to sectional and regional than to class differences. The fundamental divide was between the 'military' or 'democratic' party, as represented by such figures as Kolokotronis and Odysseus Androutsos, and the 'civilian' or 'aristocratic' party, centring on the Peloponnesian primates, the notables of the 'Nautical Islands' and the Phanariot politicians such as Mavrokordatos, Ypsilantis and Negris. This cleavage was by no means absolute. The Peloponnesian primates, for instance, formed tactical alliances sometimes with, sometimes against, the military chieftains. Moreover the 'military' party represented popular aspirations more by default than by conscious design. The overriding concern of the military chieftains was to enhance their own personal power and prestige and avail themselves of the opportunities open to them for plunder. Moreover, matters were further complicated by regional antagonisms. Then, as now, local patriotism was very strongly developed among the Greeks, the concept of *patrida* relating more to birthplace than to motherland. Antagonisms existed between Rumeliots, Peloponnesians and islanders, between individual islands, even between neighbouring villages. These sectional antagonisms were further aggravated by tensions between those from the heartland of the revolt, namely the Peloponnese and western and eastern mainland Greece, and those who had migrated to the areas under the control of the insurgents from the very substantial areas of Greek population that remained under Ottoman rule, either following the suppression of sympathetic revolts, or to volunteer in the insurgent cause, or to escape from Ottoman reprisals. These antagonisms were to remain even after the final achievement of independence, when these refugee groups were to experience considerable difficulties in gaining the acceptance of the indigenous inhabitants.

These inter-regional loyalties and rivalries inhibited attempts to develop a wider loyalty to the cause of insurgent Greece, to the idea of *patrida* as the Greek motherland. But slowly, as the war progressed, a more encompassing nationalism did develop, a trend that was indeed, somewhat paradoxically, strengthened by the factional fighting over the control of the central government. Moreover the ideological character of these internal differences became increasingly apparent. For the conflict between the 'military' and 'civilian' parties reflected differences both as to how the war was to be prosecuted and over the kind of governmental institutions which would be appropriate to liberated Greece. The 'military' party thought in terms of the traditional guerrilla warfare of the klephts, the 'civilian' in terms of a regular army organised on the European model, fighting pitched battles. The 'military' thought in terms of a religious war against the Turks, the 'civilian' in terms of a conscious nationalism. The 'military' party essentially sought to substitute its own oligarchical rule for that of the Turks, retaining the Church as one of the ruling institutions of Greek society. The 'civilian' party, on the other hand, wanted to Westernise traditional Greek society, to subordinate the Church to the state, to impose on Greece all the trappings of liberal constitutionalism. This fundamental divide was also reflected in life style and dress, the Westernisers dressing in the Western fashion, *alafranga*, the traditionalists in the *foustanella* or kilt.*

The distinction between these two main groupings should not be drawn too rigidly. The position of the Peloponnesian primates, for instance, was ambiguous. They constituted one of the traditional élites of Greek society, yet the more far-sighted of them saw in the secular institutions so beloved of the Westernisers an opportunity to retain, and even to strengthen, their existing influence in Greek society. The Westernisers were very much in a minority. Yet their superior education and political experience, their control over the executive through which the loans raised in London in 1824 and 1825 were disbursed, and the general recognition of the need to develop Western-type institutions if the support of European public opinion was to be maintained and the hostility of European governments diminished, enabled them to impose their concept of an appropriate polity for the Greek state on the majority. It was this grafting of the forms, but not the substance, of Western constitutional government onto an essentially traditional society, with a very different value system from that prevailing in the West, that was to create within Greece a fundamental political tension that has continued for much of its post-independence history.

While the Greeks indulged in the luxury of allowing their

* For an illuminating discussion of these basic tensions in Greek society, see John A. Petropulos, *Politics and Statecraft in the Kingdom of Greece 1833–1843* (Princeton 1968) 19 ff.

internal antagonisms to degenerate into civil war, the military climate, after the successes of the early years, was turning markedly against them. Some, despairing of the success of the Greek cause, defected to the enemy and actually fought alongside Ottoman troops. Others, in the tradition of klephtic warfare, made temporary truces, or *kapakia*. The situation took a serious turn for the worse when Sultan Mahmud II, a tough and energetic ruler, managed to secure the assistance of Mehmet Ali, the pasha of Egypt and a man who treated the nominal suzerainty of the Sultan lightly. The price of Mehmet Ali's co-operation was high, the pashalik of Crete for himself and that of the Peloponnese for his son, Ibrahim. After suppressing in 1824 the last vestiges of resistance in Crete, Ibrahim early in 1825 landed his well-trained and equipped army at Modon, one of five strongpoints in the Peloponnese that remained in Turkish hands. Once this bridgehead had been secured Ibrahim engaged in a 'scorched earth' campaign which dramatically altered the balance of force in the Peloponnese in favour of the Turks. Even Kolokotronis, newly released from prison, was unable to stem the tide of Ibrahim's advance. Their parlous military situation forced the Greeks increasingly to look to the Powers for their salvation.

As the Greek insurgents had, against all the odds, managed to maintain their struggle against the Ottoman Empire the attitude of the Powers had undergone a significant change. From an attitude of strict non-intervention and openly expressed disapproval they gradually, if hesitantly, moved towards an interventionist position. The lucrative Russian Black Sea grain trade and British and French commercial interests in the Levant had suffered considerably on account of the hostilities, while the governments of Britain, Russia and France suspected each other of seeking to exploit the crisis to further their own concerns in the region. The first significant breakthrough from the Greek point of view was the decision of the British foreign secretary, George Canning, to recognise the Greeks as belligerents in 1823. By this he accepted the Greek right to search neutral ships for war supplies, an important concession, justified on the ground that it was impossible to treat 'as pirates a population of a million souls'.

A year later the Russians put forward a proposal for the creation of three semi-autonomous principalities, similar in status to the Danubian principalities, which would continue to recognise the suzerainty of the Ottoman sultan. This proposal, however, was to prove unacceptable to both the Greeks and the Turks. Although he had moved towards a *de facto* recognition of the insurgents Canning rejected the Act of Submission of June 1825, a petition which sought to place insurgent Greece under the sole protection of Great Britain. This petition was drawn up by the 'English' party, which consisted of those Greeks who, encouraged by a group of British philhellenes, among them the eccentric Earl of Guilford, placed their hopes in British intervention. They believed that Britain's naval power in the Mediterranean made her the obvious external patron of Greece. Equally 'French' and 'Russian' parties came into existence, whose protagonists looked to France and Russia respectively for salvation, although at this juncture of the war it was the 'English' party that was predominant. The proponents of this dramatic appeal were well aware that in levelling it exclusively at Britain, they would inevitably arouse the jealousies of the other Powers with interests in the region.

Despite Canning's rejection of the Act of Submission he was nonetheless moving towards direct involvement in the hostilities. Mindful as always of the danger of a new Russo-Turkish conflict, which might lead to a further extension of Russian influence in the region, and suspicious of Austrian and French intentions, Canning resolved to frame a policy in co-operation with the Russians, designed to bring about some kind of mediation in the war. The Duke of Wellington was accordingly despatched on a special mission to Russia which resulted in the Protocol of St Petersburg of April 1826. The three autonomous principalities under Ottoman suzerainty proposed by Russia in 1824 were reduced to one, whose future boundaries were left vague. Britain and Russia agreed to offer mediation in the struggle, a move in which the French, Austrians and Prussians were to be invited to participate. Only France, however, joined Britain and Russia in signing the resulting Treaty of London of July 1827. This envisaged, as had the Protocol of St Petersburg, the creation of an autonomous, though not sovereign, Greek state, but now the three Powers undertook to impose mediation on the belligerents. The allied fleets in the Mediterranean were instructed to secure an armistice but without engaging in hostilities, an ambivalent policy aptly described by Canning as one of 'peaceful interference'.

While these protracted negotiations were taking place on the international scene the military situation in Greece had continued to deteriorate. In April 1826 an attempt by the inhabitants of Mesolonghi to lift Ibrahim Pasha's siege had resulted in a massacre, and in August of the same year Athens fell to the Egyptian army, although the Acropolis remained in Greek hands. The seriousness of the military situation did not prevent the formation of an assembly at Kastri to rival the third national assembly that had convened at Epidaurus in April 1826. But thanks to the intervention of General Sir Richard Church and of Admiral Lord Cochrane the two assemblies agreed to unite at the site of the ancient Troezene in April 1827. The Greeks had accepted the principle of foreign mediation, and the Troezene assembly, appreciating that his diplomatic skills and experience would be of paramount importance as the Greek question entered the plane of Great Power diplomacy, elected Capodistrias as *kyvernitis*, or president, of Greece for a seven-year term. Pending his arrival in Greece, power was to be exercised by a small governmental committee. Another strong point in Capodistrias' favour was that he had been careful not to become implicated in the factional intrigues of the insurgent Greeks.

Although Capodistrias' diplomatic expertise was widely acknowledged, many Greeks harboured suspicions of a man whose political experience had been gained in the school of Russian autocracy. For this reason the Troezene assembly framed in May 1827 yet another constitution, the third since the outbreak of hostilities. Like its predecessors this was a remarkably liberal document. Sovereignty was declared to inhere in the nation, from which all power derived. In a move to restrict Capodistrias' powers a clear distinction was made between the functions of the executive, legislature and judiciary. The assembly also appointed Church and Cochrane as supreme commanders of Greece's land

and naval forces respectively, but they were able to make little headway against Ibrahim's Egyptian troops. Indeed in June 1827, the Turks managed to recapture the Acropolis of Athens

But the signing of the Treaty of London in July 1827 was to result in a rapid and dramatic change in the fortunes of the Greeks. They had quickly agreed to mediation by the Powers but the Porte had refused and continued to reinforce Ibrahim's troops in the Peloponnese. When the large Ottoman fleet anchored at Navarino bay refused to renounce hostilities, the commander of the combined British, Russian and French fleet, Admiral Codrington, encouraged by Stratford Canning, the British ambassador in Constantinople, to interpret his instructions broadly, effectively destroyed it as a fighting force on 20 October 1827, in the last great battle of the age of sail. This 'untoward event', as the British prime minister, the Duke of Wellington, termed the battle of Navarino, effectively ensured that some form of at least qualified independence would be granted to the Greeks. The Porte, however, showed no greater inclination to yield and in April 1828 Russia declared war on the Ottoman Empire, having, along with Britain and France, withdrawn its ambassador from Constantinople in December 1827.

Meanwhile Capodistrias, encouraged by the news of the battle of Navarino, had arrived in Greece in January of 1828. Within a few days of his arrival he made it clear that he had no intention of being bound by the liberal constitution of Troezene. He began by abolishing the third national assembly and replacing it by a twenty-seven-member *Panhellenion*, which was directly under his control. The *Panhellenion* was in turn replaced, in July 1829, by a senate, a move ratified by the fourth national assembly which convened at Argos. These moves reflected Capodistrias' undoubtedly authoritarian outlook. He was genuinely convinced that Greece, still on a war footing, with its economy shattered, with its frontiers not yet determined and with the chronic disposition of its political and military leadership to factionalism, could ill afford the luxury of political democracy.

Capodistrias from the beginning realised that the deliberations of the Powers as to the future boundaries of Greece would be much influenced by the size of the regions actually under the physical control of the insurgents. Forces under the command of General Church and Dimitrios Ypsilantis extended the area under Greek control in western and eastern mainland Greece respectively. These moves were to have a considerable influence on the deliberations of the conference of the ambassadors of Britain, France and Russia to the Porte that had been summoned on the island of Poros to consider the recommendations on the Greek question made by the Conference of London. This conference, consisting of the British foreign secretary and the ambassadors of Russia and France, met on numerous occasions between 1827 and 1832. In 1828 it asked the ambassadors meeting at Poros to consider various proposals for the frontiers of Greece and authorised the despatch of a French expeditionary force to the Peloponnese to oversee the withdrawal of Ibrahim Pasha's troops. The ambassadors recommended a boundary, extending from Arta in the west to Volos in the east, that was considerably more favourable to Greece than the various possibilities mooted by the London Conference. The conference would only agree, however, in a protocol of March 1829, to making the Arta-Volos frontier 'a basis for negotiation' with the Porte and rejected outright the ambassadors' recommendation that the islands of Crete and Samos be included within the boundaries of the new state. The acceptance of the March 1829 protocol was one of the provisions of the Treaty of Adrianople of September 1829 which brought to an end the Russo-Turkish war, during which the Ottoman armies had suffered serious setbacks. The treaty also confirmed Russia's territorial gains in Asia and recognised her growing influence in the Danubian principalities.

Besides the problem of frontiers there was also the question of the future ruler of Greece. For Wellington, fearing after the Treaty of Adrianople that a tributary Greek state might, like the Danubian principalities, fall increasingly under Russian influence, was increasingly inclined to favour the idea of a fully sovereign Greece. The Powers being agreed that the new state should be a monarchy, the Conference of London began to search for a prospective prince among the royal houses of Europe not directly connected with those of Britain, Russia or France. In February

1830 the crown of a Greece with frontiers considerably smaller than the Arta-Volos line was offered to Prince Leopold of Saxe-Coburg. But in May, discouraged by the gloomy picture painted by Capodistrias of his new kingdom and by his failure to secure an extension of its frontiers, Leopold withdrew, and the search was renewed.

Although Capodistrias had been fully occupied with matters of foreign affairs he had also valiantly struggled to bring order to the chaotic affairs of the embryonic Greek state, where his central-ising methods were not well received by a people that had been accustomed under Ottoman rule to a considerable degree of local autonomy. He sought to create a national army, the rudiments of an administrative bureaucracy and of an educational system, to improve transport and communications, to encourage the revival of an economy that had been shattered by years of intermittent fighting, to establish a currency and the basis of a banking system and, above all, to deal with the question of the 'national lands', perhaps the most explosive issue confronting him on the domestic front. The national lands comprised the lands vacated by the Turks who had been major landholders before the outbreak of the revolt. From the beginning of the struggle they had been declared to be part of the Greek national domain, their acquisition being justified by right of conquest. Some of the national lands had been pledged as security for the loans of 1824 and 1825, others had been promised to the many refugees who had flooded into the liberated areas from regions such as Crete, Chios and Macedonia where the revolt had failed. But when Capodistrias, who was a firm believer in a landowning peasantry as the basic foundation of a stable society, sought to distribute them among the great masses of landless peasants, he found that large tracts of these supposedly national lands had been arbitrarily appropriated, often by powerful military leaders and primates. His ideal of a large-scale land dis-tribution was thus frustrated.

Like a number of subsequent would-be reformers of Greek society, Capodistrias combined a paternalistic and authoritarian style of government with a basic contempt for the élites of Greek society. The philhellene George Finlay noted that he referred to the primates as 'Christian Turks', the military chiefs as 'robbers', the men of letters as 'fools' and the Phanariots as 'Children of Satan'. With such attitudes it is not surprising that he managed to alienate a sizeable proportion of his subjects, and in particular almost all of those who were articulate and politically active. Primates, island magnates and Phanariot politicians, who felt excluded from power under the Capodistrian system of government, former *kapetanioi*, who felt that their contribution to the war effort had been insufficiently recognised, Westernising intellectuals, who genuinely believed that the war had been fought to establish constitutional democracy and freedom of the press and were appalled by Capodistrias' ill-disguised distaste for such notions, and disgruntled philhellenes, all combined in their opposition to Capodistrias' authoritarian ways. How the mass of his new subjects viewed their president is difficult to say, but they undoubtedly regarded him more favourably than those who believed that they were entitled as of right to a prominent role in the government of the new state. Characteristically, Capodistrias' demise was not brought about by the opposition of the 'constitutionalists' but as a result of a feud with the powerful Mavromichalis clan of the Mani, some of whose members Capodistrias had had the temerity to imprison. He was assassinated by George and Constantine Mavromichalis as he was entering a church in Nafplion on 9 October 1831.

With Capodistrias' death Greece once more relapsed into anarchy, with power nominally being exercised by a three man committee composed of Kolokotronis, one of the few veterans of the war who had not fallen out with Capodistrias, Kolettis and Capodistrias' brother, Agostino. Within a few months the agile Kolettis had ousted Agostino Capodistrias in a renewed civil war. As the various factions in Greece once more resorted to internecine strife, the Powers made a number of ineffectual efforts to restore order. But they were able to resolve the issue of the monarchy by concluding the Convention of May 1832 between Britain, Russia, France and Bavaria. This confirmed the offer of the 'hereditary sovereignty' of Greece to Prince Frederick Otto of Wittelsbach, the seventeen-year-old second son of King Ludwig of Bavaria.

The new 'monarchical and independent state' was placed under the guarantee of Britain, Russia and France, who also agreed to guarantee a loan of 60,000,000 francs, payable in instalments, to the new king. Greece was to pay an indemnity to the Porte and its definitive frontiers were to be settled by negotiations already commenced between the guarantor Powers and the Porte, negotiations in which the Greeks had no part. Until Otto came of age Greece was to be ruled by a regency council of three Bavarians, who were also to be accompanied by a Bavarian army of 3,500 troops. After eleven years in which the bitter struggle against the Turks had frequently been accompanied by internecine strife the Greeks had at last achieved, against all the odds, formal independence. In reality, however, as events were to demonstrate, the hard-won independence of the Greeks was to be qualified in a number of important respects.

4

Independence, nation building and irredentism, 1833-1913

When the young King Otto arrived on board a British ship at the provisional capital of Nafplion early in February 1833 he was greeted with a rapturous welcome by his new subjects. His inheritance, however, was not a promising one. More than ten years of intermittent struggle against the external enemy coupled with recurrent civil strife had shattered the country, dislocating an economy that for centuries had been weakened by limited markets, poor communications and the migration of the population from the fertile but disease-ridden plains to the mountains. The attempts by the wartime governments and by Capodistrias to create the rudiments of a state structure and to inspire a sense of corporate loyalty to the Greek state, overriding sectional and individual interests, had met with little success. The country was overrun with armed irregular troops, many of them resentful that their efforts during the war had been insufficiently rewarded, and many of them tempted once again to resort to their traditional livelihood of banditry. Moreover, none of the great centres of Greek commerce in the Ottoman Empire, Smyrna, Salonica, Alexandria and Constantinople, was contained within the boundaries of the new state, a fact that goes far to explain the seemingly paradoxical phenomenon of the migration of Greeks from the kingdom to the Ottoman Empire from the earliest years of its independent existence. Most significant of all, the new state embraced within its frontiers only some three quarters of a million of the more than two million Greeks under Ottoman rule, or under British protection in the Ionian Islands. Inevitably the fact that so many Greeks still remained under alien rule was to have the most profound influence on the policies, both domestic and foreign, of the independent state.

The three-man regency council, consisting of Count Joseph von Armansperg, Professor Georg von Maurer and General Karl Heideck (the only member with any previous experience of the realities of Greece), lost no time in seeking to cast the institutional structures of the new state in a conservative European mould, in the process riding roughshod over the traditional forms of communal government that had developed under the Ottomans. In a move that symbolised the extent to which the cultural orientation of the new state was to be influenced, and indeed distorted, by the burden of Greece's classical past, the capital was moved from Nafplion to Athens. The country's administrative structure was defined, following precedents established by Capodistrias. Greece was divided into ten *nomarchies*, or provinces. These were divided into *eparchies*, which in turn were subdivided into *demes*. Nomarchs and eparchs were designated by the crown and a deliberate effort was made to appoint administrators to areas where they had no ties and thus break the grip on local power exercised by provincial primates and military leaders. Rural disorder occasioned by bands of irregular troops and out-and-out bandits was a particular problem in the early years of Otto's reign. Efforts to enlist some of these irregulars into a new regular army, which was dominated by Bavarians, met with little success.

The landlessness of the overwhelming majority of the peasantry was a further cause of rural discontent. In an attempt to alleviate this source of instability, provision was made for peasants to buy smallholdings from the national lands. Yet these efforts were largely negated by a harsh and inequitable system of tax collection, which resulted in the peasants' burdens being little, if at all, easier than they had been under the Turks. Criminal and civil law codes, which were based on the European inheritance of Roman law (one of the regents, Maurer, had been a professor of law at Heidelberg) and which took little account of the well-rooted tradition of customary law, were introduced in 1833 and 1834. The educational system of the new state was based on French and German models and, to remedy the dire shortage of teachers, a training college was established at Nafplion in 1834. In 1837 a university, housed in a handsome neo-classical building designed by the Danish architect Christian Hansen, was established in Athens. This prompted the prophetic aside of Kolokotronis that one day the university would gobble up the nearby royal palace. In the course of the century the university and other educational establishments were richly endowed, often by expatriate Greeks. In keeping with the whole cultural orientation of the new state great emphasis was placed both in the schools and in the universities on the study of the classics of ancient Greek literature and in inculcating a knowledge of the *katharevousa*, or 'purified' form of the language, an artificial construct far removed from the demotic Greek of everyday speech.

European influences also underlay the Church settlement which was enacted in July 1833. It was held to be unbefitting the dignity of the newly sovereign state that the Church should remain under the jurisdiction of the ecumenical patriarch, himself highly susceptible to the pressures of a sultan with whom Greece had recently been engaged in bitter conflict. The Greek Church was declared to be independent, or autocephalous, and the Catholic Otto, to the scandal of many of his subjects, was declared to be head of the Church. Authority in matters of administration and discipline, but not doctrine, was vested in a synod of five bishops, whose enactments were subject to approval by a government commissioner. At the same time 412 out of a total of 593 monasteries in the country were suppressed and their properties forfeited to the crown. From the beginning the Church was firmly subordinated to the state, a situation much resented by conservative-minded Greeks, particularly those of the 'Russian' party, who looked to Russia as their principal external patron. Relations with the ecumenical patriarchate were not formally restored until 1850, when Constantinople was obliged to recognise the essentials of the 1833 settlement.

Count Armansperg soon emerged as the dominant force in the regency council, securing in 1834 the recall of Maurer and of Karl Abel, its secretary. By a clever manipulation of the powers of patronage inherent in his office and of the rivalries of the representatives of the Protecting Powers, Armansperg managed to retain his influence for some time after the formal termination of the regency in 1835. The representatives of the Protecting Powers had become the natural foci of the various political groupings that had emerged during the course of the war and had crystallised in the early years of Otto's reign. Mavrokordatos, the leader of the 'English' party, favoured constitutional rule, although Otto showed no enthusiasm for granting his subjects the constitution that had been envisaged in the settlement of 1832. Kolettis, the leader of the 'French' party, also broadly favoured constitutional government and was identified with an irredentist foreign policy. The rallying cry of the 'Russian' party (a prominent member of which was Kolokotronis), on the other hand, was Orthodoxy not liberalism. These political groupings were essentially fluid in character and for a time Armansperg was able to thwart their intrigues by the judicious distribution of office to members of all parties. Office holding constituted a considerable bait in a society in which opportunities for profit or advancement outside the government service were few. A number of important politicians, among them Mavrokordatos and Kolettis, were temporarily neutralised by being given posts in the diplomatic service outside Greece.

Inevitably, however, Armansperg's manipulations aroused hostility and in 1837 Otto was prevailed upon to replace him. His Bavarian successor, Ignaz von Rudhart, was a nondescript figure, and within a few months Otto had himself assumed the presidency of the ministerial council. Otto, however, despite the urgings of the influential British minister, Sir Edmund Lyons, still showed no greater inclination to grant a constitution, much to the chagrin of the constitutionalists. At the same time he managed to alienate the Napists, members of the 'Russian' party, who were behind the obscure 'Philorthodox' conspiracy which came to light in 1839. This appears to have aimed at the abduction of the Catholic Otto, whereupon he would have been offered the alternative of embracing Orthodoxy or abdication. In February 1841, hoping to reduce diplomatic pressure in the aftermath of his first major crisis with the Ottoman Porte, and in dire need of financial support, Otto went some way to appease Lyons and his domestic critics by recalling Mavrokordatos, the leader of the 'English' party, from London to become minister of foreign affairs and alternate president of the council. But Mavrokordatos' cautious attempts to devolve more power onto existing government institutions managed to alienate Otto without satisfying the constitutionalists and, after holding office for only six weeks, he was replaced by the pro-French Dimitrios Christidis.

These moves did little to still the mounting wave of criticism directed at Otto by all the various factions in Greece. Constitutionalists were frustrated by his failure to concede a constitution, Orthodox zealots by the Church settlement and by the fact that he remained a Catholic, while his lack of children created doubts over the succession. Almost all Greeks were alienated by the continuing presence of Bavarians in influential positions. Although the last Bavarian troops had left Greece in 1838 the minister of war, for instance, remained a Bavarian. There was resentment, too, of the 'heterochthons'. These were the Greeks who had migrated to the kingdom only after the end of hostilities and by virtue of their often superior education had acquired a disproportionate number of lucrative offices This particularly aroused the wrath of the war veterans who felt cheated of the due reward for their efforts. One such, Yannis Makriyannis, contemptuously dismissed these latecomers as 'the scum of Constantinople and of Europe', who enjoyed large ministerial salaries while widows and orphans of the heroes of 1821 were reduced to begging for bread. All Greeks, too, were affected by the chaotic state of the country's finances and the consequent burden of taxation. Virtually the whole of the loan guaranteed on Otto's accession by the Protecting Powers was absorbed by repayments of interest and capital and by expenditure on the army and administration. The measures of retrenchment forced on Otto in the 1840s by the Powers in an attempt to restore financial order and secure repayment of the loan created unrest among office holders and in the army, while throughout this period there was a distinct possibility of the imposition of outright financial control by the Powers.

These various strands of discontent coalesced into a widely based conspiracy against Otto. The lead was taken by a number of politicians who enlisted the help of some high-ranking army officers in Athens. The uprising was originally planned for 25 March 1844, the traditional anniversary of the outbreak of the War of Independence. Because of fears that Otto had got wind of the plot it was advanced to 3 September 1843, when troops of the Athens garrison and large crowds demonstrated before the palace demanding that Otto concede a constitution. For the first, but by no means last, time in Greece's independent history the army was prompted to involve itself directly in the Greek political arena. Following this confrontation Otto agreed to appoint a provisional government and to convene a national assembly to frame the long-sought constitution, the actual drafting of which was entrusted to a twenty-one-man committee.

As both the king and the national assembly looked upon the new constitution as a 'compact' between king and people and as the more radical elements were unable to articulate their demands, it is not surprising that the document that emerged from the assembly's deliberations was scarcely liberal in its provisions. Promulgated in March 1844, the new constitution provided for a two-chamber assembly, with the lower house (*vouli*) being elected on a wide franchise and the senate (*gerousia*), with a minimum of twenty-seven senators, being appointed for life by the king. Legislative power was vested concurrently in the king, the lower house and the senate. Only the king, however, was authorised to appoint or dismiss ministers and to dissolve parliament. Justice was also declared to originate with the king, who appointed judges. But taxes had to be voted by parliament and it was decreed that the successor to the throne must be of the Orthodox religion. Having grudgingly been forced to concede a constitution, King Otto soon made it clear that he was determined to exploit it to further his own authoritarian inclinations. After Mavrokordatos had exercised power for a few months in the summer of 1844, Otto's chosen instrument for this purpose was Kolettis. Until his death in 1847, Kolettis, by a judicious admixture of persuasion, patronage and, where necessary, brute force, demonstrated that the existence of a parliament need afford no serious obstacle to the exercise of the royal prerogative. The appointed senators, paradoxically, proved more of a hindrance to Otto than the elected deputies. Otto's blatant chicanery made him unpopular with the constitutionalists and their English patrons but for a time he was able to whip up popular support by his enthusiastic espousal of the cause of Greek irredentism.

Otto became one of the most ardent champions of the *Megali Idea*, or Great Idea, the vision of the redemption of the 'unredeemed' Greeks of the Ottoman Empire by bringing them within the confines of a single Greek state. One of the most cogent expositions of what he termed 'this Great Idea' was contained in a speech of 1844 made before the constituent assembly by Kolettis, one of its most militant advocates:

The Kingdom of Greece is not Greece. [Greece] constitutes only one part, the smallest and poorest. A Greek is not only a man who lives within this kingdom but also one who lives in Jannina, in Salonica, in Serres, in Adrianople, in Constantinople, in Smyrna, in Trebizond, in Crete, in Samos and in any land associated with Greek history or the Greek race. . . There are two main centres of Hellenism: Athens, the capital of the Greek kingdom, [and] 'The City' [Constantinople], the dream and hope of all Greeks.

Almost all Greeks subscribed to this vision, the only argument being as to how it might best be implemented. In the kingdom itself there were two basic schools of thought. The militant proponents of the Great Idea would have agreed that the Kingdom of Greece was poor, backward and essentially non-viable. But Greece's admitted inadequacies were, they argued, due precisely to the fact that the most wealthy and productive regions of the Greek world lay outside the narrow bounds of the kingdom. If only the cherished ideal of a 'Greater Greece' could be implemented, then Greece's manifest weaknesses would be remedied at a stroke. Until the Greek people had been united there could be no real hope of progress and the struggle for their unification should take priority over all else. The more cautious advocates of the Great Idea, on the other hand, argued that it was unwise to underestimate the residual strength of the Ottoman Empire, the 'sick man of Europe', as the Tsar Nicholas I once called it. To pursue an adventurist foreign policy, before the existing Greek state had been consolidated in terms of its economic and military resources, could only lead to disaster. Moreover, unless the Greek Kingdom possessed the military capability to match its grandiose irredentist ambitions, then the Ottoman Greeks would inevitably be subject to reprisals. In any case, they argued, Britain, the strongest naval power in the Mediterranean, was always likely to intervene to preserve the existing *status quo*, regarding the Ottoman Empire as a bulwark against Russian expansionism.

How did the large Greek populations still under Ottoman rule regard these irredentist aspirations? Many of them, and in particular the Turkish-speaking Greeks of Anatolia, had little consciousness of being Greek. Strenuous efforts, which met with little hindrance from the Ottoman authorities, were made in the course of the nineteenth century to 're-hellenise' them. This campaign was conducted through the agency of school teachers, many of them Ottoman Greeks, trained at the very fount of Hellenism, the University of Athens, and also by means of cultural and educational societies known as *syllogoi*. These apostles of Hellenism experienced varying degrees of success and were hampered in their efforts by their insistence on teaching the archaising *katharevousa*, then the intellectual fashion in the kingdom, rather than the spoken language. These efforts, often underwritten by the government of the kingdom, proved incapable of stemming the transition from the use of Greek to Turkish that occurred in a number of Orthodox communities of central Anatolia during the course of the nineteenth century. On the other hand, many Ottoman Greeks, particularly those in the large and prosperous communities of the coastal cities of the empire, with their excellent and richly endowed schools, were fully conscious of their Greek heritage. How did they look upon the irredentist fervour of the kingdom? Again two basic currents of thought can be detected. On the one hand there were those, mainly teachers, doctors and lawyers, who fully shared in the irredentist aspirations of the kingdom, and placed their hopes in the early fulfilment of the Great Idea. On the other, there were those who argued that the hostile policies of the kingdom towards the Ottoman Empire were wholly misguided.

Rather, they believed, the Ottoman Greeks should work towards a gradual and peaceable hellenisation of the Ottoman Empire from within.

These latter pointed to the remarkable fashion in which the Ottoman Greeks, after the setbacks of the 1820s, had by the second half of the nineteenth century largely regained the economic, and to a somewhat lesser degree, the political influence in the affairs of the Ottoman Empire that they had enjoyed before 1821. Greeks were among the principal beneficiaries of the Tanzimat reforms, and in particular the great Ottoman reforming decrees, the Hatt-i Sherif of Gülhane of 1839 and the Hatt-i Hümayun of 1856, which established an unevenly enforced equality of rights between Muslim and non-Muslim. Greeks were well represented in banking (Sultan Abdul Hamid's banker Zarifis was one of them), shipping, railways, manufacturing, commerce and the free professions (Spyridon Mavroyenis was Sultan Abdul Aziz's doctor) while Greek traders and shopkeepers were to be found throughout the empire. Indeed Greeks of the kingdom were anxious to partake of the economic opportunities afforded by the vast markets of the Ottoman Empire. In the 1850s, for instance, there were more citizens of the kingdom in Smyrna than in Piraeus, the port of Athens, while in the 1890s there were well over thirty thousand Greek nationals in Constantinople alone. Greeks also figured prominently in the Ottoman bureaucracy and, in particular, the diplomatic service. The first Ottoman ambassador to the Greek Kingdom, Kostaki Mousouros Pasha, was a Greek, as was Alexander Karatheodory Pasha, for many years deputy foreign minister. Such men found no conflict between their ethnic identity and their acting as loyal servants of the Ottoman Porte. Another factor working in favour of the Ottoman Greeks was their unusual population growth in comparison with that of the Turks. Between 1830 and 1860, for instance, the Turkish population of Smyrna declined from an estimated 80,000 to 41,000, while the Greek rose from 20,000 to 75,000. The underlying tension between those Ottoman Greeks who supported a forward policy on the part of the kingdom, a vocal minority in the mid-nineteenth century, and those who believed that the irredentism of the kingdom could only do irreparable damage to the wider interests of Hellenism, was never to be resolved.

The nationalists of the kingdom, however, were determined to redeem their brethren under Ottoman rule, even if many of the latter were quite content with the existing *status quo*, and throughout the nineteenth century proponents of the Great Idea in the kingdom were quick to exploit the Ottoman Empire's external difficulties in pursuit of their irredentist aims. The first such opportunity arose during the Near Eastern crisis of 1839–41, when it briefly looked as though Mehmet Ali's Syrian victories might presage the collapse of the Ottoman Empire at a time when the prophecies of Agathangelos were widely held to vouchsafe the reunification in 1840 of the Ottoman Empire under a Greek prince. Agitation in Crete for *enosis*, or union with the kingdom, was accompanied by the infiltration of nationalist bands across the borders into Ottoman Thessaly in 1840–41. Anti-Turkish fervour in the kingdom prevented Otto from ratifying in 1840 a Greek-Turkish commercial treaty favourable to the Porte. Tension increased when the Porte, in retaliation, banned Greek ships from its harbours. But British troops put an end to Mehmet Ali's challenge and following British, Russian and Austrian remonstrations (France having manifested support for Mehmet Ali) the crisis was defused. Otto's chronic need for finance made him particularly responsive to such external pressures.

This first crisis was to set the pattern for the persistent Great Power intervention in Greek affairs that was to characterise the struggle to extend her frontiers. This intervention sometimes reached almost absurd proportions as in the Don Pacifico incident, the high-water mark of Palmerstonian gun-boat diplomacy. This arose when anti-Jewish riots in Athens at Easter 1847 had resulted in the plundering of the property of Don Pacifico, a Maltese Jew who was Portuguese vice-consul and a British subject. Palmerston, the British foreign secretary, demanded compensation, raising in addition a number of other minor bilateral issues. When this was not forthcoming, giving vent to his personal dislike of Otto, he ordered a blockade of Piraeus in January 1850. Following French mediation, this somewhat farcical incident ended with Greece agreeing to pay a meagre £8000 in compensation. Such a heavy-handed display of force served only to boost Otto's popularity and to give credence to his inclination towards Russia in the dispute that was brewing between France and Russia over their conflicting interests in the Levant. The Russians based their claim to exercise a right of protection over the Orthodox Christians of the Ottoman Empire on a wilful misinterpretation of the terms of the Treaty of Kutchuk Kaynardja of 1774. In furtherance of this claim in 1853 Russia occupied the Danubian principalities, thus provoking hostilities with the Porte. Britain and France, anxious to resist any challenge to the integrity of the Ottoman Empire, demanded that the Russians withdraw and, when this was refused, declared war on the Russians at the end of March 1854.

The outbreak of yet another Russo-Turkish war was interpreted by the Greeks as a literally heaven-sent opportunity for furthering their expansionist aims, although they were mistaken in their belief that Tsar Nicholas I supported their irredentist claims. Nonetheless, in Greece itself nationalist fever was running high. Greek guerilla bands, several thousand strong, and joined by enthusiastic students from the University of Athens, infiltrated across the rugged Greek-Turkish frontier and began to foment unrest in a wide area of Thessaly, Epirus and Macedonia. One band penetrated as far as Jannina. In reprisal Greek nationals were expelled from Constantinople and Smyrna. Britain and France, who had been joined by Austria and Piedmont in their defence of the Ottoman Empire against the Russians, feared that Greece might actually declare war against Turkey. The Porte broke off relations with Greece and early in 1854 Louis Napoleon notified Otto that an attack on the Ottoman Empire would be construed as an attack on France. Otto retorted that, as the sole Christian king in the East, he was confident that he could rely on divine support in the fulfilment of his mission. In reply British and French troops occupied Piraeus in May 1854 and Greece was obliged to adhere to a policy of 'strict and complete neutrality'. Otto was also obliged to appoint a new administration under Mavrokordatos who was thought to be responsive to British wishes. This Anglo-French occupation was particularly resented as it coincided with a severe outbreak of cholera in Athens and Piraeus. Although relations between Greece and the Porte were restored in May 1855, the Anglo-French occupation was to last until February 1857, when a commission was appointed to enquire into the administration of Greek finances, reporting two years later.

For as long as this blatant intervention lasted Otto was able to capitalise on the resentment which it naturally engendered. As the hostilities ended, however, and the occupation troops withdrew, all the old antagonisms between Otto and his subjects began to revive. Otto still had no children, and none of his brothers had converted to Orthodoxy, which the 1844 Constitution had made a condition of inheriting the throne. There was thus uncertainty as to the succession and it appears that Otto had deliberately shirked this issue, out of the understandable fear that any successor would most likely have become a focus for intrigue by opposition elements. Moreover, Otto had aroused widespread resentment by openly voicing support for Austria in its struggle with Garibaldi and the Italian nationalists. Inevitably, most Greeks, nurtured as they were on a diet of romantic nationalism, sided with the Garibaldians. His subjects, too, could hardly fail to notice that for all Otto's passionate espousal of the cause of Greek irredentism, he had so far notably failed to achieve any extension of Greece's borders. There was growing criticism, too, at his cynical manipulation of the 1844 Constitution. A new generation of Greeks, including the articulate but frequently under-employed graduates of the University of Athens, was coming to political maturity, a generation that had not fought in the War of Independence and was increasingly conscious of the large gap between constitutional theory and the arbitrary and corrupt practice of the Ottonian system of government. The blatant manipulation of the elections of 1859 added fuel to these criticisms.

In the early 1860s tension increased. In September 1861 there was an attempt on Queen Amalia's life and a visit by Otto to Karlsbad to discuss the succession question with his relatives still left the issue wide open. Otto managed to suppress a revolt by the Nafplion garrison in February 1862 but when he and Amalia left in October for a tour of the Peloponnese another uprising of the people and garrison erupted in Athens. His reign was declared to be at an end, a provisional government appointed and a constitutional convention summoned to frame a new constitution and elect a new ruler. Otto, on the advice of the ambassadors of the Protecting Powers, decided not to resist and left Greece, without formally abdicating, as he had arrived, on a British ship. He never returned to Greece and died, cherishing to the last his affection for his adopted country, seven years later in his native Bavaria. Otto's devotion to Greece was never in doubt but he had proved himself incapable of creating the basis of stable government. That this was so was not perhaps surprising given the difficulties inherent in trying to graft the forms of constitutional government onto a society whose values and historical experience were alien to such a concept.

Although the constitutional convention had taken upon itself the task of choosing a successor to Otto, the Protecting Powers soon made it clear that they intended to reserve this role to themselves. In Greece itself there was much enthusiasm for the candidacy of Prince Alfred, the second son of Queen Victoria, who, so it was believed, might bring in his train British support for Greece's territorial aspirations and, more specifically, the cession of the Ionian Islands. In a plebiscite held in December Alfred received 230,016 votes out of 241,202. But as a member of the British royal family, Alfred was not acceptable to the Protecting Powers and his mother objected as well. After much searching, for potential candidates were deterred by Otto's tribulations, the Powers' choice fell on Prince Christian William Ferdinand Adolphus George of Holstein-Sonderborg-Glücksburg, whose father subsequently became King of Denmark. His accession was confirmed by the Protecting Powers in the Treaty of London of July 1863. His title of George I King of the Hellenes was in deference to Ottoman objections to the original formulation 'King of the Greeks', which was held to imply sovereignty over the Ottoman Greeks. The Powers also arranged for George to receive, in addition to the normal civil list, a personal pension to be paid out of the repayments due on the 1833 loan. King George had many influential relatives and he was to keep these dynastic connections in good repair by his practice of spending a large part of each year travelling outside Greece. Although something of an absentee monarch he was able from time to time to put these family ties to good effect on behalf of his adopted country.

In a goodwill gesture towards the new monarch Britain, by a treaty of March 1864, ceded to Greece the Ionian Islands, which had been under her protection since 1815. Pressure for union of the islands with the kingdom had been building up, particularly since 1848, when the great revolutionary wave of that year which had swept Europe had had some echo in the islands. The concession in 1849 of a new and more liberal constitution served only to fuel enosist agitation. As the islands were deemed by the British, by that time, to be of little strategic significance (Malta and Gibraltar were more important as naval bases), there was little interest in maintaining the protectorate. Moreover, it was hoped that their cession would encourage George in his private undertaking to the British to exercise a moderating influence over Greece's irredentist demands. The principal legacies of fifty years of British rule were good roads, a rather eccentric form of cricket and a drink known locally as *tsitsibira* or ginger beer. The cession of the islands added approximately a quarter of a million new subjects to the kingdom, which by the early 1860s had a population of some 1,100,000. The Ionian Islands had generally enjoyed a higher cultural and educational level than the mainland and a number of politicians of Ionian origin were to rise to positions of prominence in the kingdom.

Once the Ionian delegates had been sworn in by the constitutional convention, discussion of a revised constitution began in earnest. The 1864 constitution, by which Greece became a 'crowned democracy', was a considerably more democratic document than that of 1844. All power was declared to derive from the people and the king's powers were limited to those explicitly granted by the constitution. These were, however, considerable and included the right to dissolve parliament, to appoint and dismiss ministers, to declare war and to contract treaties. The senate introduced in 1844 was abolished and legislative power was exercised in a single chamber, directly and secretly elected by male suffrage. All male Greeks aged over 21, who possessed some property or followed a trade or profession, were entitled to the vote. An oddity of the franchise, which was for its times highly democratic, was that serving officers were entitled to stand for parliament, a practice that did not make for good discipline in the armed forces.

The principle of popular sovereignty was firmly enshrined in the new constitution but the politics of the early years of George's reign scarcely differed from those of his predecessor. Political parties remained highly personal, coalescing around powerful personalities rather than platforms. A forebear who had fought in the War of Independence was still a useful boost to a political career. The perpetual pursuit of office, the possession of which was essential if a politician was to have any hope of meeting the insatiable demands of his voters cum clients, made the formation of stable and long-lasting governments well-nigh impossible. There were, for instance, four elections and nine administrations between 1870 and 1875. With each change of government almost all those in government employ were liable to dismissal, to be replaced by the clients of the incoming administration. The demands of place seeking meant that the bureaucracy was much larger than was strictly necessary and, given the slow pace of economic development and the consequent paucity of other job opportunities, state employment assumed a disproportionate importance.

The state and its attendant offices were essentially regarded as prizes to be captured by rival cliques of politicians, and it is scarcely surprising that as a consequence there was little sense of collective loyalty to, or trust in, the state and its institutions. Voters expected those for whom they had voted to help them to secure employment, to intercede when necessary with a cumbersome, inefficient and unresponsive bureaucracy and generally to dispense favours and to be available at all times. Foreign visitors frequently commented on the accessibility of all those in government, including the prime minister. The many lawyers among parliamentary deputies were expected to plead free of charge for

their clients, while some deputies came near to bankrupting themselves by acting as *koumbaroi* (or godparents) to the children of
their voters. Some deputies assumed this onerous responsibility
on behalf of as many as a thousand children.

The wheels of the Greek political machine were oiled not only
by the lavish dispensation of favours but also by open bribery,
electoral manipulation and fraud. The gendarmerie and armed
forces were frequently employed as a means of intimidating re-
calcitrant voters. Some Greek politicians were quick to grasp the
political potential afforded by the brigandage that was an endemic
feature of nineteenth-century Greece. Between January 1869 and
June 1870, for instance, it was officially declared that 109 cases of
brigandage had been recorded. International attention was focus-
sed on brigandage and its political ramifications by the kidnapping
and subsequent murder in 1870 of a party of well-connected
English aristocrats on an excursion to Marathon, a tragedy known
as the Dilessi murders. Brigands proved a useful means of exerting
political pressure at the local level and, in turn, they benefited
from political patronage at the centre. In the course of the
trial of a deputy from Thessaly in 1894 it emerged that the spoils
of a band of Thessalian brigands had been divided three ways,
with one share for the brigands, one for the church and one for
the local deputy and his two brothers.

But for all the turbulence, factionalism and corruption of
Greek politics the picture was by no means entirely negative. Few
politicians personally enriched themselves with the spoils of office.
Indeed the reverse was often the case. The Greek press enjoyed a
freedom that bordered on licence and the flourishing newspapers
of the capital, most of which were directly controlled by political
parties, were quick to exploit the merest hint of scandal and
corruption. In Athens alone, during the second half of the century,
ten morning and three afternoon newspapers were needed to cater
for the insatiable demand for news and political gossip. Foreign
travellers were frequently astonished to come across Greeks in the
most unlikely of places with a lively and informed knowledge of
world affairs, even if they were prone to believe that the whole of
international politics revolved around Greece. Moreover, the

Greek political system was to undergo an important transformation during the last thirty years of the nineteenth century with the rise to power of one of the most remarkable statesmen of independent Greece, Charilaos Trikoupis.

Born in 1832, Trikoupis had spent fourteen years in England, where his father served as Greek minister. This was popularly believed to account for his phlegmatic and unemotional character. He first came to prominence when he became foreign minister in 1866 in the Koumoundouros administration. But Trikoupis' most lasting achievement lay in the reinvigoration of Greece's domestic politics. In July 1874 he wrote, anonymously, a famous article, entitled 'Who is to blame?' in the newspaper *Kairoi*, in the course of a newspaper debate as to whether it was the king and his advisers or the politicians who bore the primary responsibility for the continuing crisis in Greece's political life. Greece, Trikoupis said, was ruled as an absolute monarchy. He laid the blame squarely on King George for entrusting minority parties with the formation of governments. If only the king, he argued, would state categorically that he would ask only the leader of the party enjoying a majority in parliament to form a government, then the various parliamentary groupings would more readily form coalitions so as to achieve power. A new stability would thus enter Greek politics, and the reasons for the plethora of small parties would disappear. The article caused uproar and its supposed author was arrested, whereupon Trikoupis admitted to having written it. He was then promptly arrested for attempting to undermine the constitutional order, but was released after three days amid general public acclaim, and subsequently acquitted.

King George harboured no ill will towards Trikoupis and indeed asked him to form a government in May 1875. But in what were among the fairest elections to be held in Greece up to that time Trikoupis failed to achieve a majority. He had won his point, however, for in the speech from the throne made in August 1875 King George clearly accepted the principle of the *'dedilomeni'*, namely that the leader of the party enjoying the 'declared' support of a majority in parliament would in future be invariably called upon to form a government. Acceptance of this principle was to have a far-reaching influence on Greek politics but it was not until January 1882 that Trikoupis himself achieved a clear majority in parliament. In the meanwhile Greece had experienced at close quarters the great eastern crisis of 1875–8, which was to stretch to the full the diplomatic skills of King George.

George I's first test of statesmanship had occurred during the renewed Cretan crisis of 1866–9. A revolt in 1858 had been followed by a more serious uprising in 1866. Greek volunteers, openly encouraged by the Koumoundouros government, made their way to the 'Great Island', while Greeks abroad despatched funds for the support of the Cretan insurgents. Members of the prosperous Greek community of Manchester, for instance, subscribed for the purchase of the *Arkadi*, which was used to run volunteers and supplies through the Turkish blockade of the island. At the same time an attempt was made to form a Balkan front against the Ottomans with the signing of a treaty of alliance with Serbia in 1867, which was followed by a military convention in 1868. Although this move had little concrete result it had considerable symbolic significance as it was Greece's first treaty with one of its Balkan neighbours. British pressure led King George to dismiss the belligerent Koumoundouros while, in an effort to appease the Powers, the Porte conceded the Organic Law of 1868 which gave Christians a greater role in the administration of the island. After the collapse of the revolt in 1869 Crete was to remain relatively quiescent until crisis once again erupted in the late 1880s, apart from agitation during the eastern crisis of 1875–8.

The recurrent crises occasioned by the Cretans' demand for *enosis* inevitably brought Greece into conflict with the Porte and, given Greece's dependent relationship towards the Protecting Powers, equally inevitably led to Great Power involvement. From the 1870s onwards, however, Greece's irredentist ambitions in Macedonia were to bring her into conflict not only with the Porte but also with the rival nationalisms of the Bulgarians and Serbs. The catalyst for these growing antagonisms was the creation in 1870 by the Porte of an autocephalous Bulgarian Church headed by an exarch. Pursuing a deliberate policy of 'divide and rule', the Porte conceded the long-standing demand of the

Bulgarians for their own Church hierarchy which would free them of the much resented hegemony and cultural insensitiveness of Greek ecclesiastics. Henceforward communities in Macedonia could opt for the jurisdiction of the exarchate rather than that of the patriarchate, provided that two-thirds of the inhabitants were in favour. This move prompted the patriarchate in 1872 to declare the Bulgarian hierarchy to be schismatic, an anathema that was not to be lifted until 1945.

The establishment of the Bulgarian exarchate, an important stage in the progress of the Bulgarians towards nationhood, prompted a significant change in the attitude of the Greeks towards Russia. At the time of the Crimean War the Greeks had continued, somewhat misguidedly, to believe in an identity of interest with the Russians *vis-à-vis* the Ottoman Empire. Now, however, they began to see Russian-inspired Panslavism in the Balkans as posing as serious a threat to the interests of Hellenism as the continuance of Ottoman rule. Thus the Greeks showed little inclination to join with the Serbs and Montenegrins who in 1876 took advantage of a revolt in Bosnia and Hercegovina, which subsequently spread to the Bulgarian provinces, to wage war on the Turks. The Serbs were roundly defeated, and after protracted diplomatic manoeuvrings and denunciations of Ottoman reprisals against the Bulgarians, Russia in April 1877 declared war on the Porte.

Up to this point the attitude of King George and his government had been one of restraint towards what was seen as essentially a Slav-Turkish quarrel. But with Russia's declaration of war, popular clamour in Greece to take advantage of the Porte's difficulties and give encouragement to their enslaved compatriots in Thessaly, Epirus, Macedonia and Crete mounted. Fearful that Slav gains were likely to be at the expense of Greek interests, the attitude of the government perceptibly changed. Greek troops were moved to the frontier, irregular bands began to carry out raids in Thessaly and Macedonia and revolt broke out in Crete. Early in 1878 King George ordered a partial mobilisation and at the beginning of February he authorised Koumoundouros to move troops into Thessaly. But Greece had acted too late, for this move coincided almost exactly with the conclusion of an armistice between the Russians and the Turks. Greek troops were now withdrawn from Ottoman territory, although Greek irregulars continued their activities in Macedonia. News of the Treaty of San Stefano of 3 March 1878, which formally concluded the Russo-Turkish war, occasioned great alarm in Greece, for it provided for the creation of a 'Greater Bulgaria', incorporating virtually the whole of Macedonia, with an outlet to the Aegean and stretching almost to the Adriatic. The Bulgaria of San Stefano clearly represented a major threat to Greek claims in the region. But it was not only Greece that was thoroughly alarmed. Both Austria, with her own increasing Balkan ambitions, and the British, who feared the creation of such a massive Russian client state, vigorously opposed the settlement.

At the ensuing Congress of Berlin of June/July 1878, at which the chief Ottoman delegate was an Ottoman Greek, Alexander Karatheodory Pasha, the Bulgaria of San Stefano was considerably reduced in size. North of the Balkan mountains an autonomous Bulgarian principality was created, and to the south the province of Eastern Rumelia was to be ruled by a Christian governor appointed by the Porte. The formal independence of Serbia, Montenegro and Romania was also recognised. As a counterweight to Russian expansion in Asia, Britain, by the separate Cyprus Convention of June 1878, assumed the administration of Cyprus but not sovereignty over her and undertook to pay the surplus of revenue over expenditure to the Porte. Greece was not formally represented at the Congress of Berlin but was allowed to state her claim to Thessaly, Epirus and Crete. She received little satisfaction beyond a further promise of reforms, including the appointment of a Christian governor, in the administration of Crete. These were embodied in the Pact of Halepa of October 1878. The Powers at the same time invited the Porte to consider modifications of her frontiers in favour of Greece. After the Porte had shown little inclination to honour this invitation, the Greeks mobilised in 1880. Following pressure by the Powers, the Turks then agreed, at a conference of ambassadors in Constantinople in 1881, to yield the fertile province of Thessaly and the Arta region of Epirus to Greece.

It was the support of thirty out of thirty-five deputies of the newly annexed province of Thessaly, combined with the salutary effects of a new electoral law, that contributed significantly to Trikoupis' clear parliamentary majority in the elections of January 1882. A number of members of the old guard of Greek politicians had died in the previous few years, among them Voulgaris in 1877, Deligeorgis in 1879 and Zaimis in 1880, while Koumoundouros was to die in 1883. For much of the next twenty years Greece was to enjoy the semblance of a two-party system, as Trikoupis alternated in power with Theodore Deliyannis. Trikoupis was prime minister and minister of foreign affairs between 1882 and 1885, 1887 and 1890, and 1892 and 1895; Deliyannis between 1885 and 1887, 1890 and 1892, and 1895 and 1897. The contrast between the two politicians could not have been stronger. Trikoupis was a reform-minded Westerniser, anxious to consolidate and develop Greece economically and politically before becoming involved in irredentist adventures. Deliyannis, on the other hand, the scion of a prominent family of Peloponnesian primates, was a determined champion of the cause of 'Greater Greece'. His domestic policies encompassed little more than the negation of Trikoupis' reforms. Indeed he once declared that he was against everything that Trikoupis was for.

Trikoupis, with the support of business interests, engaged in a vigorous and not unsuccessful attempt to develop the country's economy, and in particular to improve communications. This programme was financed by contracting external loans, by increasing the yield of taxation through more rigorous collection, by raising taxes, which were almost exclusively indirect, and customs duties, and by exploiting state monopolies such as salt and matches. Before 1878, when Greece's outstanding debts in connection with the loans of 1824, 1825 and 1833 were regularised, Greece had found it virtually impossible to raise money in the international money markets. Trikoupis' moderation, however, inspired a qualified confidence in foreign investors and between 1879 and 1890 six external loans were raised, with a nominal value of 630 million drachmas, although, because Greece was still not regarded as a good risk, these had to be discounted by up to 30 per cent. Moreover, by 1887, 40 per cent of the annual budget was devoted to debt service, and, by the time expenditure on the armed forces had been allowed for, only a very small proportion of these external loans was available to finance Trikoupis' public works programmes. The need to maintain Greece's external credit sometimes inhibited the process of domestic reform. Trikoupis shied away, for instance, from introducing land reform in the newly acquired province of Thessaly, where agriculture was characterised by large *chiftliks*, or estates worked by landless labourers, to avoid offending the susceptibilities of foreign capital and of wealthy expatriate Greeks who were increasingly inclined to invest in the mother country.

Despite these problems, however, a modest economic progress was registered in the 1880s and 1890s. When Trikoupis assumed office in 1882 there were only seven miles of railway linking Athens with its port of Piraeus. By 1893 some 568 miles of railway were in operation, with a further 305 miles in the course of construction, although not until 1916 was the Greek railway system to be linked with that of the rest of Europe. There were also some 4000 miles of telegraph lines. Steamship tonnage under Greek ownership rose from 8241 tons in 1875 to 144,975 tons in 1895. Wealthy Greeks, often living abroad, began to buy up large numbers of old steamships, which were captained and crewed by their fellow islanders, thus beginning a tradition that was to make Greece one of the foremost shipping nations in the present century. The Corinth canal was opened in 1893, although it did not bring the immediate economic benefits that had been expected. In the early 1890s there were seventeen cotton mills and three large woollen mills in the country. The draining of Lake Copais, completed by a British company, recovered some 30,000 acres of highly fertile land for cultivation. Greek exports were few, however, and almost entirely agricultural. The most important export, currants, was dangerously dependent on fluctuations in world prices.

Trikoupis' endeavours were by no means restricted to the economic sphere. He sought to raise the minimum educational requirements for positions in the civil service and at least to diminish the wholesale dismissals of public servants that accompanied each change of administration. He took measures to curb the recurring problem of brigandage, to improve policing, to increase the size of Greece's armed forces and to improve the quality of their training and equipment. A French military mission was invited to Greece and new ships were ordered for the navy. In an effort to reduce the grip of local magnates he increased the size of parliamentary constituencies in 1886 by reducing their number to 150, the minimum prescribed in the constitution of 1864.

Much of the positive achievement of Trikoupis, however, was undone when Deliyannis came to power. Deliyannis reintroduced, for instance, smaller constituencies, a move which increased the possibilities of electoral manipulation. He gained easy popularity by reducing the burden of taxation which Trikoupis' ambitious schemes made necessary. Above all his demagogic exploitation of Greek irredentism merely compounded the country's economic difficulties without securing any of the desired goals of Greek foreign policy. When, for instance, Bulgaria in 1885 annexed Eastern Rumelia, Greece, like Serbia, demanded territorial compensation. Deliyannis mobilised, but after the imposition in 1886 of a naval blockade by the Powers, Greece was forced to demobilise and Deliyannis was ousted from office. His sabre rattling had produced no tangible result and the great cost of the mobilisation burdened Trikoupis' subsequent administration. In an effort to bring order to Greece's finances and to restore her credit-worthiness he was obliged to raise taxation, a move which in turn gave renewed scope to Deliyannis' demagogic populism.

By the time of Trikoupis' last administration, 1892–5, Greece's financial situation had become desperate. A catastrophic fall in the world price of currants revealed the essential frailty of the Greek economy, heavily dependent as it was on a limited number of agricultural exports. The declining value of the drachma resulted in as much as a half of state revenues being devoted to servicing external debts, which were payable in gold. In 1893, the year of the major crisis, imports amounted in value to 119,306,000 francs, while exports amounted to only 82,261,000 francs.

Trikoupis was in effect forced to declare bankruptcy, reducing by 70 per cent the interest payments on foreign loans, while revenues that had been earmarked for the repayment of specific loans were channelled directly into the treasury. The seriousness of the collapse of international confidence can be gauged from the fact that the 5 per cent loan of 1881 which in April 1893 stood at £76 had by December of the same year fallen to £30. The dire straits of the Greek economy gave a decisive impetus to emigration, which henceforth was to become an important safety valve in times of economic distress. Between 1890 and 1914 some 350,000 Greeks, amounting almost to one sixth of the entire population, migrated, principally to the United States. The remittances which these frugal and industrious migrants sent back to their families were to assume an ever-increasing importance for the Greek balance of payments.

The distress consequent on the financial collapse of 1893 and the measures of austerity forced on Trikoupis made a Deliyannist victory in the next elections, those of 1895, inevitable. Trikoupis forthwith retired to Paris where he died the following year and was thus spared the humiliation inflicted upon Greece in 1897 as a result of defeat at the hands of Turkey. The great crisis of that year had its origins in one of the recurrent Cretan crises. Unrest in the late 1880s had been temporarily repressed through harsh measures imposed by the Turkish authorities, but revolt had once again broken out in 1895. The insurgents were given aid and encouragement by the ultra nationalists of the *Ethniki Etairia*, or National Society, although, despite popular pressure, Deliyannis withheld government support, for the Powers had already sent a fleet to the island. But early in 1897, responding to popular pressure and the enthusiasm of King George for the annexation of the island, he despatched ships and troops. Rejecting a Turkish offer of autonomy under Ottoman sovereignty for the island and encouraged by the inability of the Powers to concert action to contain the crisis, Deliyannis in March 1897 ordered a mobilisation. In the following month hostilities erupted in Thessaly but the Greek army was no match for the reinvigorated Turkish forces and within a month it had been overwhelmingly defeated.

93

The contrast between Greece's voracious irredentist appetites and her modest military capabilities had never been more starkly revealed. It was clear that she could never challenge the Ottoman Empire single-handed and hope to win. The king and his eldest son, Crown Prince Constantine, who had commanded the Greek armies in Thessaly, were made the scapegoats for defeat as anti-dynastic feeling built up. Greeks turned their backs on Queen Olga in the streets of Athens, and there was an unsuccessful attempt on the king's life. For a time King George seriously considered abdication.

Although Greece had suffered a crushing military defeat, the terms of the peace settlement were relatively lenient thanks to the influence of the Powers which on this occasion at least was benign. Greece was obliged to pay a war indemnity of four million Turkish pounds and to concede a number of minor frontier rectifications. Perhaps the most humiliating provision of the peace settlement was the setting up of an International Financial Control Commission, with representatives of Great Britain, France, Russia, Germany, Austria-Hungary and Italy charged with overseeing the payment of the interest on Greece's large external debts. The commission's revenues derived from the state monopolies of salt, kerosene, matches and playing cards, the duties on tobacco, cigarette paper and stamps, together with the import duties levied at Piraeus, Greece's principal port. A relatively favourable settlement was obtained over Crete. The island was granted an autonomous status under Ottoman suzerainty. Prince George, King George's second son, was appointed High Commissioner on the island, which he was to rule with the assistance of a partly elected, partly appointed assembly, with both Christian and Muslim delegates.

The decade following the defeat of 1897 was one of confusion, isolation, introspection and questioning in Greece. Greece's isolation was emphasised in 1897, and her search for allies met with little success. The Cretan settlement had, temporarily at least, brought peace to the island but the situation in Macedonia remained critical. Rivalry between Greece, Bulgaria and Serbia over the inheritance of Turkey in Europe had reached a high point in the 1890s. Initially the struggle to inculcate a sense of national consciousness into populations that were frequently aware only that they were Christian was conducted through ecclesiastical, cultural and educational propaganda. The *Ethniki Etairia* played a leading role in seeking to hellenise the Orthodox populations of Macedonia and Epirus. By the turn of the century there were some 1000 Greek schools in Macedonia, with a total attendance of some 75,000 pupils, approximately twice the number of those attending schools owing allegiance to the Bulgarian exarchate. The Serbian society of Saint Sava controlled about half as many schools as the Bulgarians, while the Romanians also began to develop an increasing interest in the Vlach populations scattered throughout Macedonia and Epirus.

It was not long before these rivalries erupted in violence. The founding of the Internal Macedonian Revolutionary Organisation (IMRO) in 1893 marked an important stage in the escalation of the conflict. Initially founded to fight for the principle of 'Macedonia for the Macedonians', its autonomist aspirations were soon to be challenged by the Supreme Macedonian Committee which advocated the annexation of Macedonia by Bulgaria. The Greeks were not slow to meet force with force and a period of protracted guerrilla warfare between rival Greek and Slav bands now commenced, with encouragement and material support being given to the Greeks by the Church authorities (particularly after the appointment of Germanos Karavangelis as metropolitan of Kastoria in 1900), and by Greek consular officials in the disputed territories. It was by no means unknown for the Greeks to collaborate with the Turks to get the better of their detested Bulgarian rivals.

Inevitably Macedonia, with its extraordinary patchwork of ethnic groups and its fierce antagonisms, became an increasing source of concern to the Powers, who feared that at any time a local conflict could flare up into a major international crisis, as had happened in 1878. After the suppression of the IMRO-inspired uprising of Ilinden in the summer of 1903, the Powers were moved once again to propose reforms for the troubled province. These were enshrined in what was known as the

Mürzsteg programme. This provided for Great Power supervision of the Ottoman gendarmerie. The Powers also 'expected' that the Porte would reshape its territorial boundaries and administrative units, 'with a view to a more regular grouping of the different nationalities', an expectation that was immediately seen by the contending Greeks, Bulgarians and Serbs as implying an extension of their own territorial boundaries. The Mürzsteg programme, like so many earlier reform programmes imposed by the Powers on the Porte, largely proved to be a dead letter, and the feuds of the patriarchalists, exarchists and autonomists continued unabated. A new element was the increasing militancy of the Albanians. Significantly, and ominously for the future integrity of the Ottoman Empire, they were predominantly Muslim. Their early demands for autonomy were soon followed by armed struggle for outright independence from the Porte.

The emergence of a form of two-party system during the period of the ascendancy of Trikoupis and Deliyannis was to prove a false dawn, and with Trikoupis' death in 1896 Greek politics reverted to their traditional anarchic pattern. Trikoupis' political heir, Theotokis, in difficult circumstances lacked the talents of his predecessor, while Deliyannis, who made something of a comeback in the early years of the century with his demagogic promises to slash public expenditure, was assassinated in 1905 by a disgruntled gambler, angered among other things at Deliyannis' proposals to curb gambling. The reformist impetus that had characterised the Trikoupis administrations was now absent but, in the wake of 1897, some measures were introduced to improve Greece's military preparedness. Funds were set up to re-equip the army and fleet. One immensely wealthy Vlach from Metsovo, George Averoff, who had amassed a fortune, along with a good many other Greeks in Egypt under British administration, subscribed a large part of the sum required to purchase a battleship. But overall the continued jobbery and demagogy of Greek politics were to create a widespread disillusion with traditional politics. The manifest structural weaknesses of the Greek political system and the inadequacies of its politicians were an increasing affront to a small but growing educated middle class. Demands for political renewal were increasing.

The muddle and incompetence of the politicians was to be shaken by the Young Turk Revolution of 1908. This resulted in the restoration of the short-lived Ottoman constitution of 1876 and the eventual overthrow of Sultan Abdul Hamid, and appeared to presage an upturn in the fortunes of the 'Sick Man' of Europe. The Young Turks, with their promises of equality for all inhabitants of the empire whether Christian, Jewish or Muslim, were initially greeted with rapture not only by the Ottoman Greeks but by the Greeks of the kingdom as well. But this enthusiasm soon faded. For the Young Turks, smarting under the Austrian annexation of Bosnia and Hercegovina, which had been under her administration since 1878, at Bulgaria's renunciation of Ottoman suzerainty and at the unilateral proclamation (somewhat to the embarrassment of the Athens government) by the Cretan assembly on 8 October 1908 of *enosis* with the Greek motherland, began a policy of forced 'Ottomanisation' of their non-Muslim subjects. It was the cautious reaction of King George and his government to the agitation in Crete that was to be one of the factors helping to precipitate the most serious internal crisis in Greece since independence.

The coincidence of nationalist ferment over Crete, and the fear of losing Macedonia, with mounting economic difficulties had helped to catalyse resentment against the traditional political world. As emigration had increased and as Greeks had sought outlets for their talents in the United States, Egypt and elsewhere, so the Greek economy had become, through the increasing flow of emigrants' remittances, increasingly susceptible to the fluctuations of other economies, and both the United States and Egypt had suffered serious economic setbacks in 1908. At home overproduction of currants, combined with poor olive, wheat and tobacco crops, had resulted in economic stagnation and growing unemployment. More ominously, domestic unrest was coupled with rumblings of discontent within the army. As so often these had their roots in purely professional grievances. NCOs were aggrieved at legislation which would have weakened their chances of promotion to commissioned rank and it was widely felt that Crown Prince Constantine, as commander-in-chief, had shown undue favouritism towards his own protégés. Three clandestine groups developed within the army to give expression to these various grievances and, in July 1909, these came together to form the *Stratiotikos Syndesmos*, or Military League, whose leader was Colonel Nicholas Zorbas and whose membership amounted to some 1300 officers, mainly of junior rank.

With the successful example of the Young Turk conspiracy before them, the Military League drafted a memorandum addressed to the king, the government and the Greek people. This demanded the ousting of the Crown Prince and other members of the royal family from the armed forces, the appointment of serving officers as ministers of war and the navy, and a programme of military and naval reform. Money was to be voted by parliament for this, the country's finances were to be put on a sound footing and the burden of taxation reduced. A number of other unexceptionable demands were made. Theotokis had resigned in July 1909 under fire for his handling of the Cretan question and had been succeeded by Dimitrios Rallis. Despite his initial sympathy towards the Military League's objectives, Rallis on 27 August declined to receive a deputation which sought to hand over the League's memorandum of reform. Following this rebuff, a large proportion of the Athens garrison marched out to Goudi. From Goudi they issued an ultimatum threatening to march on Athens if various demands were not met. These included the formal acknowledgement by the government that it had accepted the reform memorandum, an amnesty for all involved in the Goudi *kinima*, or putsch, and the reinstatement of non-commissioned officers who had been dismissed from the army for protesting about the limitation of promotion prospects.

These demands were scarcely very radical but Rallis nonetheless resigned, to be replaced by Kyriakoulis Mavromichalis, with whom the Military League had had some previous contact and who accepted its demands. The Goudi events aroused little public excitement although the League's platform was enthusiastically endorsed at a huge demonstration at the end of September. In

October 1909, with the king's support, Mavromichalis set about gaining parliamentary authority for its various reform proposals. Following a threat to impose an outright military dictatorship, parliamentary objections to the reforms were overcome and, under pressure from the League, a large number of mildly reformist bills were enacted. But by early in 1910 members of the League had lost faith in working through the existing political oligarchy and were increasingly inclined to look for political leadership to the Cretan Eleftherios Venizelos, who called for constitutional reform. Venizelos, born in Crete in 1864, had returned to the island after studying at the University of Athens and had participated in the uprisings of 1889 and 1896–7. After 1897 he had become a member of the Cretan assembly and minister of justice to Prince George, the High Commissioner. An ardent champion of *enosis* of the island with the mainland, he had the great virtue in the eyes of the Military League of not being compromised by any close involvement with the oligarchy of mainland politicians and their aura of chaos, jobbery and incompetence. This enabled the League to step down from power without appearing to capitulate to the old politicians and, in a rare instance of military self-abnegation, to dissolve itself in March 1910.

Overcoming his initial reluctance, King George agreed to the holding of elections in August 1910 for a national assembly empowered to revise the 1864 constitution. As this was a revisionary assembly, double the normal number of deputies were elected. Venizelos did not directly contest the elections but many of the reformist independents, who gained 146 seats, looked to him as their leader. Supporters of Theotokis won 112, of Rallis 67, with the remaining 37 deputies being followers of Mavromichalis and Zaimis. Venizelos returned to the mainland in September amid rapturous public acclaim and, the following month, became prime minister of a minority government. As the new assembly continued to be dominated by the old politicians, Venizelos called for new elections in December. In these he received a handsome majority of almost 300 out of 362 seats, with most of the opposition parties abstaining. Having convincingly demonstrated his popular support and having secured an overwhelming dominance of the revisionary assembly, Venizelos was free to embark on an ambitious policy of domestic renewal. In this he was supported by King George, who was shrewd enough to see in Venizelos the best hope of stemming the anti-dynasticism that had surfaced in 1897 and gained renewed momentum during the great crisis of 1908–9.

Although the Military League had played a crucial role in projecting him to the forefront of the political stage in Greece, Venizelos was anxious to demonstrate that he was no mere puppet of the military. He released the officers who had been arrested for trying to thwart the Goudi *kinima* and, despite the army's resentment at the role of the royal princes, he created a new position of inspector-general of the army for Crown Prince Constantine. One of his first priorities was constitutional reform and in 1911 more than fifty amendments to the non-essential provisions of the 1864 constitution were enacted. One of the most important of these provided for the expropriation of land and property where this was held to be in the national interest. This amendment provided the legal basis for Venizelos' subsequent land reforms in Thessaly, where, after 1917, the big Thessalian *chiftliks*, or estates, were broken up. To reduce the possibility of filibustering, the parliamentary quorum was reduced from one half to one third of all deputies and greater security of tenure was vouchsafed to judges and public officials.

A number of other important reform measures were introduced. Entrance to the civil service was made conditional on public examinations, primary education was made free and compulsory, local government was reorganised. Interest rates were reduced, minimum wages introduced for women and children, a progressive income tax was introduced to diminish the heavy reliance on indirect taxes which bore disproportionately severely on the poor. A ministry of national economy was created, trades unions were officially recognised and company 'unions' declared illegal. It was during this period that the first serious manifestations of interest in socialism appeared in Greece, but the low level of industrial development, and the consequent small size of the industrial proletariat, inhibited the development of a serious working-class movement. Socialist ideas found a more fertile ground among Greeks in the great cities of the Ottoman Empire such as Constantinople, Salonica and Smyrna. But here the development of a socialist movement was impeded by disputes as to whether socialist organisation should be based on class or ethnic lines. Venizelos, who had personally taken charge of the ministries of the army and the navy, also devoted considerable attention and energy to the reorganisation and re-equipment of Greece's armed forces, an endeavour assisted by the achievement, after many years of deficit, of a budgetary surplus in 1910 and 1911. A French military, and a British naval, mission contributed to the growing efficiency of the Greek armed forces, which by 1912 had a mobilised strength of some 150,000.

The liberal reforms introduced by Venizelos may have blunted the development of strong socialist and agrarian movements such as appeared in other Balkan countries. They certainly proved to be popular with the Greek electorate and in elections in March 1912 for a 181 seat parliament Venizelos won 146 seats. This was a striking indication of Venizelos' popularity and of the degree of unity that he had engendered in the Greek people. This high degree of domestic consensus was to stand the Greek people in good stead during the dramatic developments that were to take place during the next eighteen months on the external front. Given the conflicting irredentist ambitions of the Balkan states and the upsurge of Turkish nationalism consequent on the Young Turk revolution, a clash in the Balkans sooner or later seemed inevitable. When Italy, seeking a colonial empire of her own, declared war on the Ottoman Empire in 1911, and armed revolt broke out among the Albanians, the Slav states of the Balkans, the Serbs, Montenegrins and Bulgarians, were anxious to exploit the discomfiture of the Young Turks. Venizelos was not so sure, for unlike the other protagonists, the Greeks had large populations in Asia Minor, amounting to well over a million, who were vulnerable to the increasingly aggressive nationalism of the Young Turks. On the other hand if Greece did not act together with the Slavs then she might find herself presented with a fait accompli in Macedonia.

Greece and Serbia had both learnt the hard way that single-handed onslaughts on the Ottoman Empire by small Balkan states were doomed to failure. Joint action clearly recommended itself, but radical differences over Macedonia continued to divide Greece, Serbia and Bulgaria. Nonetheless a Serb-Bulgarian treaty was signed in March 1912, with a secret annexe relating to Macedonia. A Greek-Bulgarian agreement was concluded in May of 1912. This provided for mutual assistance if either country were attacked by the Turks. Negotiations also got under way between the Greeks and Serbs. Despite a declaration by the Powers that they would not tolerate any disturbance of the existing territorial arrangements in the Balkans, Greece, Serbia and Bulgaria on 18 October 1912 declared war on the Ottoman Empire, Montenegro having by prior agreement already attacked the Turks ten days previously.

The new Balkan allies made sweeping gains at the expense of the Turks, as well they might have considering that the forces at the disposal of the Turks amounted to 400,000 while the combined Balkan armies, to which Greece contributed some 200,000 troops, totalled 1,300,000. Greece's improved navy gave her control of the Aegean and enabled her to liberate Chios, Mytilini and Samos, although the Italians had already, during the Italo-Turkish war of 1911, captured and occupied the Dodecanese islands, the largest of which was Rhodes. The Greek armies made spectacular advances in Macedonia, capturing Salonica on 9 November, arriving a few hours before the Bulgarian troops and thus averting a potentially explosive confrontation between the allies. As it happened sephardic Jews, the descendants of the Jews expelled from Spain in the fifteenth century and still Spanish speaking, heavily outnumbered either the Greek or Slav inhabitants of the great Macedonian port. The Serb and Bulgarian armies made equally spectacular gains. In early December the Turks put out peace feelers. These were accepted by the Serbs, Bulgarians and Montenegrins but rejected by the Greeks who were still laying siege to Jannina, the capital of Epirus. Greece did, however, agree to participate in a conference held in London in December 1912 to discuss peace terms. At the same time, a concurrent meeting of the ambassadors of the Powers was convened in London, chaired by Sir Edward Grey, the British foreign secretary.

A new element of uncertainty, however, was added by a coup in Constantinople in January 1913 in which the hard line Enver Pasha and his Young Turk colleagues regained power. The new Turkish regime was not prepared to offer sweeping enough concessions to the victorious allies and early in February 1913 hostilities once more broke out. The Greeks were now able to capture Jannina and push further up into Epirus. Once again the Turks sued for peace and were obliged to recognise the territorial acquisitions of the Balkan allies by the Treaty of London of May 1913. But the somewhat artificial Balkan alliance was beginning to show signs of strain. Greece and Serbia in a treaty of June 1913 agreed as to the division of the spoils in Macedonia, and, in an article clearly directed against Bulgaria, agreed to support each other, by force if necessary, to impose their agreed settlement. Bulgaria, which had borne the brunt of the fighting against the Turks, had gained least. In resentment she attacked her erstwhile allies Greece and Serbia, while Romania now decided to enter the fray by occupying the Dobrudja, which had hitherto been a part of Bulgaria. Greece pushed on beyond Salonica to take Drama, Serres and Kavalla while Turkey counter-attacked and recaptured Adrianople (Edirne). This second Balkan war was of short duration and the Bulgarians, thoroughly beaten, were forced to negotiate. By the Treaty of Bucharest of August 1913 Bulgaria was obliged to cede much of Macedonia to Greece and Serbia, although she did retain the Aegean outlet she had won at Dedeagatch (Alexandroupolis). Greek sovereignty over Crete was accepted although her ambition to annexe Northern Epirus had been thwarted by the creation of an independent Albania. The Powers agreed that Greek sovereignty over the Aegean islands should be recognised but this was rejected by the Turks.

Under the inspiring leadership of Venizelos, Greece's gains during the first and second Balkan wars had been spectacular indeed. Her land area had increased by almost 70 per cent. While her population increased from approximately 2,800,000 to 4,800,000, by no means all of these new inhabitants were Greeks, as substantial numbers of Slavs and Turks inhabited her newly acquired Macedonian territories. Moreover a shadow had been cast over the Greek triumph by the assassination of King George I by a madman in Salonica in March 1913. George, by the standards of the time, and certainly in contrast to his predecessor and successor on the throne, had manifested a commitment to constitutional rule that had done much to inject an element of stability into Greek politics. His successor, Crown Prince Constantine, was to lack the same sure touch. Despite this setback, however, Venizelos as the prime architect of Greece's spectacular victories, was at the peak of his popularity. If the Greeks could only remain united among themselves, or so it seemed, then their most cherished irredentist ambitions lay within their grasp. The widely believed prophecy that the Greeks would recapture Constantinople when a Constantine once again sat on the throne of Hellas no longer seemed all that far-fetched. There was even excited talk that he would take the title of Constantine XII in succession to Constantine XI Palaiologos, the last Emperor of Byzantium.

5

Schism, defeat, republic and restoration, 1913-1935

Greece's triumphant successes in the Balkan wars had resulted in her emergence as a significant Mediterranean power and had been accompanied by a remarkable degree of national unity. The First World War, however, was to place intolerable strains on the cohesion of Greek society and Greece was to emerge from the war and her subsequent adventure in Asia Minor a country divided against herself. The consequences of this division were to distort the whole course of Greece's political development during the inter-war period. The immediate cause of what came to be known as the *Ethnikos Dichasmos*, or National Schism, lay in the differences that emerged between King Constantine I and his prime minister, Venizelos, over the policy to be adopted by Greece following the outbreak of hostilities between the Entente (Britain, France and Russia) and the Central Powers (Germany and Austria-Hungary) in August 1914.

Venizelos, an enthusiastic champion of Greece's traditional British connection, had developed a strong personal rapport with the British Liberal statesman Lloyd George during a visit to London in 1912, and was from the beginning a strong supporter of the Entente. Yet the fact that Serbia's assailant in 1914 was Austria-Hungary did not necessarily oblige Greece to go to her assistance under the terms of the Greek-Serbian treaty of June 1913, which was essentially a pact against possible Bulgarian aggression. Nonetheless within a matter of days after the outbreak of hostilities Venizelos offered to commit Greek troops to fight alongside the Entente. The British foreign secretary, Sir Edward Grey, was not inclined to take up the offer, however, for at this initial stage of the war his overriding concern in the Balkans was to thwart a possible alignment of the Ottoman Empire and of Bulgaria with the Central Powers. Greece had only recently emerged from a bitter conflict with both states and for the Entente precipitately to have embraced Greek support might simply have served to push them into alliance with the Central Powers. Moreover, King Constantine did not share his prime minister's pro-Entente zeal. Impressed by the military strength of the Central Powers, and less in awe of Britain's naval superiority in the Mediterranean than Venizelos, Constantine believed that Greece's interests would best be served by a policy of neutrality. His opponents argued that his training at the Prussian Military Academy and his marriage in 1889 to Sophia, the sister of Kaiser Wilhelm II, predisposed him towards the Central Powers but his advocacy of Greek neutrality seems to have been based on a sincere appraisal of the likely outcome of the conflict. After his summary expulsion from Greece in 1917, however, he openly manifested pro-German sentiments.

Grey's policy received a setback when the Ottoman Empire formally aligned itself with the Central Powers on 5 November, whereupon Britain formally annexed Cyprus, which since 1878 had been administered by Britain while remaining under Ottoman sovereignty. But Turkey's entry into the war only served to strengthen Grey's resolve to keep Bulgaria out and thus block land communications between the Central Powers and their new ally. As an inducement to Bulgaria to remain neutral, Grey considered a proposal that Greece should cede the recently acquired region of Kavalla, Drama and Serres. To this end he offered in January 1915 to Venizelos 'important' but unspecified 'territorial concessions on the coast of Asia Minor'. Venizelos was prepared to accept the offer as it stood but King Constantine and the Greek general staff insisted on a more specific promise of compensation for the yielding of territory so recently and hardly won. This Grey was reluctant to give for he had also offered territory in Asia Minor to Italy. This offer was embodied in the Treaty of London of April 1915 by which Italy was brought into the war on the side of the Entente.

Venizelos saw a further opportunity of demonstrating his

support for the Entente in the ill-fated Dardanelles campaign. If the attack against the Straits were to be followed by a successful thrust against Constantinople he wanted to ensure that Greece was entitled to her share of the spoils, although it had been agreed by the Entente Powers that in such an eventuality Constantinople would go to Russia. Venizelos persuaded King Constantine to commit Greek troops to the campaign, albeit on a smaller scale than he had originally envisaged. But the acting chief-of-staff, Colonel John Metaxas, resigned, arguing that such a move would lay Greece open to Bulgarian attack. He also warned of the military difficulties inherent in holding on to any territory acquired by Greece in Asia Minor. Metaxas' resignation caused the king to reconsider his decision. Moreover the king was well aware that even if the campaign succeeded Russia would be likely to veto any Greek presence at the Straits, control of which she had long coveted. As a result of this royal volte-face Venizelos resigned in March 1915. His resignation marked the beginning of the National Schism, the division of the country into two fiercely antagonistic camps. The one consisted of Venizelos' supporters, who were convinced that King Constantine was intent on preserving Greece's neutrality under any circumstances, the other of his opponents, who were no less convinced that Venizelos was bent on dragging Greece into the war on the side of the Entente under one pretext or another.* Both views were distortions, but they were fervently maintained by their protagonists and the country slid remorselessly towards a state of virtual civil war. Moreover, underlying the disputes over foreign affairs was a fundamental cleavage between those who viewed with favour Venizelos' reformist policies and those conservatives who strongly opposed them.

King Constantine replaced Venizelos as prime minister by Dimitrios Gounaris, who was reputed to be pro-German, although his foreign minister, Zographos, was regarded as being pro-Entente. Gounaris by no means pursued an anti-Entente policy. But he did seek firm assurances from Grey and the Entente that

* Michael Llewellyn Smith, *Ionian Vision: Greece in Asia Minor 1919–1922* (London 1973) 54.

Bulgaria, which had still not entered the war, should attack Turkey. Alternatively he wanted the Entente to guarantee Greece against a possible Bulgarian attack. But the Entente Powers, still anxiously courting Bulgaria, were reluctant to take any steps that could be construed as anti-Bulgarian. King Constantine sought a way out of the growing political impasse by holding new elections in June of 1915. Venizelos won a clear, although somewhat reduced, majority of 184 out of 317 seats. He did not actually assume office, however, until August, it being argued that the king's illness precluded the transfer of power at such a critical juncture.

No sooner had Venizelos once again become prime minister than a new crisis developed. This was occasioned by Bulgarian mobilisation on 22 September, following a secret treaty between King Ferdinand of Bulgaria and the Central Powers. Since the Bulgarian mobilisation was largely aimed at Serbia, it raised in an acute form the question of Greece's obligations to Serbia under the treaty of June 1913. Venizelists held that Greece was now obliged to go to the assistance of Serbia. Anti-Venizelists, on the other hand, argued that Greece was only committed to go to the aid of Serbia if she were attacked by Bulgaria alone, and that the treaty was not binding in the event of Great Power involvement. King Constantine, while agreeing to Venizelos' demand for Greek mobilisation, continued to insist on Greek neutrality. For this reason, after initially approving, he opposed the despatch of troops by Britain and France to northern Greece in support of the Serbs, a move which Venizelos had invited. Venizelos in turn won support in parliament for the despatch of Greek troops to fight alongside the Serbs. As a consequence King Constantine once again called upon Venizelos to resign, although the landings in October of Entente troops in the Salonica region went ahead.

Venizelos' supporters regarded the king's insistence that he resign as flagrantly unconstitutional, for he clearly retained the support of the majority in a parliament that had been elected only a few months previously. In the king's defence, however, it was, not altogether convincingly, argued that Greek monarchs had traditionally exercised a considerable discretion in matters of foreign policy and that, under the constitution, the sovereign had wide prerogatives in appointing and dismissing ministers and dissolving parliaments. But whatever the constitutional rights and wrongs of the situation Venizelos' second resignation on 5 October 1915 signified a total breakdown in relations between the king and his elected prime minister. Britain and France, however, had not yet given up Greece for lost and held out to Venizelos' successor, Alexander Zaimis, the prospect of the cession of Cyprus to Greece in return for aid to Serbia, whose forces were now under severe pressure. Zaimis soon afterwards resigned, to be succeeded by a more overtly anti-Entente government.

Venizelos and his supporters, arguing that the Constantinists were bent on thwarting the popular will, now withdrew from active participation in the political process. Venizelos called for a boycott of the elections held in December 1915 and the turn-out was barely a quarter of that in the elections of the previous June. The Venizelists' boycott of political life was paralleled in 1916 by a further serious deterioration in relations between the neutralist royal government in Athens and the Entente. In the landings at Salonica in October 1915, the British and French had shown scant respect for Greek sovereignty and relations were further exacerbated with their seizure in January 1916 of Corfu, through which the defeated Serbian army was evacuated after a gruelling retreat across the mountains of Albania. The Entente was further angered by the royal government's refusal to allow these Serbian troops to cross overland from Corfu before regrouping on the Salonica front and by its surrender to the Germans and Bulgarians of the strategically important Fort Rupel in Macedonia on 22 May 1916.

On 30 August 1916 a group of pro-Venizelos officers launched a coup in Salonica against the official government. They were backed by the pro-Entente *Ethniki Amyna* (National Defence) which had been founded by a group of prominent citizens in the city at the end of December 1915. A month later, Venizelos, despairing of the existing political system, left on 26 September for his native island of Crete. He followed this by a triumphal procession through the Aegean islands, arriving in Salonica in early October 1916. Here he created his own provisional government and set about transforming the *Ethniki Amyna* into a fully fledged army. The Entente allies initially withheld recognition from the new regime for fear of triggering off open civil war, but they continued their pressure on the royal government in Athens which was manifesting an increasingly benevolent neutrality towards the Central Powers. This pressure culminated in December 1916 with the landing of British and French troops in Athens to back up Entente demands for weapons and war materials and in order to secure control of railway communication with the north. This was perhaps the most flagrant of the many interventions of the Protecting Powers in the internal affairs of Greece. The allies were met with armed resistance and the landing force, which suffered serious casualties, was forced to retreat. This clash was followed by large-scale reprisals against supporters of Venizelos in areas under the control of the royal government.

Britain and France now formally recognised the Venizelos government and mounted a blockade of those substantial areas of the kingdom, namely the Peloponnese and southern Rumeli, that remained loyal to the king. New Greece, the areas that had only recently been incorporated in the Greek state, on the other hand, enthusiastically supported the Salonica government. The Entente allies, smarting under the humiliation inflicted on their troops in Athens, demanded reparations for the casualties they had suffered, and only lifted their blockade when Constantine in June 1917 bowed to Entente pressure to give up his throne. Constantine, without formally abdicating, went into exile, accompanied by his eldest son George. He was succeeded by his second son Alexander. On the departure of Constantine, Venizelos became prime minister of a reunited Greece, and moved the seat of his government to Athens. One of his first acts was to reconvene the 'Lazarus' parliament elected in June 1915, so called because it had been raised from the dead. With the opposition boycotting its affairs, Venizelos secured a massive vote of confidence in the newly reconstituted parliament.

Once firmly installed in Athens, Venizelos' supporters set about revenging themselves for the humiliations they had suffered at the hands of the royalists. Some thirty prominent anti-Venizelists were exiled to Corsica as Germanophiles, while far-reaching purges were initiated in all levels of the civil service. Setting a convenient but dangerous precedent for future administrations, the permanent tenure of members of the judiciary was suspended and dismissals of judges and judicial officials made by the provisional government were retrospectively confirmed. The purge was also extended to the ranks of the Church. A number of bishops who in anathematising Venizelos had invoked the 'sores of Job' against him, were deposed, while an enthusiastic Venizelist, Meletios Metaxakis, became Archbishop of Athens and Metropolitan of Greece. Perhaps the most significant of the purges took place in the armed forces where many royalist officers were removed and replaced by officers loyal to Venizelos. This was to create a discontent within the ranks of the officer corps which was to have major repercussions on Greek politics during the interwar period, when each rival faction, on gaining power, purged the officer corps of Venizelists or royalists as the case might be. But there was more to Venizelos' domestic policies during this period than mere reprisals against his opponents. Between 1917 and his defeat in the elections of November 1920 some significant reforms were introduced, particularly in the field of education, in which a number of prominent Greek intellectuals played an important role.

Once in firm control of all of Greece Venizelos committed a total of some nine divisions to the Macedonian front. These were deployed in the determined attack launched on the Salonica front in September 1918 by the allied commander, the French General Franchet d'Espérey. This overwhelmed the opposing Austrian, German and Bulgarian forces and contributed in large measure to the decision of the German High Command to sue for peace. Venizelos gave further convincing proof of his devotion to the Entente cause when he committed two Greek divisions to the ill-fated Western attempt to 'strangle Bolshevism at birth'. Anxiety to make plain his devotion to the allied cause and a fear of bolshevism were undoubtedly the mainsprings of this decision, but there were also several hundred thousand Greeks in southern Russia and the Pontos region.

With the signing of the general armistice on 11 November 1918 (the Turks having already signed an armistice at Mudros on 30 October), Venizelos was determined to reap the reward for his record of unflinching support for the allies, and he soon arrived in Paris as Greece's principal negotiator at the Versailles Peace Conference. One basic problem facing the peacemakers was posed by conflicting Greek and Italian territorial claims in Asia Minor. By the Treaty of London of 1915, by which she had been induced to enter the war, Italy had been given the Antalya region. This concession had been widened by the agreement of St Jean de Maurienne of April 1917 to include the Smyrna region, which was of course the principal focus of Greece's territorial aspirations. So important were Greece's ambitions in this respect that Venizelos had even been prepared to cede newly won territory in Macedonia to the Bulgarians, if necessary, for the Smyrna region. He might at the peace conference be prepared to be flexible over Greek claims to the Dodecanese, Italian sovereignty over which had been recognised at the Treaty of London of 1915, and to Northern Epirus, the region, largely Orthodox in population, that had been incorporated into Albania in 1913. He might also be prepared to see Constantinople and the Straits placed under some form of international control together with the creation of an independent or autonomous Armenia, in which the sizeable Greek population of the Pontos could be incorporated. Over Smyrna, however, there could be no compromise. For the incorporation of Smyrna and its hinterland within the bounds of the independent Greek state had long been a cherished element of the Great Idea. Population figures compiled independently by the Ottoman authorities and by the ecumenical patriarchate shortly before the First World War had given the Turks (some 950,000) a majority over the Greeks (some 620,000) in the *vilayet*, or province, of Aydin which incorporated the Smyrna region. Nevertheless Venizelos was confident that the inevitable influx of Greeks from other regions of Asia Minor, combined with the high natural rate of population increase of the Anatolian Greeks, would soon lead to an overwhelming Greek preponderance in the area. By 1919 Venizelos had an additional reason to seek to consolidate the Greek population of Asia Minor, which amounted to perhaps as many as a million and a half, under Greek protection. For, from the time of the Balkan wars onwards, during most of which time Greece and Turkey had been ranged on opposing sides, the Anatolian Greeks had been subjected to discriminatory and often harsh treatment, although, unlike the Armenians, they had not been the object of genocide.

Greek annexation of Smyrna and its hinterland was, then, the key Greek demand at the peace conference. Although as yet there was no prospect of a peace settlement with the Ottoman Empire, in March 1919 the Italians began landing substantial contingents of troops in the Antalya region. By early May they were moving in the direction of Smyrna, to the manifest alarm not only of the Greeks, but of the British, French and Americans as well. For it was clear that Greek and Italian claims in Asia Minor were in direct conflict. Although no concrete agreement had yet been reached among the allies as to the shape of any final settlement with the Turks over the liquidation of the Ottoman Empire in general and over the future over Asia Minor in particular, Lloyd George, the British prime minister, secured the agreement of his French counterpart, Clemenceau, and of President Wilson of the United States to Venizelos' proposal to land Greek troops for the protection of the local population. The Greek occupation force, under the protection of allied warships, began to disembark at Smyrna on 15 May. In this somewhat haphazard and casual way began the Greek occupation of western Asia Minor, an occupation that was to culminate three years later in a disaster of truly tragic dimensions.

Lloyd George had little understanding of the geo-political realities of the enterprise to which he had given his encouragement. His foreign secretary, Lord Curzon, and his military advisers took a less sanguine view of the venture. Moreover, the Greek landings were marred by fighting between Greek troops and elements in the local Turkish population, which resulted in substantial casualties on the Turkish side. The arrival a few days later of Aristeides

Stergiadis, a stern disciplinarian genuinely committed to the notion of Christian-Muslim equality, as the Greek High Commissioner, ensured that ugly incidents of this kind were not repeated. But a severe blow had from the beginning been struck at the confidence of the local Turkish population in the fairness of the Greek administration. Stergiadis' attempt to dispense even-handed justice to Muslim and non-Muslim alike resulted in the alienation of many members of the local Greek community and did little to win over the local Turks.

Rival bands of Greek and Turkish irregulars were soon at each other's throats and within a matter of months British military observers were drawing attention to an ominous revival of Turkish national feeling in Anatolia, for the resurgence of which the Greek occupation of the Smyrna region had acted as the catalyst. In the National Pact of February 1920, Mustafa Kemal (Atatürk) and his increasingly powerful and representative Turkish nationalist followers had declared their independence from the supine, pro-Allied Turkish government centred in Istanbul. They made it clear that they would not tolerate a foreign occupation of Anatolia, which they considered to be the heartland of the Turkish people. The defiance of the Anatolian nationalists also began to influence the hitherto quiescent Turks of the capital. This prompted the allies, in March 1920, to tighten their grip on Istanbul.

The Italians soon began to appreciate the potential of a revived Turkish nationalism and reached an accommodation with the nationalists. The French, too, whose own claim to exercise a protectorate over Cilicia conflicted with Kemal's determination not to yield an inch of the Anatolian homeland, began to have increasing doubts about the wisdom and durability of the Greek occupation. Few doubting voices were raised in Greece, however, where the news that the peace treaty with Turkey had been signed on 10 August 1920 at Sèvres was greeted with rapturous enthusiasm as signalling a massive step towards the fulfilment of the Great Idea. Under the treaty, Smyrna and its hinterland, while remaining under Turkish sovereignty, was for five years to be administered by Greece. It might then be formally united with Greece if a local parliament or plebiscite voted for such a union. Greek sovereignty over the Aegean islands acquired during the Balkan wars was to be recognised, although Imvros and Tenedos, on account of their strategic position straddling the entrance to the Dardanelles, were to be demilitarised. In a separate agreement the Italians had already undertaken to cede the Dodecanese, with the exception of Rhodes, to Greece. Greece was to receive virtually the whole of western and eastern Thrace, although Bulgaria was to have special rights in the port of Dedeagatch (Alexandroupolis). Istanbul was to remain the Turkish capital but with an allied garrison. The Straits were to be administered by an international commission dominated by the Powers but on which Greece and Turkey were to be represented. By a separate treaty Britain and France formally abandoned the guarantee of Greece that they had assumed in 1832. Although Cyprus, Pontos and Northern Epirus were not included in the settlement, Venizelos' supporters could truly claim that he had created a Greece of 'the two continents and of the five seas'.

In fact, however, the provisions of the Treaty of Sèvres were to remain a dead letter, and the euphoria briefly engendered in Greece by the signing of the treaty was soon to be dissipated by political confusion. Inter-party squabbles now began to threaten the whole edifice of Greek irredentism. On 25 October 1920 King Alexander, who had succeeded his father in 1917, died of a bite from a pet monkey. The refusal of his older and younger brothers, George and Paul, to accept the crown had the effect of transforming the elections scheduled for November 1920 into a contest between the supporters of the exiled King Constantine and those of Venizelos. The latter were confident that Venizelos' impressive diplomatic triumphs in Paris would be enough to guarantee victory. In fact, however, his opponents secured 246 seats in a 370 seat parliament and his supporters only 120. Venizelos in disgust went into self-imposed exile. He and his followers had drastically underestimated the degree of residual support that existed for the crown, the resentment which had been created by the activities of Venizelist zealots and the continuing bitterness over the allies' flagrant meddling in Greece's internal affairs during the war. They failed, moreover, to appreciate that apparent foreign policy triumphs were no compensation for the weariness of a population that had been on a war footing for the best part of eight years. With a population of some 5½ million, Greece was maintaining some 200,000 men under arms, of whom many were stationed in Asia Minor. The royalists had sought to exploit opposition to the war in their campaign but once in power they made it clear that they were determined to pursue a forward policy in Asia Minor.

Britain and France, thoroughly alarmed at the prospect of a Constantinist restoration, warned in a note that the return of King Constantine would be regarded with strong disfavour and have serious financial consequences. On 5 December, however, a plebiscite recorded an overwhelming vote for his return. The official figures were 999,960 in favour, 10,383 against. These figures had obviously been manipulated, but nonetheless there seems to have been a majority in favour of Constantine's return and he was warmly received when he landed in Greece on 19 December 1920. Those purged by the Venizelists were reinstated and efforts were made to restore the seniority of army officers ousted in 1917. Venizelist officers as such were not purged from the army, but command posts were reshuffled, some officers resigned and others were kept from front-line positions. These changes had an unsettling effect on army morale at a time when the international situation was changing to Greece's disadvantage.

The French and Italians saw in the restoration of Constantine a useful pretext for coming to terms with Mustafa Kemal. At a conference of the parties to the Anatolian entanglement, in London in February 1921, the French and Italians both took the opportunity to make private deals with the Turkish nationalists, the French agreeing to a revision of their Cilician frontiers, the Italians withdrawing their claim to territory in Anatolia. These agreements were a prelude to France's later abandonment of her claim to Cilicia and the Italian evacuation of Asia Minor. Soon afterwards Kemal signed a treaty of friendship with the fledgling Soviet republic, both parties seeing themselves as victims of foreign intervention.

Although now abandoned by their erstwhile allies France and Italy, the Greeks nonetheless gained the impression that Lloyd George would look with favour on a further Greek offensive in Asia Minor, which the military position now called for. Towards the end of March 1921 a major offensive was launched, and by the end of the summer the Greek armies, now nominally commanded by King Constantine himself, had reached the Sakarya river, some forty miles from the Turkish nationalist stronghold of Ankara. The Greek offensive, however, was critically impeded by their inability to purchase arms in Britain, following the proclamation in April 1921 by the allies of a policy of strict neutrality, although the French and Italians showed few inhibitions in supplying arms to the Turkish nationalists. By the early autumn of 1921 the Greeks had been pushed back to the line of the Afyonkarahisar-Eskishehir railway and an uneasy military stalemate ensued, with the Greek lines of communication being dangerously extended.

On the Greek side there was a growing realisation that the Greek position in Asia Minor was untenable both politically and militarily. For this reason proposals put forward by Curzon at the Paris conference of March 1922 for a compromise peace which would involve the withdrawal of the Greek armies from Asia Minor and the placing of the Greek populations under League of Nations protection, were acceptable to the Greeks. But the Turks, sensing victory, insisted on an unconditional evacuation of the Greek forces, a demand unacceptable to the Greeks. The Greeks, moreover, continued to derive comfort from Lloyd George's ambivalent statements of encouragement, and in July 1922 unsuccessfully sought permission from the allies to enter Istanbul. Meanwhile Mustafa Kemal was preparing a devastating counter-attack along the two-hundred-mile Greek front at a time when the fighting capabilities of the Greek army had been seriously impeded by the replacement as commander-in-chief in Asia Minor of General Papoulas by the idiosyncratic General Hadjianestis, who had had no battle experience since the Balkan wars.

Mustafa Kemal launched his offensive on 26 August 1922 in the region of Afyonkarahisar. The Turkish attack rapidly turned into a Greek rout, with the Greek forces retreating in disarray to

Smyrna and the coast. On 8 September the Greek army evacuated the city, which the Turkish army entered the following day. Initially the Turkish occupation of the city was relatively orderly but on the evening of the 9th outbreaks of killing and looting began. This was followed by a full-scale massacre of the Christian population, in which the Armenians suffered the greatest casualties. Some 30,000 Christians perished, and in the great fire that ensued the Armenian, Greek and Frankish quarters were very largely destroyed. Only the Turkish and Jewish quarters survived the holocaust. 'Gâvur Izmir' or 'Infidel Izmir', as the Turks called the city, was no more. A quarter of a million people fled to the waterfront to escape the inferno, but the allied troops and ships stationed in the port for the most part maintained an attitude of studied neutrality. Within a few days the last Greek troops had abandoned the soil of Asia Minor and withdrawn to the Greek islands and mainland. A 2500-year Greek presence on the western littoral of Asia Minor had been abruptly terminated in conditions of total disaster. If the Greek defeat in the Greco-Turkish war of 1897 had proved a major psychological shock, then the 'catastrophe', as the Greeks termed the Asia Minor débâcle, was to administer both a profound physical as well as psychological shock. For not only did it signify the end of the Great Idea but the 'catastrophe' was also to result in the arrival in Greece of well over a million Greeks, many of them destitute, bearing with them little more than their holy icons and other religious relics, a significant number of them indeed knowing no other language than Turkish.

Not surprisingly, a setback of this magnitude had profound repercussions on the domestic politics of Greece. On 10 September King Constantine dismissed his government but the political pace was now being made by a revolutionary committee formed from the defeated rump of the Asia Minor army. The committee's leaders were Colonels Plastiras and Gonatas and the naval Captain Phokas. The revolutionary committee arranged for leaflets to be dropped by plane over Athens on 26 September, an early example of the use of aircraft in a military *coup d'état*. These called for the abdication of the king and the resignation of his government. These demands were backed up by the arrival of a battleship, with the revolutionary committee and a contingent of troops on board, at Lavrion near Athens. Backed by armed force the revolutionary committee assumed power, although a token civilian government was set up. King Constantine abdicated, to be replaced by his eldest son George, and eight politicians and senior officers were arrested, along with many others. Venizelos, at this time outside Greece, declined to participate in the revolutionary government, but agreed to act as its representative abroad in the hope of being able to salvage something from the wreckage of a truly catastrophic military defeat.

Declaring itself to be above party politics, the revolutionary government announced in mid-October the setting up of a commission of inquiry to determine responsibility for the Asia Minor disaster. On the basis of the commission's findings the eight politicians and military commanders arrested by the junta were tried in November by court martial on charges of high treason. As the court martial progressed Britain threatened to break off diplomatic relations if death sentences were carried out. This threat led to the resignation of the nominal civilian government and the revolutionary committee formed a government headed by Colonel Gonatas, with General Pangalos as minister of war. Plastiras stayed outside the government as 'Leader of the Revolution'. On 27 November all eight on trial were found guilty of high treason and six of the defendants were condemned to death. Despite strenuous British intervention on their behalf and a belated and somewhat half-hearted plea for clemency by Venizelos, the six, Gounaris, Protopapadakis, Baltazzis, Stratos, Theotokis and General Hadjianestis, were executed on 28 November. Gounaris, who was ill, had to be helped to the place of execution. This was in effect judicial murder, for whatever their failings and errors of judgement, the six could manifestly not be accused of deliberate acts of treason. The execution of the six, which led to the immediate withdrawal of the British minister, was to cast a long shadow over subsequent political developments in Greece and gave to the antagonism between Venizelists and royalists something of the quality of a blood feud. But, if the long-term consequences were grave, in the short term the traumatic shock induced by the executions may well have had the effect of averting the real possibility of civil war and it contributed powerfully to the restoration of discipline in the army.

The revolutionary government briefly considered launching an attack on Turkish Thrace, for the substantial Greek forces on this front had quickly been re-grouped. But this was essentially a bluff, for it was clear that only a negotiated settlement with the Turks was possible and that all Venizelos' diplomatic skills would be needed in the negotiations which resulted in the Treaty of Lausanne of July 1923. By the terms of the Treaty, Greece forfeited virtually all the gains she had won at the Treaty of Sèvres, e.g. the Smyrna enclave, eastern Thrace and the islands of Imvros and Tenedos, while Italy reneged on her undertaking to cede the Dodecanese to Greece. Greek sovereignty over Mytilini, Chios and Samos was, however, recognised by the Turks, although restrictions were placed on the garrisoning and fortifying of the islands which lay only a few miles from the Turkish coast.

At the end of January 1923 a separate convention on an exchange of populations was signed between Venizelos and Ismet (Inönü), the Turkish representative. This provided that there should be 'a compulsory exchange of Turkish nationals of the Greek Orthodox religion established in Turkish territory, and of Greek nationals of the Moslem religion established in Greek territory'. Some odd anomalies resulted from this decision to consider religion as the basic criterion of nationality. It meant, for instance, that the substantial populations of Turkish-speaking Orthodox Christians of Asia Minor, the *karamanlis*, were included in the exchange. Many of these, particularly the womenfolk, knew no Greek at all. Likewise, the Greek-speaking Muslims of Crete, the descendants of Christian families who had apostasised *en masse* to Islam in the seventeenth century, were also uprooted. The only exceptions to the exchange were those members of the substantial Greek population of Istanbul who could prove that they were established in the city prior to October 1918 (hence the appellation *établis*), together with the inhabitants of the largely Greek populated islands of Imvros and Tenedos. The ecumenical patriarchate, the focus of world Orthodoxy, was also permitted to remain in the Phanar in

Istanbul. In return the Muslim population of western Thrace was allowed to remain *in situ*.

The actual exchange was weighted very heavily in Turkey's favour, for some 380,000 Muslims were exchanged for something like 1,100,000 Christians, although most of the Greeks had already fled to Greece before the refugee convention had been signed. Plenty of land had been vacated by the departing Greeks for the incoming Turks, and Turkey was in any case underpopulated. Greece, on the other hand, was scarcely capable of maintaining its existing population, and was obliged to take in a total influx of refugees, including those from Russia and Bulgaria, approaching 1,300,000. Some uncertainty exists as to the precise numbers. The 1928 census gave the following figures: refugees from Turkey, 1,104,216; refugees from Russia, 58,526; refugees from Bulgaria, 49,027. The overall population of Greece rose between 1907 and 1928 from 2,600,000 to 6,200,000. The population of Athens alone nearly doubled between 1920 and 1928, the city being encircled by refugee shanty towns which survived for many decades afterwards.

Although the exchange of populations necessarily occasioned a great deal of human misery it did largely remove what would have undoubtedly remained a permanent and potent source of tension between Greece and Turkey and it did ensure that Greece itself became an ethnically homogeneous society. After the Greek advances of 1912, for instance, the Greek element in Greek Macedonia had constituted only some 43 per cent of the population. By 1926, with the resettlement of the refugees, the Greek element had risen to 89 per cent. In western Thrace the Greeks in 1919 had constituted a mere 17 per cent of the population. By 1924 this figure had risen to 62 per cent. The result was that Greece was transformed into a country virtually without minority problems, by Balkan standards at least, although the existence of the Turkish minority in western Thrace and of the slavophone population of Macedonia was from time to time to occasion friction with Turkey, Yugoslavia and Bulgaria.

Inevitably an influx of this magnitude into a poor, backward and essentially non-industrialised country was to have profound socio-political consequences. Implementation of the 1917 legislation completed the process of breaking up the large landed estates which reached a peak in 1923. The extensive properties of the monasteries of Mount Athos were also expropriated. These lands, together with those of the departing Muslims, were made available to the incoming Greeks. A Refugee Settlement Commission, chaired by an American citizen, oversaw the process of resettlement with remarkable efficiency, raising international loans for the purpose. The successful resettlement of the refugees of rural origins and the breaking up of the large estates was to ensure that Greece, even if its agriculture was to remain fragmented and inefficient, was to be spared the problems associated with a pauperised, landless, rural peasantry such as Romania, for instance, experienced. It helps to explain, too, why Greece has never developed any real agrarian movement on the Romanian or Bulgarian pattern.

The settlement of the refugees with an urban background proved to be more of an intractable problem. Cities such as Smyrna had possessed very large and highly stratified Greek populations, ranging from wealthy entrepreneurs to a rudimentary industrial proletariat. Few of the middle-class Anatolian Greeks had been able to bring with them any but their most portable possessions. Some were to deploy their entrepreneurial skills in Greece and give a much needed boost to the country's industrial development. But others, who constituted with the workers a source of cheap labour, were reduced to eking out a miserable existence on the fringes of Athens and Salonica, and contributed to the top heavy urban development of the country. On the whole, however, Greece coped remarkably well with the enormous strains placed on the fabric of its society by the arrival of the refugees. One likely influence of the refugees was on the decision to abolish the monarchy in 1924. A plebiscite in that year resulted in a 70 (758,742) per cent vote in favour of a republic, against a 30 (325,322) per cent vote for the monarchy. Analysis of these votes indicates that New Greece, and the refugee districts of Athens and Piraeus, voted overwhelmingly for a republic, with Old Greece remaining faithful to the monarchy. It has often been observed that a number of leading cadres of the Communist Party of Greece (KKE), originally founded in 1918 as the Socialist Labour Party, were of Anatolian origin. These included Nikos Zakhariadis, the party's secretary-general between 1931 and 1956. It is not surprising that the communists should have made some headway in recruiting among the *déraciné* refugees. Indeed in 1924 the KKE declared that its struggle for power was aimed at 'the bourgeois fascist-republic in order that we impose by arms. a workers' and peasants' and refugees' government'. The KKE was, however, critically impeded in its recruitment effort by the decision imposed upon it by the Comintern in 1924 that it should advocate the creation of an autonomous Macedonian state. In 1935 the party line switched to one of support for the principle of the equality of all nationalities within Greece. Despite this it was easy for the party's opponents to stigmatise the KKE as unpatriotic, prepared to cede territory for which Greek blood had been shed. Such jibes carried particular weight with the refugees, a large number of whom were settled in Greek Macedonia and who, having once been dispossessed, were disinclined to repeat the experience. Generally the refugees continued to blame the royalists for their misfortunes and, despite all their privations, remained loyal to Venizelos and his supporters.

The revolutionary government of Gonatas retained its grip on power throughout 1923, and survived without difficulty a counter-revolution in October 1923 organised by Generals Leonardopoulos, Gargalides and Colonel Ziras. Although there was no evidence that King George was implicated in the attempted coup, suggestions that he was were to prove disastrous for the monarchy. The royalists largely abstained from the elections held in December, anti-Venizelists winning a mere 7 seats to the Venizelists' 401. Following the election King George went abroad on 'leave of absence', pending a plebiscite on the constitutional issue, while Venizelos, responding to the urgent pleas of his followers, returned to Greece early in January 1924. He was prime minister, however, for barely a month before handing over the premiership to Kaphandaris on the pretext of health. Kaphandaris in turn was succeeded as prime minister by Alexander Papanastasiou, the leader of the republican and mildly socialist wing of the Liberal party. Despite the holding of elections, the Papanastasiou cabinet retained a distinct military flavour. Although there was a convincing vote for a republic in the April 1924 plebiscite, a new republican constitution was not voted until 1927.

A series of somewhat ineffective republican governments, all to some degree beholden to the military, culminated in General Pangalos' *opéra bouffe* military dictatorship of 1925–6, which he established with the help of a mere twenty-eight fellow conspirators. After a short period of quasi-parliamentary rule, Pangalos openly proclaimed himself dictator in January 1926. Having exiled a number of prominent politicians he had himself elected president in elections in which he was the sole candidate. Two civil servants were publicly hanged for embezzlement but otherwise Pangalos left little impression on Greek public life other than his over-reaction to a minor border incident which led to a short-lived invasion of Greece's traditional enemy Bulgaria, and a decree forbidding women to raise their skirts more than a specified distance from the ground. In August 1926 he was overthrown in a putsch, led by General Kondylis and Colonel Napoleon Zervas, an erstwhile supporter.

Admiral Koundouriotis, a member of a distinguished Greco-Albanian family from Hydra, resumed the presidency. Following elections in November 1926 an 'ecumenical government' was formed, consisting of representatives of the republican parties (143 seats) and their opponents (127 seats). Under the aegis of this coalition cabinet the republican constitution was finally promulgated in 1927. This provided for a two-chamber parliament, consisting of a senate (*gerousia*) and lower house (*vouli*), and further extended civil liberties. On the resignation of the coalition in February 1928, Venizelos made a come-back as leader of the Liberals when President Koundouriotis appointed him prime minister in July 1928. Venizelos promptly called new elections in August. He won a massive majority but the peremptory manner in which he did away with proportional representation alienated his former close collaborators, Kondylis, Kaphandaris and Papanastasiou. Although Venizelos' four-year premiership between

1928 and 1932 was to provide a welcome element of stability after the political turmoil of the twenties, it cannot be compared for reforming impetus with his administration on the eve of the First World War. It was not merely the case that Venizelos was now an older man, whose views on social questions had failed to keep pace with the times, but more that he was ill-equipped by training and temperament to deal with the severe strains placed on the Greek economy by the world depression following the Great Crash of 1929. His essential conservatism was reflected in the 'idionym' law of the same year which made attempts to undermine the existing social order illegal.

Greece was particularly badly affected by the world crisis, for her principal exports were luxury products such as tobacco, currants and olive oil, whose prices slumped with reduced demand in a depressed world economy. By 1934 the value of Greek exports amounted to only half the value of imports. Moreover, the total value of Greek exports had fallen from a yearly average of $125 million between 1922 and 1930 to a mere $49 million in 1933. At the same time there was a sharp decrease in emigrant remittances and in receipts from shipping, the principal means by which Greece had traditionally overcome its chronic balance of payments deficits. Greek emigrants in the United States were naturally affected by the recession, while emigration to the United States, a traditional safety valve in times of economic discontent, had been effectively cut off by the Johnson-Reed Act of 1924, which particularly discriminated against southern Europeans by establishing an entry quota based on the size of existing ethnic groups in proportion to the total American population. Inevitably the international financial crisis weighed heavily on Greece which had large external debts and had raised further substantial loans on the international money markets to finance the resettlement of the refugees. By 1933 something like two thirds of state expenditures were devoted to servicing Greece's massive foreign debts and as a consequence she was obliged to default on her interest payments, as had happened in 1893.

But if Venizelos showed little grasp of the complexities of international trade and finance and increasingly resorted to illiberal measures to contain domestic unrest, his expertise in matters of foreign policy was undiminished. The 'catastrophe' in Asia Minor had demonstrated that the era of an adventurist foreign policy was clearly over. Indeed, Mussolini had exploited Greece's weak international position after 1922 by using the pretext of the murder of the Italian members of the Greek-Albanian frontier commission to bombard and occupy the island of Corfu in 1923. League of Nations pressure brought about an Italian withdrawal although Greece was obliged to pay a substantial indemnity. Relations with Bulgaria, traditionally bad, were seriously impaired by the Greek-Bulgarian frontier incident of 1925, which again resulted in Greece, following League of Nations mediation, paying an indemnity. Relations with the new Turkish republic were inevitably strained in the aftermath of the 'catastrophe', and they were further exacerbated by disputes arising out of the status of the *établis* and of the ecumenical patriarchate, over compensation for immovable property left behind by the refugees and as a result of General Pangalos' brief outburst of anti-Turkish belligerency.

On returning to office in 1928 Venizelos embarked on a determined policy of mending fences with Greece's neighbours. Relations with Italy were normalised by the conclusion of a treaty of friendship in September 1928. In 1929 a treaty of friendship was negotiated with Yugoslavia, Greece's traditional good relations with her northern neighbour having been soured by disputes over Yugoslav access to a free zone in Salonica and over Greece's slavophone minority. Relations with Albania and Bulgaria also improved. But the greatest of Venizelos' diplomatic triumphs during this period undoubtedly lay in his successful rapprochement with Turkey, a mere eight years after the Asia Minor débâcle. In 1930 Venizelos paid an official visit to Turkey during which he called at the ecumenical patriarchate in the Phanar, the first such visit by a Greek prime minister. By the Ankara convention Venizelos reached agreement on the vexed question of compensation for immovable refugee property. The terms he negotiated greatly upset the refugees themselves, but in agreeing them Venizelos was preparing the ground for a Greco-Turkish treaty of friendship signed in the same year. This treaty was to usher in a decade of good relations between Greece and Turkey.

During the early 1930s Venizelos was also able to assist in laying the groundwork for what in 1934 was to emerge as the Balkan Entente. The Balkan Entente was developed from a series of conferences convened, largely on Greek initiative, in Athens (1930), Istanbul (1931), Bucharest (1932) and Salonica (1933). There was much talk of Balkan unity, some substance was given to the enthusiastic rhetoric of the politicians by the creation of a number of inter-Balkan organisations, and some real progress was made in the sphere of inter-Balkan cultural relations. A persistent theme of the various conferences was the creation of a Balkan Pact, although matters were complicated by Bulgaria's refusal to accept as permanent the frontiers established by the Treaty of Neuilly (1919) and by Albania's insistence, along with Bulgaria, in raising the question of the status of minorities. Bulgaria and Albania were not signatories to the Balkan Pact that was eventually signed in Athens in 1934, but the 'anti-revisionist' states of the Balkans, Greece, Yugoslavia, Romania and Turkey, agreed on a mutual guarantee of their existing frontiers. The high hopes initially raised by the Balkan Pact were later to crumble under the impact of German and Italian penetration of south-east Europe. On the outbreak of the Second World War the Balkan Pact proved to be a dead letter, but it nonetheless stands to Venizelos' credit that it was largely due to his initiatives that a genuine effort was made to diminish the traditional rivalries and mutual antagonisms of the Balkan states.

In elections held in September 1932, at the end of his four-year parliamentary term, Venizelos' Liberals secured a narrow victory over Panayis Tsaldaris' Populists, the bulk of whom were royalists, although Tsaldaris himself had undertaken to work within the framework of the republican constitution. Lacking an overall majority Venizelos was unable to form a government, and in November Tsaldaris formed a minority government. Venizelos soon brought this down and summoned new elections for March 1933. But this tactic backfired, for the Populists won 135 seats to the Liberals' 96, although the senate, elected on a complicated franchise, remained under Venizelist control. Venizelos' defeat prompted General Nicholas Plastiras, the main protagonist of the putsch of 1922, to mount a coup on the night of 5/6 March. This failed miserably and inevitably there were suspicions that Venizelos had connived at, if not actually encouraged, the coup. Equally inevitably the failed putsch was followed by an anti-Venizelist backlash. The Plastiras coup, opening up as it did all the old wounds caused by the National Schism, was to have a disastrous effect on the stability of the Greek political system. A number of Venizelos' former supporters, among them Kondylis, had by this time become bitter opponents. On 6 June 1933 there was an attempt on Venizelos' life in the course of an extraordinary car chase down the Kifissia–Athens road. Venizelos' bodyguard was killed and his wife wounded and the inertia of the Athens police in investigating the assassination attempt led to suspicions of government complicity.

Despite Tsaldaris' willingness to accept the republican regime there was now increasing talk in government circles of a restoration of the monarchy. This in turn helped to precipitate a further anti-government coup on 1 March 1935, planned largely by republican officers who had either been compulsorily retired or feared such retirement in the wake of the abortive 1933 coup. Although mounted on a larger scale than that of 1933, the *kinima*, or putsch, of 1935 also ended in ignominious failure. Three army officers were executed for their involvement, and more than a thousand were purged from the army, navy and air force. Overall these were the most extensive purges so far undertaken in the Greek armed forces. Many hundreds of Venizelists in the civil service and the universities were also purged. Venizelos, who had accepted the leadership of the coup, was forced into exile where he joined General Plastiras in France. They were subsequently sentenced to death in absentia. Venizelos died in Paris the following year, and Plastiras was to remain in France until summoned back to Greece at British behest ten years later. A significant number of officers purged for their role in the 1935 coup, among them Colonels Bakirdzis, Saraphis, Psarros and (naval) Commander

Koutsogiannopoulos, were subsequently to play a major role in the wartime resistance to the Axis.

The failed coup strengthened the hand of those seeking a royalist restoration. In April the republican-controlled senate was abolished and the Venizelists abstained from the elections of June 1935 in protest at the continuance of martial law and of press censorship imposed in the aftermath of the March coup. This made a Populist landslide a foregone conclusion. Tsaldaris' Populists duly won 287 seats in a 300-seat parliament and Metaxas' Royalist Union 7. Tsaldaris now promised a plebiscite on the issue of monarchy versus republic. This was not enough, however, for the more extreme champions of a royalist restoration, who were led by Venizelos' erstwhile supporter Kondylis. On 10 October a group of high-ranking officers stopped Tsaldaris' car and demanded either an immediate restoration or his resignation. Tsaldaris resigned, to be replaced by Kondylis as prime minister. Kondylis now declared the abolition of the republic in the fifth national assembly, from which Tsaldaris and his supporters withdrew. On 3 November a plebiscite was held on the issue. This resulted in the patently rigged result of 1,491,992 votes for a restoration to 32,454 against. Even in the Venizelist heartland of Crete there was an overwhelming vote for a restoration. Although the results had clearly been crudely falsified, nonetheless it is likely that many Greeks had favoured a restoration, hoping that it would bring about a measure of stability after the confusions and uncertainties of recent years.

Moreover King George II himself, who had spent the years of his exile in England, seems to have returned to Greece with the genuine intention of bringing about reconciliation and a healing of the wounds occasioned by the National Schism. Indeed, even Venizelos, who was never a doctrinaire republican, shortly before his death in exile in France in March 1936 urged a 'benevolent toleration' of the monarchy, provided that his supporters were not victimised. It was the king's wish to pardon the military, and amnesty the civilian, participants in the abortive 1935 putsch that led to the removal of the hard-liner Kondylis as prime minister. At the beginning of December 1935 the king appointed Constantine

Demertzis, professor of civil law at the University of Athens and a moderate royalist, to head a caretaker government to oversee elections. These elections, held on 26 January 1936, were fairly conducted under a system of proportional representation and had a disastrously inconclusive result. The Populists and their royalist allies gained 143 seats, the Liberal party and its allies 141 seats, and the communist dominated Popular Front 15. The communists, holding the balance between the two main blocs, were now projected from relative obscurity to the forefront of the political stage. Demertzis remained as prime minister while the politicians sought to negotiate a way out of the political impasse.

Tsaldaris, the Populist leader, and his Liberal counterpart, Themistocles Sophoulis, were aware of a growing groundswell of public disillusion with the politicians and their seemingly incessant intrigues and were both personally inclined to form some sort of coalition, although their freedom of manoeuvre was impeded by hardliners in their respective parties and pressure from the military. While negotiations got under way between Populists and Liberals, each of the main blocs secretly talked with the communists. When news of these secret discussions was leaked, apparently by the communists themselves, there were rumblings of discontent within the army. The minister of war, General Papagos, warned the king that the army would not stand for any deal with the communists, whereupon General John Metaxas was appointed in his place. Following his involvement in the 1923 putsch against the Revolutionary Government, Metaxas had been very much on the fringe of Greek politics and his disenchantment with parliamentarianism had been growing apace. Although he lacked any kind of public following, an odd quirk of fate was to give Metaxas his chance of wreaking revenge on the politicians he so despised. For Demertzis died on 13 April, and as there was still no end in sight to the political impasse, King George now appointed Metaxas prime minister. Within the space of a few months not only did Demertzis die but so also did Venizelos, Papanastasiou, a widely respected reformist politician, General Kondylis, and two former presidents of the republic, Koundouriotis and

Zaimis. At such a critical juncture Greece could ill afford the loss
of such experienced politicians.

The politicians continued their discussions, but their chances
of agreement were critically diminished by differences over the
vital question of the reinstatement in the armed forces of the
republican officers cashiered in 1935. Moreover, although
Sophoulis now made it clear that he ruled out the possibility of a
deal with the communists, the news that he had been negotiating
with them added further to the climate of disillusionment with
the politicians. Seeking a temporary way out of the impasse, the
deputies agreed to a proposal of Metaxas that parliament should
be adjourned for five months until 30 September. Parliament's
legislative functions were meanwhile to be transferred to a forty-
man commission, on which the parties were to be represented in
proportion to their overall strength in parliament. But in agreeing
to this manoeuvre the politicians were effectively cutting their
own throats, for it soon became clear that Metaxas never had any
intention of allowing parliament to reconvene. Moreover, the
parliamentary commission solved nothing. As the British minister
to Greece, Sir Sydney Waterlow, noted in one of his despatches,
the commission was 'a body which . . . merely reproduced in
miniature the political stalemate paralysing the Chamber and the
country'.

This feverish politicking in Athens was accompanied by unrest
in the country at large. Greece was still suffering grievously from
the effects of the world economic depression and this occasioned
a considerable amount of labour unrest. A large demonstration in
Salonica on 9/10 May by tobacco workers, who had been particularly badly hit by the collapse in world demand for Greek
tobacco, resulted in the death of 12 strikers. Some of the conscript
troops used to maintain order, along with elements in the police,
broke ranks and had to be confined to barracks to prevent further
fraternisation with the strikers. Mounting labour unrest, coupled
with the continued political impasse in Athens, increased the
king's sympathy towards Metaxas' plans for a 'strong' government. Although he had returned to Greece six months earlier
with conciliatory intentions, King George was rapidly losing

patience with the politicians and initially accepted, only to reject, a proposal for a coalition made on 22 July by Sophoulis, for the Liberals, and Theotokis, for the majority of the Populists, an agreement that could have ended the political deadlock. Matters reached a climax when the communists called a twenty-four-hour general strike for 5 August to protest against proposed legislation to impose compulsory arbitration in labour disputes. To pre-empt what he regarded as a direct communist challenge to his authority Metaxas secured the king's assent to the suspension on 4 August of a number of key articles of the constitution. Workers were mobilised to maintain essential services, press censorship was introduced, and parliament was formally dissolved, with no date being set for its recall. In the time-honoured fashion of military usurpers Metaxas claimed that these were merely temporary measures, to head off a threatened communist seizure of power. In fact, however, parliament was not to reconvene until 1946, after ten of the most stormy years in Greece's turbulent history.

6

Dictatorship, occupation, resistance and civil war, 1936–1949

Metaxas, having removed the last constraints on his authority, enjoying the active support of King George II, and able through him to count on the loyalty of the armed forces, now set about his long-cherished ambition of reshaping the Greek character and re-moulding Greek society. Since his days as a young army officer at the Prussian military academy he had nurtured an admiration for *ernst*, 'the serious German spirit', which he contrasted with the Greeks' excessive individualism and lack of a sense of corporate loyalty. In pursuit of this basic objective of 'disciplining' the Greek people he aped many of the trappings of German Nazism and Italian Fascism. In conscious imitation of Hitler's Third Reich he evolved the concept of the Third Hellenic Civilisation. The first was the pagan civilisation of ancient Greece, the second the Christian civilisation of Byzantium. The third, which would be fashioned under his aegis, would combine the virtues of both. In pursuit of his essentially paternalistic, authoritarian style of government he had himself proclaimed in 1937 'First Peasant' and 'First Worker', and also liked to be known as 'Leader' or 'National Father'. He declared a moratorium on peasant debts and introduced labour legislation that sounded progressive on paper, but much of his populist, anti-plutocratic rhetoric was belied by his practice. Workers particularly resented his introduction of compulsory arbitration of labour disputes.

Metaxas placed great store by the country's youth, and to this end created the National Youth Organisation (EON), which was intended to be the standard bearer of his ideals after his death. Membership of EON was made mandatory and rival organisations such as the Boy Scouts were suppressed. EON, too, was seen by Metaxas as providing a substitute for the lack of any kind of mass party base for his power, the most obvious difference between the Metaxas regime and the fascist regimes that he so admired. He shared to the full, however, their hostility towards liberalism, communism and parliamentary government, and indeed their nationalism, although his nationalism was of the non-aggressive variety. Nor, moreover, was his ideology, such as it was, based on theories of racial superiority.

Metaxas met with little opposition to the establishment of his dictatorship but equally with little enthusiasm. The reaction of the Greek people was one of resigned acquiescence. The general feeling was that the politicians, with their interminable feuds and intrigues, had not served the country well in recent years. Moreover, their inadequacies continued to reveal themselves under the dictatorship and their ineffectual and unco-ordinated conspiracies were easily frustrated by Metaxas and the ruthlessly efficient Constantine Maniadakis, who, as the minister responsible for public order, despatched many leading politicians to exile in the islands. The one serious manifestation of opposition to the regime, the uprising in the Venizelist stronghold of Crete in July 1938, quickly collapsed and the island was placed under martial law. The communists, despite their small numbers, proved a tougher nut to crack, owing to their greater experience of clandestine political activity. But Maniadakis achieved a remarkable degree of success in penetrating their underground party organisation and was able to produce a version of the party newspaper *Rizospastis* which outsiders had difficulty in distinguishing from the genuine article. Another successful tactic in undermining party morale was his practice of releasing communists from detention provided that they would sign a humiliating declaration, renouncing not only their political past but also denouncing their erstwhile comrades. Some of these declarations were extracted by brute force, for the communists were treated altogether more harshly than the politicians, whom Maniadakis handled relatively benignly. Some were signed on party orders to enable particular individuals to resume underground activity. Nonetheless, an aura of suspicion attached to those who, for whatever reason, did sign, and they were never subsequently able to shake it off.

Metaxas' ideological attachment to fascism was paralleled by an increasing German penetration of the Greek economy. Between 1930 and 1938 the proportion of Greek exports shipped to Germany rose from 24 per cent to 39 per cent of the total, while imports from Germany rose from 10 per cent to 29 per cent. By 1938 Germany was importing 40 per cent of the Greek tobacco crop, one of Greece's major exports. Yet despite Metaxas' admiration for the domestic policies of Nazi Germany and Fascist Italy, in matters of foreign policy, conscious of British sea power and of King George's attachment to Britain, he was anxious not to disturb the existing British connection. Indeed in 1938 he proposed an alliance with Britain. The British government, anxious to avoid new commitments, declined the offer, although it did extend extra credits to the Greek government. In April 1939, however, a few days after the Italian occupation of Albania, Britain and France did offer Greece, together with Romania, a guarantee of her territorial integrity, if she chose to resist aggression.

On the outbreak of the Second World War in September 1939 Metaxas sought to maintain a benevolent neutrality towards Britain while turning a blind eye to a series of Italian provocations. These culminated in August 1940 in the Italian torpedoing of the cruiser *Elli* which was anchored off Tinos for the traditional celebration of the Feast of the Dormition (Assumption) of the Virgin. But Metaxas' patience did have limits. When Mussolini, piqued at Hitler's lack of consultation with his principal ally and aiming at an independent Mediterranean and Balkan policy for Italy, ordered his minister in Athens to deliver at 3 a.m. on the morning of 28 October 1940 a humiliating ultimatum to the Greeks, Metaxas' reply was immediate and uncompromising. 'This means war', he told the Italian minister, rejecting out of hand an ultimatum which constituted a direct challenge to Greek sovereignty and which was to expire at 6 a.m. the same morning.

Mussolini had in part been tempted to single Greece out as a victim by intelligence reports that morale in the Greek army was low and equipment poor. But one of Metaxas' major achievements had been to bring about the reorganisation and re-equipment of the Greek armed forces under their chief-of-staff, General Papagos. Moreover, his dignified rejection of the Italian ultimatum was followed by an intense wave of national exaltation, and the Italian invading force that began to pour across the Albanian frontier met with fierce resistance. Greeks flocked to the colours, although Metaxas refused to relax his vendetta against prominent Venizelists and no officer of senior rank who had been cashiered in the abortive Venizelist coups of 1933 and 1935 was allowed to re-enlist. These rejects, many of them soldiers of high professional competence, fiercely patriotic and staunchly pro-British, were left kicking their heels in Athens and Salonica where they formed natural recruits for the British Special Operations Executive, which, unknown to the Greek authorities, had already been charged with secretly laying the groundwork for a post-occupation resistance network in Greece.

Although it is clear that the imbalance between the Greek and Italian forces in numbers and equipment was not as great as it seemed at the time, the spectacle of the Greek David worsting the Italian Goliath gave a great boost to the anti-Axis struggle during the dark winter of 1940–41. Greece, indeed, was Britain's only active ally at the time and the Greeks gave convincing proof that the Axis armies were not invincible. Within a matter of days the Greek army had not only pushed the Italians back to the Albanian border but had counter-attacked across it, capturing Korcë (Korytsa) on 22 November, Sarandë (Ayioi Saranda) on 6 December and Gjirokastër (Argyrokastro) on 8 December. These victories had a particularly strong emotive appeal to the Greeks for these were the three principal towns of Northern Epirus, the partially Greek-inhabited area of southern Albania on which Greek nationalists had long cast a covetous eye. The victorious Greek armies were poised to push on to the port of Vlorë (Valona), a crucial Italian supply base, when atrocious weather conditions in an area of poor communications led to a military stalemate.

From the moment of the Italian attack Churchill had made it

clear that Britain was prepared to go to the assistance of Greece, telling the war cabinet in early November 1940 that Britain could not afford the stigma of allowing another small nation, solemnly guaranteed by Britain, to fall to the Axis. The chiefs-of-staff, however, reluctantly allowed only four squadrons of Blenheims and Gladiators to be despatched to Greece. Moreover, Churchill's offer to commit troops in January 1941 was declined by Metaxas, who was unwilling to offer anything that might be considered as a provocation to Hitler. The Greek attitude changed, however, with Metaxas' death at the end of January and with mounting evidence that Hitler was tightening his grip on the other Balkan countries. The British also began at this time to take a more sanguine view of the possibilities of stemming a German invasion of Greece, although it is clear that the primary motive in sending British troops into Greece was to bolster the Yugoslavs, at this time coming under intense German pressure to adhere to the Tripartite Pact, and the Turks to stand up to the Germans. On 22/23 February a top-level British mission, including Anthony Eden, the foreign secretary, Field-Marshal Dill, the Chief of the Imperial General Staff, and General Wavell, the Commander-in-Chief, Middle East, visited Athens and met with King George, the new prime minister Alexander Koryzis and General Papagos, now the Greek commander-in-chief. They received assurances that Greece was prepared to fight on, despite mounting evidence of Germany's aggressive intentions towards the country.

At the Tatoi meeting, however, a catastrophic misunderstanding occurred. Eden, Dill and Wavell gained the impression that Papagos had agreed to withdraw forces from the Metaxas defensive line on the Bulgarian frontier to the more easily defensible line of the Aliakmon river in western Macedonia, where they would be reinforced by the British and Dominion forces being despatched to Greece. Papagos on the other hand, anxious not to leave Macedonia undefended, understood that such a withdrawal was to be contingent on determining Yugoslav willingness to resist the Germans. This confusion resulted in a critical delay in redeploying the Greek forces and effectively doomed operation *Lustre*, as the British expeditionary force was code-named, to failure in advance. Moreover, the German Legation was able to monitor the landing of the British force while, at Greek insistence, General 'Jumbo' Wilson, its commander, was obliged to move around in civilian clothes under a pseudonym. When Hitler, anxious to secure his Balkan flank before attacking the Soviet Union, launched operation *Marita*, the invasion of Greece, on 6 April, the misunderstanding over the Aliakmon line meant that the Greek forces, and their British allies, had little chance of mounting a successful defensive action. There were, moreover, signs of defeatism in high Greek military and government circles. These contributed to the suicide of the prime minister, Koryzis, on 18 April. His successor was another banker, the Cretan Emmanuel Tsouderos. But by this time Greek resistance on the mainland was crumbling beyond repair. General Tsolakoglou, the commander of the western Macedonian army, without government authorisation negotiated an armistice on 20 April, and, as the Germans closed in on Athens, the king and government withdrew to Crete. At the same time some 42,000 out of the 58,000 British troops that had been despatched to Greece were evacuated. It was intended to hold Crete as an impregnable fortress but, following a massive German airborne attack (20 May) and fierce fighting, Crete was overrun and the king, his government and British and Greek forces were obliged to withdraw to Egypt. Thus by the beginning of June 1941 the whole of Greece had been overrun and was firmly in the grip of a tripartite German, Italian and Bulgarian occupation, with the Germans holding only the most strategically sensitive areas, i.e. Athens and Salonica, some of the islands, and a strip of land on the Turkish frontier. General Tsolakoglou became prime minister of a puppet government (to be succeeded by the civilians Constantine Logothetopoulos and John Rallis), while the Greek government-in-exile and the king established themselves in London.

Inevitably, the overriding concern of most Greeks during the harsh years of the occupation was the struggle for sheer physical survival for themselves and their families amidst appalling hardships and deprivations. Nevertheless, the will to resist an alien and brutal occupier was present from the beginning. Moreover, occupation and resistance were to have the most profound consequences on the political life of Greece, and the impress of these dramatic events was to influence the whole subsequent course of Greek history. Within a matter of weeks of the occupation acts of resistance to the occupiers were recorded. On 31 May, for instance, the Nazi flag flying over the Acropolis in Athens was torn down. The lead in organising more co-ordinated resistance was taken by the communist party, which, in the anomalous circumstances of the occupation, was to emerge as a major force in the political life of Greece. During the inter-war period the Greek communists had been a negligible force, torn by internal disputes and never gaining more than 9 per cent of the vote in elections. The Italian invasion of Greece had thrown the party into confusion. Although the current Comintern line was that the war was essentially a struggle between rival imperialisms, the imprisoned secretary-general of the KKE, Nikos Zakhariadis, hailed the Greek resistance to the Italian invasion as 'a war of national liberation' and urged the Greeks to rally round Metaxas in the common cause. He was subsequently to denounce the war as imperialist, but this first pronouncement was the one that most Greeks remembered and it helped to restore the KKE's reputation as a patriotic party after its advocacy between 1924 and 1935 of an autonomous Macedonia. At the time of the occupation much of the leadership of the KKE was in prison. Some escaped, a handful were released by the occupation forces, while many more remained in confinement. Zakhariadis, for instance, was to spend the rest of the war in Dachau. Although the KKE had suffered more than the non-communist politicians during the Metaxas dictatorship it was able to take advantage of its internal discipline and exploit its greater experience of clandestine activity to good effect during the occupation. The non-communist politicians, by contrast, were for the most part on the periphery of the dramatic events of the war years.

At the end of June 1941, a few days after the launching of operation *Barbarossa*, Hitler's invasion of Russia, the sixth plenum of the central committee of the KKE met to formulate the party line now that an imperialist war had been transformed into the great patriotic war for the defence of the Soviet motherland.

The sixth plenum resolved that it was the fundamental duty of Greek communists to organise for the defence of the Soviet Union and for the overthrow of the foreign fascist yoke. To this end the Greek people were invited to join in the formation of the National Liberation Front (EAM), which was founded in September 1941. Although the communists were dominant in EAM from the beginning, nonetheless the impression that it represented a genuine coalition of the KKE with a number of other small left wing and agrarian parties was carefully maintained. In its propaganda EAM took care not to scare off potential recruits, in what was fundamentally a conservative and traditional society, with wild talk of land collectivisation or nationalisation. It stressed instead its patriotic role as a focus for resistance to the Axis. It also demanded that, on liberation, a constituent assembly should be summoned so that the sovereign Greek people might decide on their future form of government.

Within a short time a number of offshoots of EAM came into existence. EEAM, or the Workers' National Liberation Front, concentrated its efforts on the urban working class and was instrumental in organising some impressive strikes, particularly those of February and March 1943, which effectively put an end to German plans to draft Greek workers for compulsory labour service. Mutual Solidarity (EA) organised relief for the many victims of the Albanian war and of the appalling famine in Athens during the winter of 1941–2, when Greeks died by the thousand of starvation. EAM's youth wing, the United Panhellenic Organisation of Youth (EPON), built up a wide membership among young people. But by far the most important offshoot of EAM was its military arm, the National Popular Liberation Army, universally known by its initials ELAS which, when pronounced, sounded exactly like the Greek word for Greece, Ellas. ELAS was founded towards the end of December 1941 and its first guerrilla bands took to the hills in the early summer of 1942. The most important of these was led by Athanasios Klaras, known under the pseudonym Ares (the God of War) Veloukhiotis. A man of great drive and ruthlessness, Ares was perhaps the ablest military commander of ELAS.

In the winter of 1941–2 a number of non-communist resistance organisations also came into being, the National Republican Greek League (EDES) being the most important. The nominal leader of EDES was General Nicholas Plastiras, the prime mover of the military coup of 1922. But he remained in France, where he had gone in exile after the failed putsch of 1933, for most of the war. EDES' actual leader in Greece was General Napoleon Zervas, who had been involved in both the establishment and the overthrow of the Pangalos dictatorship in 1926. EDES' programme was reformist and, at this stage of the war, republican. Zervas, after strong pressure by a key British agent in Athens, took to the hills in the early summer of 1942. Another republican and reformist resistance organisation was Colonel Dimitrios Psarros' National and Social Liberation (EKKA), which did not send men to the mountains until the spring of 1943. While the groundwork for resistance was being laid within Greece, the king and the government-in-exile in London, out of contact with the realities of occupied Greece, somewhat grudgingly purged the government of those tainted by association with the Metaxas regime and promised the restoration of constitutional liberties at the end of the war. The government-in-exile was more concerned with the question of Greece's post-war territorial claims than with the question of resistance to the occupation forces, the importance of which it consistently underestimated, believing that the risk of reprisals outweighed any possible military advantage.

The concern of the government-in-exile not to add to the miseries of the Greek people was understandable, for the occupation, especially in the areas of German and Bulgarian jurisdiction, was extremely harsh. The Bulgarian occupation forces imported Bulgarian settlers into Greek Macedonia, while the Germans showed no compunction in destroying villages and massacring their inhabitants in reprisal for acts of resistance. The wanton destruction in December 1943 of a number of villages in the Kalavryta region and the execution of almost seven hundred villagers was a particularly horrifying example of such terror tactics. Moreover, the German policy of requisitioning food and other supplies had quickly resulted in catastrophic inflation and appalling food shortages, which had a special impact on city dwellers. The situation in Athens during the winter of 1941–2 was so desperate that the Tsouderos government was able to persuade the British authorities to lift their blockade of Greece and to allow food supplies to be shipped in via Turkey for distribution by the Swedish Red Cross. One tragic consequence of the occupation was the virtual elimination of Greek Jewry. The very substantial sephardic Jewish population of Salonica was almost wiped out. The situation of the Jews in Athens was marginally better, and many were helped to escape by EAM. A particularly distressing consequence of famine and the forced sale or confiscation of Jewish property was the exploitation by black marketeers of the misery of their compatriots.

Despite the occupation, Great Britain remained closely involved in Greek affairs. Official British policy towards Greece was to support the return of the king on liberation. This was partly because it was believed in the Foreign Office that constitutional monarchy would provide the best guarantee of a friendly post-war Greece. This in turn was regarded as being an essential British interest in view of Greece's strategic position straddling Britain's imperial sea communications and the routes to her vital supplies of oil in the Middle East. Partly, too, and particularly so in the case of Churchill, British support for the monarchy derived from a sense of personal obligation to King George for his courageous behaviour in the critical early months of 1941. Yet almost all the evidence emerging from occupied Greece pointed to a massive groundswell of republican sentiment, a development that was to pose major problems to British policy-makers.

Through its agents in Greece, the Special Operations Executive, the wartime body charged with fomenting resistance in occupied Europe, was kept well informed of developments in 1941 and 1942, even if it did not always share its information with the Foreign Office, and in the autumn of 1942 it became directly involved in the politics of occupied Greece. In an effort to staunch the flow of supplies reaching Rommel's North African armies, the British military authorities in the Middle East decided to send a sabotage team into Greece, commanded by Brigadier E. C. W.

Myers, to cut the railway line from Salonica to Athens. This mission, known under the code name *Harling*, was then to withdraw, leaving its second in command, Colonel C. M. Woodhouse, to form a permanent liaison with the Greek guerrillas. The *Harling* party, which had been told virtually nothing of the politics of the resistance, was parachuted into Greece at the end of September 1942 and soon made contact with both Zervas and Ares Veloukhiotis. Zervas showed great willingness for EDES guerrillas to take part in the operation. Ares, however, was less enthusiastic, for EAM policy at this time was to concentrate its activities in the towns and, unlike Tito and his partisans in Yugoslavia, EAM never fully appreciated the revolutionary potential of peasant-based resistance in the countryside. But after some initial hesitation, Ares, acting apparently on his own initiative, and without the authority of the Central Committee of EAM in Athens, decided to commit ELAS forces to the operation. The combined efforts of the *Harling* party and of the contingents of EDES and ELAS had a triumphant outcome on the night of 25 November with the destruction of the Gorgopotamos viaduct, thus severing a vital German supply line for several weeks.

The Gorgopotamos operation was a spectacular demonstration of the military potential of armed resistance. As a result the British military authorities ordered the entire *Harling* mission to remain in Greece to co-ordinate further resistance activity. But the Gorgopotamos operation was to prove the only significant example of co-operation between EDES and ELAS throughout the entire occupation. Within a month, sporadic skirmishes had broken out between units of EDES and ELAS, after Zervas had declined the offer of the military command of ELAS. In March 1943 ELAS broke up a small resistance group known by the initials AAA and took captive its military leader, Colonel Stephanos Saraphis, who had played a prominent role in the abortive Venizelist coup of 1935. In a remarkable volte-face Saraphis agreed to become the military commander of ELAS. In an effort to ensure communist control EAM imposed a tripartite command structure on ELAS, and Saraphis' exercise of his authority was subject to the approval of both the political commissar of ELAS, a Vlach called Andreas Tzimas, and its *kapetanios*, or politico-military adviser, Ares Veloukhiotis. This tripartite command structure was repeated throughout ELAS at all levels, with the posts of commissar invariably, and those of *kapetanios* usually, being held by communists.

By the time of Saraphis' adherence to ELAS, Myers and Woodhouse had had time to form their own conclusions as to the political situation in occupied Greece. Myers reported back to Cairo that EAM/ELAS was by far the largest resistance organisation in Greece, and that preparation for a post-war bid for power ranked as high in the objectives of its communist leadership as did resistance. Myers also stressed the depth of the feeling that his mission had encountered, among all sections of the people, against a restoration of the monarchy. He pointed to the almost universal demand that King George should not return to Greece after the liberation unless and until there had been a plebiscite on the constitutional issue. This reporting went very much against the grain of official British policy and Myers' advice was largely ignored. Instead, Zervas was prevailed upon in March 1943 to make a statement, unknown to his followers, in support of King George, and in the next month Churchill issued a directive to all British liaison officers in Greece that subject to 'special operational necessity' they were to co-operate where possible with resistance groups prepared to recognise the authority of the king and his government. By this stage of the occupation, however, there were very few active in the resistance who placed faith either in King George or in his government which, following disturbances in the Greek armed forces in the Middle East, had moved from London to Cairo in March of 1943. The British therefore tried to contain EAM/ELAS by building up the strength of Zervas' non-communist EDES as a countervailing force.

In the summer of 1943, however, British policy underwent an important change. With the planned allied invasion of Sicily the British military authorities were anxious to deceive Hitler into expecting a repetition of the Entente strategy of the First World War, namely an allied landing in Greece. If such deception plans were to have any success then the co-operation of ELAS was essential, for by the summer of 1943 it was in control of wide areas of the Greek mainland and disposed of much greater forces than did EDES. Hence Britain switched from a policy of containment to one of co-operation. Such a switch was fully acceptable to EAM/ELAS, for its communist leadership, itself convinced that liberation was near, was anxious to legitimise its relations with the likely liberating power, Britain. In July 1943 the 'National Bands' or 'Military' agreement was negotiated. Although EAM/ELAS undertook to cease harassing rival organisations, nonetheless the terms were broadly favourable to the left. For, in the new Joint General Headquarters which was to be set up to co-ordinate resistance activity under the authority of the Commander-in-Chief, Middle East, three places were to be reserved for EAM/ELAS representatives, while EDES, EKKA and the British Military Mission were to have one each. Operation *Animals*, as the diversionary feint was known, achieved some notable successes, such as the destruction of the Asopos railway viaduct in June, and it had the desired effect of inducing the Germans to send a further two divisions to Greece to counter an expected invasion.

But the 'National Bands' agreement had not long been in force before a major crisis erupted in relations amongst the resistance, the British authorities, the king and the government-in-exile. In August 1943 a guerrilla delegation, which was accompanied by Myers and in which EAM/ELAS had secured four out of six places, flew to Cairo. The arrival of this delegation represented a unique opportunity during the occupation to bridge the ever widening gulf between the resistance on the ground in Greece, its chief source of logistical support, the British, and the king and the government-in-exile, which in the British view represented constitutional legitimacy. However, the opportunity to create a viable coalition between those fighting the Axis from within Greece and those carrying on the struggle in the Middle East was lost. The king, the Tsouderos government, and the British authorities were caught off balance by the insistent political demands of the guerrilla representatives and failed to grasp the significance of the new currents of political opinion that were emerging in

Greece under the stress of occupation and its consequent deprivations. They simply could not understand that the overwhelming
majority of those who were prepared to engage in active resistance
were not prepared to do so on behalf of what they saw as a discredited monarchy and political system.

The guerrilla delegates made two basic demands. The first was
that the king should make an unequivocal declaration that he
would not return to Greece before a plebiscite. With this first
demand the exile government, by now largely republican in com-
position, concurred. But King George was reluctant to enlarge
upon his somewhat noncommittal undertaking of July 1943 to
hold elections for a constituent assembly within six months of
liberation. He sought the advice of Churchill and President
Roosevelt, then in conference in Quebec, who unequivocally
urged him to stand firm in the face of guerrilla demands. The
second demand, at which not only the king but his government
also took fright, was that guerrilla nominees should be given three
key government portfolios, those of the interior, war and justice,
and that these ministers should actually exercise authority within
'Mountain Greece', as the liberated portions of Greece were
known. At this point the British authorities panicked and made
a clumsy attempt to ship the guerrilla delegation back to Greece
against their will, at the same time preventing Myers from returning to Greece. When the guerrillas did return, with none of their
basic demands met, they were in a thoroughly disgruntled frame
of mind. EAM's claim to the effect that the British were bent on
imposing King George on the Greek people by force of arms, if
need be, gained new plausibility.

Even before the Cairo mission civil war in the resistance had
been a possibility, and the meeting itself represented the last chance
to avert such a calamity. But after the failure of the mission civil
war moved from the realms of possibility to those of probability.
Within a matter of weeks ELAS, determined to remove any
threat to its domination of the resistance, accused EDES of collaboration, with some justification as it subsequently transpired,
and fighting broke out between the two guerrilla armies. The
internecine fighting of the winter of 1943/4, which had many of

the characteristics of a civil war and in which EKKA was not involved, is often referred to as the 'First Round' in the communist bid to achieve power in Greece. Once again, as during their War of Independence and as during the First World War, the Greeks were fighting among themselves as well as against their external enemies. In an effort to staunch the bloodletting, Britain cut off arms supplies to ELAS, but this proved to be little more than a gesture, for after the surrender of the Italian Pinerolo division in the wake of the Italian armistice in September, ELAS had access to a large source of weaponry. At the same time British moral and material support for EDES was stepped up. At Christmas 1943, a British, American and Russian appeal was made to the warring parties to resolve their differences. The Russians only reluctantly agreed to associate themselves with this initiative, for it would seem that at this time they were genuinely uncertain as to what was going on in Greece. Eventually after arduous negotiations a truce, known as the Plaka agreement, was patched up between ELAS and EDES at the end of February 1944. The basic terms of the agreement defined the area of operations of the two organisations, with EDES being confined to its heartland of Epirus.

But no sooner had peace of a sort returned to the 'Mountain' than EAM sprang a new surprise by announcing, in mid-March 1944, the creation of a Political Committee of National Liberation (PEEA). PEEA, under the leadership of the much respected and non-communist university professor Alexander Svolos, was to oversee the administration of those large areas of rural Greece now under EAM control. While PEEA was careful formally not to usurp the functions of the government-in-exile, its creation nonetheless clearly constituted a direct challenge to Tsouderos and his ministers in Cairo. Indeed, within two weeks pro-EAM elements had fomented mutinies within the Greek armed forces stationed in Egypt, demanding the creation of a government of national unity to be based on PEEA. Churchill ordered firm action to deal with the mutinies, which were suppressed with the loss of a single British life. Death sentences were passed on a number of the leaders of the mutiny, but these were commuted for fear of the bitterness that would have been their inevitable consequence. Large numbers of those involved in the mutinies were interned.

Such a direct challenge to its authority inevitably occasioned a major crisis within the government-in-exile. Emmanuel Tsouderos, who had been prime minister since April 1941, made way for Sophocles Venizelos, the son of Eleftherios Venizelos. But Venizelos proved no more capable of handling the situation, and within a few days he was replaced by George Papandreou, who had appeared, like some *deus ex machina*, from occupied Greece at the critical moment. The British authorities were overjoyed with Papandreou's arrival in the Middle East, for as a prominent Venizelist he was untainted with monarchical associations, yet at the same time he was doggedly anti-communist and determined to prevent a communist assumption of power at the end of hostilities. Moreover, having just escaped from Athens, he had direct experience of the realities of occupied Greece.

Seeking a way out of the political impasse that had now arisen, Papandreou summoned a conference in the Lebanon in May 1944 to which representatives of all political parties and resistance groups were invited, both PEEA and EAM having meanwhile denounced the mutinies as harmful to the allied war effort. The British ambassador to the exile government was on hand throughout the proceedings. Twenty-five delegates attended the conference. EAM, ELAS, the Greek communist party and PEEA all sent delegates, but only two of these were communists, and the small left wing representation at the Lebanon conference did not reflect the true balance of political power in occupied Greece. Heavily outnumbered and outmanoeuvred by the consummate politician Papandreou, the left wing delegates were forced on the defensive and subscribed to the Lebanon agreement of 20 May 1944. The most important provision of this called for the placing of all guerrilla formations under the command of a government of national unity, in which five relatively unimportant posts were reserved for EAM representatives. But back in Greece the EAM Central Committee was not prepared to surrender its power so cheaply. It now demanded the retention of ELAS, by now almost four divisions strong and by far the largest guerrilla force, the removal of Papandreou as prime minister, and the holding, on liberated Greek soil, of key ministries such as those of the interior and justice, a demand that had first been advanced by the guerrilla delegates in Cairo in August 1943. Deadlock thus ensued between Cairo and the 'Mountain', but, unknown either to Papandreou or the Greek left, a new factor had entered the Greek political equation. Greece was to become a pawn in the power play between Churchill and Stalin.

It was the conjunction of the mutinies among the Greek forces in the Middle East with the push of the Red Army into Bessarabia that was to reinforce Churchill's by now almost obsessive desire to prevent the establishment of communist hegemony in post-liberation Greece. In minutes composed at this time he described the ELAS guerrillas as 'miserable Greek banditti' and 'the most treacherous, filthy beasts'. He was particularly outraged by the forcible dissolution of EKKA and the murder of its leader Colonel Psarros on 16 April by an ELAS detachment acting, it would seem, on its own initiative rather than on the orders of the EAM Central Committee. Some members of the defeated rump of EKKA enlisted in the anti-communist Security Battalions. These had been set up in late 1943 by the quisling government of John Rallis and were equipped by the occupation forces. Composed of outright collaborators and those who regarded the communists as posing a more serious threat to their country's future than did the Germans, the Security Battalions were particularly active in the Peloponnese. They were denounced as collaborationist by both the British authorities and the exiled Greek government.

As early as April 1944 Churchill was talking of giving the Russians the lead in Romania, in the clear expectation of securing a reciprocal facility in Greece. In May Eden approached the Russians with the proposal that if they were to take the lead in Romania, then Britain should be allowed to 'play the hand' in Greece. The Russians accepted provided that President Roosevelt had no objections. Roosevelt, overriding his Secretary of State, agreed to what he thought was a provisional wartime arrangement. The Churchill-Stalin agreement, subsequently broadened to embrace, in addition to Greece and Romania, Bulgaria, Yugoslavia and Hungary, was finalised at Churchill's meeting with Stalin in Moscow in October 1944, when the 'percentage' of British interest in Greece was put at ninety, that of the Soviet Union at ten. The percentages were precisely reversed in the case of Romania. This was the price that Churchill was prepared to pay, as he himself put it, for 'freedom of action' in Greece, and the 'percentages agreement' was to have a powerful influence on the subsequent course of events in Greece.

These high-level power politics were quite unknown to EAM, which in the summer of 1944 had every reason to hope for the fulfilment of its ultimate objective, the achievement of power on liberation. It controlled by far the largest armed formations in Greece, some four times the size of those of its only rival, EDES. Moreover, whereas EDES was confined to a small power base in Epirus, the authority of EAM/ELAS extended over much of the Greek mainland. By the end of the occupation the membership of EAM has been variously estimated at between half a million and two million. Its opponents claimed that it had built up this preponderance on the basis of terror but, although EAM/ELAS certainly did not shrink from terror tactics, nonetheless the movement did clearly enjoy genuine mass support.

Many prominent liberal figures continued to give EAM their active support even after its communist orientation had become apparent, and relatively few of the rank and file were communists. To the bulk of the Greek people, wearied by the hardships, famine and rampant inflation of the occupation, EAM offered a vision of the future that appeared to be quite beyond the capacity of the old politicians, whose arcane quarrels and intrigues seemed increasingly irrelevant to the country's real needs. Moreover, EAM was able to offer more than a mere vision of the future. In the extensive and overwhelmingly rural areas under its control it brought improved educational and health facilities, a system of popular justice that was responsive to the needs of a peasant society, improved communications, education, even theatrical performances. In short, EAM appeared to take a much closer interest in the welfare of the peasants than ever the politicians had done. Not the least of its attractions was its willingness to utilise the talents of women who, in an essentially patriarchal society, had hitherto been expected to confine themselves to exclusively domestic concerns. EAM was also careful to avoid any suggestion that it posed a threat to such deep-rooted peasant values as private property and Orthodox Christianity. One of EAM's proposals, indeed, was for an increase in the stipends of village priests, and a number of Orthodox bishops openly espoused its cause.

Given its overwhelmingly military and political strength within Greece, it is not surprising perhaps that EAM should have repudiated the substantial concessions made by the left wing representatives at the Lebanon conference. For Papandreou's authority as prime minister of a government of national unity rested not on any power base within Greece but solely on the fact that he enjoyed British support. But the deadlock that had ensued between Papandreou and the 'Mountain' was suddenly broken at the beginning of August, when EAM agreed to accept the essence of the agreement that had been negotiated at Lebanon. Just a week before this conciliatory switch in policy a Soviet military mission, the first-known direct contact between the Russians and the Greek communists during the occupation, had arrived at ELAS headquarters. Although there is no direct evidence, it is possible that the leader of this mission, Colonel Popov, passed on instructions from Stalin that EAM should both participate in the government of national unity and agree to place ELAS under its orders. Such advice would have been consistent not only with Stalin's recent understanding with Churchill but would also have been in accordance with Soviet policy in the other countries of eastern Europe. In any case, the communist leadership appears to have been unnerved by the apparent indifference of the Russians to the situation in Greece.

Whether or not EAM's retreat from its previous hard line towards Papandreou reflected Soviet instructions, by entering the government the communists had clearly forfeited what would have been the most opportune moment for an outright seizure of power. They certainly had the means of taking the country over in the confusion surrounding the German withdrawal in early

October 1944, before the government of national unity had been able either to land or to establish its authority. If they had done so, there would have been little that Churchill could have done about it, whatever his determination to frustrate EAM. Some leading communists subsequently argued that the party leadership had allowed a priceless opportunity to slip out of its hands in failing to make an all-out bid for power at this critical juncture. Be this as it may, six EAM nominees entered the government of national unity, in relatively unimportant posts, early in September, and at the end of the month, at Caserta in Italy, ELAS and EDES agreed to place their forces under Papandreou's command. He in turn placed them, with all other Greek forces, under the command of Lieutenant-General Ronald Scobie, the commander of the small British force of some 6000 combatant troops which, at Churchill's insistence, was to accompany the government back to Greece.

The Papandreou government, transformed, thanks to British support, from a rump of discredited politicians into a genuine government of national unity, landed in Greece on 18 October 1944. As the last of the German occupation forces, harassed by guerrilla units and allied raiding forces, were withdrawing from the north of the country, the Papandreou government and indeed the British liberation force, were greeted with scenes of delirious enthusiasm. But the magnitude of the problems facing the government soon became apparent. The rate of inflation, which had already reached staggering proportions during the occupation, accelerated still further. Gold sovereigns, which had been shipped into Greece in large quantities by the British authorities to finance resistance activities, were the only currency that retained confidence. Soon after liberation a sovereign could be exchanged for 170,000,000,000,000 drachmas. Massive bottlenecks developed over the distribution of relief supplies to a country whose economy had been literally shattered in the course of the occupation. Another basic problem facing the government was the punishment of collaborators, but, despite the insistent demands of the left, Papandreou showed little will to tackle this emotive question, nor did the British authorities appear to regard it as a high priority.

The most serious problem facing Papandreou was how to bring about the peaceful disarming of the guerrilla formations and their replacement by a national army, without whose backing the government could not long hope to govern the country. As long as ELAS' forces continued in existence, even if under the nominal command of Scobie, the balance of physical force undoubtedly lay with ELAS rather than the national government. During November protracted negotiations involving Papandreou and the left wing ministers appeared to have resulted in a solution acceptable to both sides. The gist of the agreement was that guerrilla bands of both ELAS and EDES were to disband on 10 December, except for a unit of ELAS, which would equal in size a unit composed of the Sacred Battalion, of the Mountain Brigade and of members of EDES. The Sacred Battalion was manned entirely by officers and the Mountain (Rimini) Brigade had been thoroughly purged in the aftermath of the April mutinies in the Middle East. The left claimed, with some justification, that only royalists and anti-communists remained. These two formations were to compose the core of a national army, which would be supplemented by the call-up of a number of age groups.

But at the end of November the communists, charging that Papandreou was going back on his earlier undertakings, demanded a total demobilisation. A tougher line now became apparent and this may have represented a victory for the hardliners within EAM, who felt that the party should have moved to seize power in October, and who were now seeking an opportunity for a direct confrontation with Papandreou. The blundering and confusion on the part of all parties, the left, the national government and the British, now began to move rapidly towards a seemingly inexorable and tragic climax. At the beginning of December George Siantos, the secretary of the KKE, made it clear that ELAS would refuse to demobilise on 10 December, whereupon General Scobie declared that he would have no hesitation in using British force if need be to defend the legally constituted government. The left wing ministers resigned from the Papandreou government and, in an atmosphere of mounting crisis, EAM called for a mass demonstration in Athens on Sunday 3 December, which was intended as the prelude to a general strike. Papandreou, after agreeing to the demonstration, subsequently withdrew permission, but nonetheless thousands of demonstrators converged on Constitution Square in the centre of the city. Panic-stricken police fired on the demonstrators, of whom about fifteen were killed and many more wounded.

The bloody repression of the 3 December demonstration was followed by attacks on police stations although, initially at least, ELAS forces were careful to avoid attacking British troops. There is evidence that the KKE, at this stage, was anxious to avoid a direct confrontation with the British, but within a few days British troops were heavily involved in the fighting. Churchill, who had certainly not flinched from the prospect of an outright confrontation with ELAS, had cabled to Scobie on 5 December that he should treat Athens as a conquered city and shoot to kill if it proved necessary to restore order. The telegram was leaked in the American press and contributed to the attitude of studied neutrality adopted by the American administration throughout the December fighting in Athens. Their ambassador, Lincoln McVeagh, went so far as to refuse to allow British troops to draw water from a well in his garden during the hostilities. The Russians, scrupulously adhering to the Churchill/Stalin agreement, refrained from offering any encouragement to the insurgents.

The small British contingent in Athens, and the pathetic forces at the disposal of the Papandreou government, were rapidly forced on the defensive and isolated in a small area of the centre of Athens. That they were not totally overrun was due to the rapid despatch of British reinforcements from the Italian front, from which they could be ill spared. But although ELAS made the initial military running in Athens, the December insurgency does not seem to have represented an all-out bid for power. If it was so intended then it was conducted on a curious basis. In the first place, the small British forces stationed in Salonica, Patras and Volos were not attacked, despite the fact that they were heavily outnumbered by ELAS troops. Secondly, ELAS' two principal military leaders, Ares Veloukhiotis and Stephanos Saraphis, were sent on an irrelevant campaign to liquidate Zervas' forces in

Epirus. The KKE itself subsequently blamed the somewhat half-hearted prosecution of the insurgency on Siantos. He was denounced, but without evidence, as a British agent who had organised the uprising to give the British the pretext they needed to smash the left. The most likely explanation, however, for the fact that ELAS refrained from making an all-out onslaught on the British presence in Greece, is that they were not aiming at a full take-over of power, but rather at securing the removal of their principal bugbear, George Papandreou, as prime minister. Since at least 1943 Papandreou had been determined to thwart an EAM bid for power and had showed a great deal of energy and determination in forestalling such an eventuality. If Papandreou could be removed from office and replaced by a more pliable politician, such as the octogenarian liberal, Themistocles Sophoulis, then EAM might well in time aspire to power in a constitutional or quasi-constitutional manner.

In the event Papandreou did, on the outbreak of hostilities, immediately offer his resignation but was ordered by Churchill to remain in office With the arrival of reinforcements from Italy the military tide began to turn in Athens. Churchill, at a critical juncture of the war, became obsessed with Greece to the exclusion of virtually all else, and flew with Eden, his foreign secretary, to Athens on Christmas Eve 1944 in the hope of reconciling the warring factions. But not even his prestige was able to bring about a settlement, although he did at last grasp the depth of feeling that existed in Greece against the monarchy on the part of both communists and non-communists. He agreed to a solution of the constitutional issue that had been bandied about for the best part of a year but which up till now he had vigorously resisted, namely the appointment of Archbishop Damaskinos of Athens as regent, pending a plebiscite on the constitutional question. Churchill, who had earlier denounced Damaskinos as 'a pestilent priest, a survival from the Middle Ages', now became a fervent admirer of the archbishop.

The appointment of Damaskinos as regent on 30 December and the replacement of Papandreou as prime minister by the veteran republican General Nicholas Plastiras on 3 January 1945, coupled with increasing evidence of British military ascendancy, led ELAS to drop its previous severe conditions and accept a ceasefire on 11 January. This was followed by a political settlement which was reached at Varkiza, on the outskirts of Athens, on 12 February. ELAS agreed to disarm, and in fact handed over rather more weapons than it was obliged to. In return the Plastiras government promised an amnesty for political crimes, a distinction that was to cause subsequent confusion, undertook to purge collaborators in the army and police with greater vigour, to guarantee democratic freedoms, and to hold a plebiscite on the monarchy, which was to be followed by elections.

The British authorities, who for several months had been virtually running the Greek government, had lighted on Plastiras in the hope that he would be a force for moderation and reconciliation in a highly polarised political atmosphere. But Plastiras proved unable to check the right wing backlash that followed the Varkiza agreement, a backlash which was fuelled by the discovery that some of the 8000 civilian hostages taken by ELAS, in the hope of staving off defeat during the last stages of the fighting in Athens, had either been killed or had died in its custody. Despite the promise of amnesty, leftists were systematically persecuted and little serious effort was made to bring collaborators to justice. But the KKE and EAM openly continued to function as such and Nikos Zakhariadis, who had spent the war in the Dachau concentration camp, was returned by the British authorities to Greece, where he resumed control of the KKE.

In April 1945 Plastiras was forced out of office by right wing pressure after the publication of a somewhat defeatist letter he had written to Tsouderos in July 1941. He was replaced by Admiral Voulgaris who, although a republican, was opposed by the left for his role in suppressing the April 1944 mutinies in Egypt. His 'non-political' government, however, proved no more capable of controlling a deteriorating economic and political situation than had that of Plastiras. Right and left wing bands continued to resort to violence; in the Peloponnese the right wing bands of the X (Khi) organisation were particularly active. Preparations were made for holding elections, although it proved impossible to produce accurate electoral registers, for the last elections had been held almost ten years previously, and there was great administrative dislocation consequent on the war. The Varkiza agreement had provided that the elections were to be held under allied supervision, but although Britain, the United States and France agreed to participate in this exercise, the Soviet Union declined, on the grounds that to do so would constitute interference in the internal affairs of Greece. Further confusion was occasioned when in September 1945 the regent, Archbishop Damaskinos, during a visit to London, secured the agreement of the British that elections would now precede the plebiscite on the monarchy and not vice versa, as had been agreed at Varkiza.

In October the Voulgaris government, under fire from both the Liberals and the (royalist) Populists, resigned. After some weeks of confusion, and further British pressure, the octogenarian Themistocles Sophoulis emerged as the prime minister of a predominantly Liberal government. In an effort to calm the situation Sophoulis decreed a wide ranging amnesty, dropped several thousand outstanding prosecutions against left wingers and announced the holding of elections, the first since 1936. These were fixed by the regent Damaskinos, acting on British instructions, for 31 March 1946. The left protested that given the prevailing climate of violence and uncertainty elections held so soon could not possibly afford an accurate reflection of opinion in the country. This was a view with which Sophoulis himself had some sympathy but Britain, anxious for domestic reasons to reduce her burdensome commitments in Greece and to see the creation of a government legitimised through elections, insisted that they proceed on schedule. As late as 21 February the politburo of the KKE had hinted that it would be prepared to participate in the elections, but in the event the left decided to abstain, arguing that there had been no improvement in the climate of political terror. This decision to abstain may have been taken in defiance of Soviet advice to the contrary and was subsequently acknowledged by the KKE to have been an error.

With the left abstaining, the elections of 31 March 1946 were essentially a contest between the right wing Populists, with their royalist allies, and the fragmented Liberal and centre right parties. In a 354-seat parliament the Populists and their various right wing allies won 206 seats; the National Political Union, an alliance of three small parties headed by Sophocles Venizelos, George Papandreou and Panayiotis Kanellopoulos respectively, won 68; Sophoulis' Liberals won 48; and the National Party, led by General Napoleon Zervas, the former leader of EDES who had now emerged as the scourge of the left, won 20. The Allied Mission for Observing the Greek Elections (known by the initials AMFOGE) declared the elections to have been a fair expression of the people's will. It put the number of politically motivated abstentions at 9·4 per cent, but the communists claimed that, as a mere 49 per cent of those on the electoral registers had voted, the remaining 51 per cent had consisted of left wing abstainers. The AMFOGE estimate was certainly too low, and the communist claims certainly too high. The true number of left wing voters who abstained must remain a matter of conjecture.

After some internal party wrangling Constantine Tsaldaris, a nephew of the pre-war Populist leader Panayis Tsaldaris, emerged as leader of a Populist government. With a very substantial majority in parliament, Tsaldaris arranged for a plebiscite on the monarchy to be held on 1 September 1946. This was duly held, and resulted in a 68 per cent (1,136,289) vote in favour of the restoring the monarchy, with 32 per cent (524,771) voting against. The plebiscite was not supervised by AMFOGE, although Britain and America did vet the electoral registers, and opposition allegations of ballot rigging were confirmed in confidential reports by allied observers. But so polarised had Greek politics now become that a significant number of non-communist anti-monarchists appear to have voted for King George's return, seeing him as the best guarantee against a communist accession to power. On 27 September King George II set foot on Greek soil for the first time since his hurried evacuation from Crete in May 1941. But after little more than six months on the throne he died in April 1947, and was succeeded by his brother Paul, who was without his dour intransigence.

Despite the holding of both elections and plebiscite, 1946

brought Greece no nearer to the political stability so ardently desired by its British patron. The costly British commitment to Greece took the form of Military, Naval and Air Force Missions that played an important role in the restructuring of the post-war Greek armed forces and were accused by the left of assisting in the purge of all but officers of impeccable royalist credentials. There was also the Economic and Financial Mission, charged with advising on ways to bring runaway inflation under control and to assist in the enormous tasks of post-war reconstruction, the Legal Mission, which reported on the legal system, the Prisons Mission, charged with advising on the prison system and finally the Police Mission, whose task was to help in the reconstruction of the city police forces.

The Tsaldaris government, unlike that of Sophoulis, showed little inclination to try to bridge the ever widening gulf between right and left. Once again leftists were subject to persecution of various forms and little attempt was made to deal with pressing problems of reconstruction. Tsaldaris, indeed, attached a higher priority to pressing Greece's territorial and other claims against her neighbours than to domestic reconciliation. Greece sought war reparations from Bulgaria as one of the occupying powers but her claims were repudiated by the new communist regime. Moreover, Russian support for the Balkan communist states meant that there was little chance of Greece achieving the frontier rectifications she sought at the expense of Albania and Bulgaria. Tsaldaris vigorously pursued Greece's claim to Northern Epirus, the region of southern Albania inhabited by Greeks and Orthodox Albanians, but this was resisted with equal vigour by Albania's new communist ruler Enver Hoxha. Tsaldaris' only success in this sphere, indeed, was in securing the promise that the Dodecanese islands, occupied by Italy since 1911, would be transferred to Greek sovereignty, an undertaking that was implemented by the Treaty of Paris of February 1947.

Tsaldaris' harsh measures against the left served only to accelerate the gradual drift towards all-out civil war in the country. Right wing reprisals since the Varkiza agreement had forced many left wingers once again to take to the hills, and, indeed, even before the March 1946 elections, the KKE had apparently resolved to seek power through armed force should this prove necessary. On the very eve of the elections there was a much publicised communist attack on the village of Litokhoro in Pierria but there had been isolated hostilities even before this and these were to gather momentum throughout the summer and autumn of 1946. In August the Tsaldaris government claimed for the first time that communist bands were being actively supported by the Bulgarians and Yugoslavs. The Soviet government then prompted the Ukraine, which had separate membership of the United Nations, to complain to the Security Council that the Greek government was responsible for frontier provocations and was persecuting minorities. In keeping with the hardening of attitudes that marked the beginning of the Cold War, the Soviet position had by this time changed from the relatively benign neutrality of December 1944 to open hostility. Already in January 1946 the Russians had called for the withdrawal of British troops from Greece. A further stage in the escalation of the conflict was the announcement in October 1946 of the creation of a communist Democratic Army, commanded by Markos Vafiadis, a communist leader of Anatolian origin.

In the winter of 1946–7 a fully fledged civil war got under way, although the communist press in Athens was not banned until October 1947 and the KKE itself not proscribed until December of that year. More uncertainty was created early in 1947 when the British government informed the American State Department that, due to her own acute economic and financial crisis, Britain could no longer shoulder the burden of propping up the Greek state. With remarkable alacrity the American administration, which during the preceding months had become increasingly involved in Greek affairs, took up the challenge, and on 12 March President Truman, in requesting $400 million of emergency aid from the Congress, enunciated what came to be known as the Truman Doctrine, by which the United States undertook to underwrite the efforts of 'free peoples' struggling to resist subversion by armed minorities.

Markos Vafiadis' hit and run tactics, together with the logistical support and cover provided by Yugoslavia, Bulgaria and Albania, put him at an advantage over the Greek regular army. Yet although the Democratic Army was able to move at will over much of mainland Greece throughout 1947 and 1948, Markos' attempts to seize such towns near Greece's northern borders as Florina, Grevena and Konitsa to serve as a provisional capital of Democratic Greece met with failure. Nonetheless, after his second unsuccessful attempt to capture Konitsa, Markos announced on Christmas Eve 1947 the formation of a Provisional Democratic Government. But despite the propaganda and material support which the Democratic Army received from the Eastern bloc countries, the Provisional Democratic Government was never recognised even by the Cominform countries. In December 1946 the Greek government had made a second complaint to the Security Council about Yugoslav, Bulgarian and Albanian assistance to the communist guerrillas. The United Nations agreed to the setting up of a commission to investigate the charges. The majority report of this commission of investigation substantially supported the Greek case, and the General Assembly created a United Nations Special Commission on the Balkans (UNSCOB) to see that the recommendations of the commission of investigation were implemented. UNSCOB in numerous reports drew attention to the various kinds of support afforded to the Democratic Army by Greece's communist neighbours, ranging from medical and rest facilities to the supply of weapons, military training, and, on occasion, the use of their territory for operational purposes.

Meanwhile, the aid afforded to the Democratic Army by Greece's northern neighbours was more than matched by the increasing amount of American military and other aid being funnelled to Greece through the American Mission for Aid to Greece (AMAG). American aid was not confined to weaponry and equipment and American military observers played an active role in advising on the conduct of military operations. A joint Greek-American general staff was created (in November 1947) and new impetus was given to the prosecution of the war by the arrival in February 1948 of General Van Fleet as commander of the Joint

US Military Advisory and Planning Group (JUSMAPG). British troops also remained in Greece in a non-combatant role, and the British Military, Naval and Air Force Missions continued to assist in the training of troops throughout the civil war. The degree of American influence on Greek affairs during this period was at least as great as, and perhaps greater than, that exercised by Britain between 1944 and 1947.

With the Democratic Army relying heavily for logistical and political support on Yugoslavia, Bulgaria and Albania, support which of course could only have been vouchsafed on the authority of Stalin himself, and the Greek national army increasingly dependent on American military aid and American and British political support, Greece had in effect become a key battleground in the Cold War. Once again she was the focus of Great Power rivalries, with the Powers fighting their battles through Greek proxies. By November 1948 the security situation had so deteriorated that martial law was proclaimed throughout the country. Land communications between the two main cities of Greece, Athens and Salonica, were virtually impossible, and train services between them were not restored until late in 1949.

Had the Democratic Army continued to pursue the classic guerrilla tactics advocated by Markos Vafiadis, and had it been able to rely on the continued co-operation of its communist neighbours, then there is little doubt that the fighting could have been prolonged almost indefinitely in terrain that was admirably suited to irregular warfare. But despite the relative success of the Democratic Army in 1947 and 1948, the odds were slowly beginning to turn against the left as a result of a number of factors, both internal and external. In the first place, Tito's split with the Cominform in 1948 was to have serious consequences for the Greek left. Stalin had become increasingly concerned with the implications of Tito's plans for a Balkan Federation, under Yugoslav aegis, and saw Tito's support for the Greek communists as a bid to consolidate Yugoslav hegemony in the area. Stalin is reported to have told leading Yugoslav and Bulgarian communists early in 1948 that the Greek civil war should be brought to an end as soon as possible, for he saw no prospect that Britain and the

United States would allow Greece to fall to the communists and
thus cut their lines of communication in the Mediterranean. As the
Soviet Union had no navy there was little she could do to prevent
the eventual crushing of the revolt.* He might have added that
the Soviet Union was not yet a nuclear power and could scarcely
afford an open confrontation with the United States. When the
KKE sided with Moscow in Tito's quarrel with the Kremlin it
could only be a matter of time before Yugoslavia closed its frontier
to the Democratic Army, which it duly did in July 1949.

The KKE, casting around for scapegoats for its defeat, subsequently claimed that it had been stabbed in the back by Tito but
the closing of the frontier, although a serious blow to the Democratic Army, was by no means the only, or even the decisive,
factor in its defeat. The massive infusion of American military aid
and advice was at last beginning to revive the fortunes of the
national army, which had received a boost to its morale when, in
January 1949, Marshal Papagos, the victor of the Albanian
campaign, took over as commander-in-chief. Moreover, as the
efficiency of the national army increased, there was mounting
dissension within the ranks of the Democratic Army itself.
Markos Vafiadis, appreciating that the Democratic Army could
never hope for victory in set-piece confrontations with a larger,
better equipped and increasingly better trained and generalled
national army, continued to pin his faith in hit and run tactics.
Zakhariadis, however, believed that the Democratic Army
should fight as a regular army. After bitter infighting Markos
was purged as a purported defeatist in February 1949, and
Zakhariadis assumed personal command of the Democratic
Army.

At the same time the KKE, following the current Cominform
line once again, as it had in the twenties and early thirties, espoused
the cause of an autonomous Macedonia within a Balkan federation.
This was a move in part prompted by the fact that by this late
stage of the war some 30 per cent of the Democratic Army was
made up of 'slavophone hellenes' from the Slav-speaking areas of
Greek Macedonia. As during the inter-war period, the party's

* Milovan Djilas, *Conversations with Stalin* (London 1962) 164.

support for the concept of an autonomous Macedonia, enabled its opponents to argue that it was fundamentally unpatriotic and that it was prepared to cede territory for which much Greek blood had in the past been shed. On the international front the KKE had also received a great deal of adverse publicity over its policy of evacuating, for protection against 'monarcho-fascist' reprisals, children aged between three and fourteen from the areas it controlled. Estimated by the Red Cross to number some 25,000, they were moved to various countries of the Eastern bloc. The Greek government denounced these evacuations as a new janissary levy but the number of parents enlisting Red Cross assistance in their return was relatively small.

By the summer of 1949 the national army, which enjoyed the great advantage of total command of the air, was definitely gaining the ascendancy over the Democratic Army and, after a series of fiercely fought battles in the Grammos and Vitsi mountains on the Albanian border, the remnants of the Democratic Army, numbering some 5000, together with the KKE leadership, fled across the border into Albania. In October the KKE proclaimed a 'temporary end' to hostilities that was in the event to prove permanent. Sporadic incidents continued for some months, but in effect the civil war was now over. Just as at the time of the First War the Greeks were on a war footing for the best part of ten years, from 1912 to 1922, so the Greeks during the period of the Second World War were to experience the ravages of war for far longer than the rest of Europe, more or less continuously between 1940 and 1949. The period of the civil war added greatly to the already massive material destruction of the occupation, but, as the fighting was now not between German, Italian, or Bulgarian and Greek but between Greek and Greek, the civil war added a whole new dimension of hatred and division to the Greek tragedy. Some 80,000 Greeks were killed during the civil war, appalling atrocities were committed by both sides, some 20,000 Greeks were sentenced for offences against the state, over 5000 of them receiving death or life sentences, some 700,000 refugees, almost 10 per cent of the population, were forced to move from their homes. The Greeks had emerged from the First World War a divided nation, they were to emerge from the Second World War and the ensuing civil war even more divided. This latest division was to leave a legacy of bitterness that was to cast a long shadow over Greece's post-war political development.

7

Uncertain democracy and military dictatorship, 1949-1974

Despite the immense strains imposed by the civil war on the Greek body politic, the temptation to resort to a non-parliamentary 'strong' government was nonetheless resisted and parliamentary institutions survived the strife intact. The Populists had won a clear victory in the elections of 1946, but for most of the three years of the civil war Greece had been ruled, largely as a result of American pressure, by a Populist/Liberal coalition. Although the Populists were clearly the dominating force, the government had been headed by the Liberal Themistocles Sophoulis, who died, aged eighty-eight, just as the civil war was coming to an end. Martial law was ended in February 1950 and in the following month the first elections were held since those of March 1946. No less than 44 parties contested 250 seats under a system of proportional representation. Tsaldaris' right wing Populists, with 62, won the largest share of the seats, but the combined vote of the three centre parties gave them 136, a hopeful vote for moderation given the bitterness engendered by the civil war. The far left vote went to the Democratic camp, which won 18 seats. The three centre parties, Sophocles Venizelos' Liberals, Nicholas Plastiras' National Progressive Centre Union (EPEK) and the George Papandreou Party (which had changed its name from the Democratic Socialist Party and was precisely what its new title suggested) agreed to sink their differences and formed a somewhat shaky centrist coalition, headed by Plastiras.

This coalition quickly collapsed after disputes about the degree of leniency to be extended to those convicted of assisting the Democratic Army. Venizelos then became prime minister, with Populist support, but in November 1950 the Populists withdrew their backing. This period of unstable coalitions led to fresh elections in September 1951. A few weeks before, Field-Marshal Papagos suddenly announced that he would contest the elections as leader of the Greek Rally, which was consciously modelled on de Gaulle's *Rassemblement du Peuple Français*. Papagos had in May peremptorily resigned all his military offices following a dispute with the palace, a move that provoked sympathetic rumblings in the army. Another significant feature of the 1951 elections was the emergence of the United Democratic Left (EDA) as a cover for the banned communist party, although not all its supporters were communists.

Despite the adoption of a modified system of proportional representation, the September 1951 elections resulted once again in parliamentary deadlock. Papagos' Greek Rally won 114 seats, in the process decimating the Populists with a mere 2. The National Progressive Centre Union received 74 and the Liberals 57. The United Democratic Left, a number of whose candidates were in prison or exile for left wing activities, received 10 seats, and the George Papandreou Party none. Papagos, professing to scorn the old politicians, refused to enter a coalition and almost immediately began to demand new elections. Once again a centre coalition government was formed, with Plastiras as prime minister, and the American administration, making no secret of its concern about the continuing instability of Greek politics, announced that American aid, on which Greece was still heavily dependent, was to be reduced from $225 to $182 million. In March 1952, in an undisguised intervention in domestic politics, the American ambassador, John Peurifoy, openly advocated a change in the electoral system from proportional representation to simple majority, implying that if this were not done then American aid might be further reduced. Such a change would clearly have benefited Papagos' Greek Rally, which not surprisingly championed the simple majority system. Venizelos, acting prime minister during the illness of Plastiras, formally criticised such a blatant intervention. Nonetheless, his government got the message and soon announced that the elections to be held in November 1952 would be on the basis of the simple majority system, although a number of other measures were taken aimed at undercutting Papagos' support.

The continuing political uncertainty impeded any serious attempt to get to grips with pressing problems of economic and financial reconstruction. At the end of 1951, parliament, following two years of deliberation, voted for a revised constitution. This came into effect in January 1952, and replaced the 1911 constitution, which had been theoretically in force since the abrogation in 1935 of the republican constitution of 1927. In certain respects the 1952 constitution was less liberal than its predecessor. Civil servants, for instance, were denied the right to strike, and 'internal danger' was made a sufficient reason for proclaiming a state of emergency and encroaching on civil liberties. Nonetheless, the 1952 constitution did guarantee the basic democratic freedoms, and given the difficult circumstances in which it had been gestated, was on paper a not illiberal document. But at the same time much of the repressive emergency legislation enacted during the years of the civil war remained in force and was used without hesitation to harass known left-wingers.

One of the most resented aspects of this emergency legislation was the insistence on a certificate of 'healthy social views' for state employment, for a driver's licence, for a passport, and, for a time, for university entrance. These certificates were granted by the police and a vast system of dossiers on the political views, real or supposed, of hundreds of thousands of Greeks was built up. Many of those responsible for implementing this oppressive system themselves had dubious records of wartime collaboration or right wing extremism. Although Plastiras himself genuinely favoured reconciliation between right and left, it was not until April 1952 that measures of leniency were taken. These resulted in the commutation of almost all the death sentences still outstanding, the reduction in the sentences of, or the pardoning of, many of the 20,000 or so prisoners convicted of subversion. Even so, Nikos Beloyiannis, who had been convicted of organising a communist spy ring, was executed in March 1952, a move which aroused a storm of protest both in Greece and abroad.

The November 1952 elections resulted in a massive parliamentary majority for Papagos' Greek Rally, much larger than its overall share of the vote. With just under a half of the popular vote it received almost five-sixths of the seats in parliament, 247 out of 300. An alliance of the National Progressive Centre Union, the Liberals and the Socialist Union of Popular Democracy attracted 34 per cent of the popular vote but received only 51 seats. The United Democratic Left, with almost 10 per cent of the popular vote, received no seats. There had been no less than 16 different administrations between 1946 and 1952 but the 1952 elections were to usher in eleven years of uninterrupted right wing rule. Despite its repressive features, this period of much needed political stability was to enable real progress to be made towards Greece's post-war reconstruction, and it was at this time that the essential foundations were laid for the consistently high, if distorted, rate of economic growth that has characterised the post-war Greek economy.

An important role in creating the conditions for the development of the consumer society of the sixties and seventies was played by Spyros Markezinis, who held the key economic ministry of co-ordination. Under Markezinis' aegis the economy was set on a free enterprise course. The drachma was drastically devalued in 1953, legislation was introduced to protect foreign capital, interest rates were reduced, import controls were relaxed and measures taken to prune the hydra-headed bureaucracy. Investment in the manufacturing sector, however, was low, and Greeks, after their experience of runaway inflation during the occupation and civil war, preferred to sink their savings into property. Hence the proliferation of apartment blocks which have disfigured not only Athens but many provincial towns as well in recent years. Economic development met with a temporary setback, however, with a serious earthquake in the Ionian Islands in August 1953, and another in Volos in the following year. In time Markezinis fell out with Papagos, and defected from the Greek Rally with 22 deputies to form the Progressive Party. This defection, however, did little to dent Papagos' massive parliamentary majority.

During Papagos' premiership important developments also took place in foreign policy. In 1951, with the Cold War at its height, Greece, although scarcely an Atlantic country, was admitted to the North Atlantic Treaty Organisation. Some improvement took place in her relations with Bulgaria and Albania, while those with Yugoslavia improved dramatically. Greece and Yugoslavia had traditionally been good neighbours, and, in a sense, the antagonism of the civil war period was an aberration in the course of a long friendship which had included alliance in two world wars. Negotiations during the winter of 1952–3 resulted in the signing in Ankara in February 1953 of a treaty of friendship and co-operation between Yugoslavia, Turkey and Greece. This was followed by the conclusion of a formal treaty of alliance of the three countries in August of the same year at Bled in Yugoslavia. These developments represented a partial attempt to revive the Balkan Entente of the 1930s and provided for a substantial degree of both military and political co-operation. This Balkan Pact, however, was to prove stillborn. This was in part because, with the thaw in Russian-Yugoslav relations in 1955, the Yugoslavs no longer placed such a high priority on Balkan security. But the primary reason for the collapse of the Balkan Pact was the rapid deterioration in Greco-Turkish relations occasioned by the Cyprus problem, which in the mid-1950s reached an acute phase.

Cyprus, with a population of 600,000, some 80 per cent of whom were Greek and 18 per cent Turkish, was the last substantial area of Greek population to remain outside the borders of the Greek state. By the 1950s the demands of the Greek majority on the island for *enosis*, or union, with the Greek motherland had become insistent. By the Cyprus Convention of 1878 the Ottoman government had agreed to British administration of the island, although Ottoman sovereignty was retained and the Cypriots were obliged to pay an annual tribute to the Porte. In 1914 Britain formally annexed the island when the Ottoman Empire entered the First World War on the side of the Central Powers. The following year Britain offered Cyprus to Greece as an inducement to enter the war on the side of the Entente Powers but the offer was rejected. By the Treaty of Lausanne of 1923 Turkey recognised British sovereignty over the island, which became a Crown Colony in 1925.

Pro-*enosis* agitation resulted in the burning down of Government House in Nicosia in 1931, whereupon the British authorities dissolved the Legislative Council, which had contained both Greek and Turkish Cypriot members, and henceforth ruled by decree. A number of prominent members of the enosist movement, including two bishops, were deported. In 1941 Eden, the British foreign secretary, fearful that the Germans might score a propaganda triumph by capturing the island and formally ceding it to Greece, was prepared to make a public declaration that Britain was prepared to consider granting *enosis* at the end of the war, subject to the retention of base facilities. The Colonial Office, however, fearful of the impact such a declaration might have on Britain's other colonial dependencies, vetoed the idea. But many Cypriots, and indeed Greeks, continued to hope that *enosis* would be granted at the war's end as a reward for the important contribution made by both Greeks and Cypriots to the allied war effort. But once again Colonial Office objections ruled out any such possibility. As long as Britain exercised her traditional hegemony over Greece no Athens government was prepared to embarrass her by making demands for *enosis* or by fomenting disaffection on the island.

When, however, in the late forties the United States assumed Britain's role as Greece's primary patron, this reluctance diminished. Moreover, *enosist* sentiment was on the increase in Cyprus itself. In January 1950, a 96 per cent vote in favour of *enosis* was recorded in a poll organised by the Orthodox Church among Greek Cypriots. A leading role in organising the plebiscite was played by Bishop Makarios (born Michael Mouskos) who, in March 1950, was elected Archbishop of Cyprus. As ethnarch of the Greek community he combined, in the tradition of the Ottoman Empire, civil as well as spiritual leadership of his flock. In 1951 Makarios met with Colonel George Grivas, a Cypriot who had led the ultra right wing X (Khi) organisation in Greece at the end of the German occupation, and who was laying the groundwork for armed resistance to British rule. Makarios' enosist aspirations also received cautious support from Papagos. But when Papagos made an informal approach to Eden, the British foreign secretary, about the possibility of *enosis*, he was rebuffed. In the House of Commons the Minister of State for the Colonies, Henry Hopkinson, incautiously declared in July 1954 that, for strategic reasons, British sovereignty over Cyprus could never be relinquished.

When a Greek attempt to raise the issue of Cyprus in the United Nations failed, there were massive demonstrations in Greece and violence, fomented by Grivas' National Organisation of Cypriot Fighters (EOKA), erupted in Cyprus in April 1955. The British authorities sought to use the Turkish community on the island as a counterweight to the demands of the Greek Cypriots and the Turkish government, which had hitherto been rather indifferent to the fate of the Turks on the island, was encouraged to consider itself as having an interest in the island comparable to that of Greece. In September 1955 violent riots erupted in Istanbul aimed at the prosperous community of some 100,000 ethnic Greeks who had been allowed to remain in the city by the Lausanne settlement of 1923. The riots were subsequently found to have been inspired by the Turkish government. In retaliation Greece withdrew its officers from the NATO headquarters in Izmir and any hope of continued Greek and Turkish co-operation in the Balkan Pact was shattered.

In this deteriorating situation Papagos died in October 1955. The most obvious contender for the leadership of his Greek Rally was Stephanos Stephanopoulos, whom Papagos had himself singled out for the succession. But before the party had had a chance to elect a new leader, King Paul passed over the more obvious candidates and asked Constantine Karamanlis, the relatively unknown Minister of Public Works, to form a government, thus prompting the resignation of Stephanopoulos. Although he had made an impact as an energetic and efficient administrator, Karamanlis, the son of a Macedonian schoolmaster turned tobacco merchant, was not a part of Greece's traditional political establishment. But he had a reputation as a firm believer in Greece's Western orientation and it could be that King Paul, himself firmly committed to the American and NATO connection, considered that Karamanlis would be more likely than some of his rivals for the leadership of the Greek Rally to agree to a settlement of the Cyprus issue acceptable to Greece's NATO partners.

One of Karamanlis' first acts was to reconstitute the Greek Rally as the National Radical Union (ERE). Essentially a continuation of the Greek Rally, ERE included almost all the leading members of Papagos' party, who had mostly begun their careers in the Populist Party, as had Karamanlis himself. Elections were scheduled for February 1956 under a highly involved electoral system, designed to strengthen ERE at the expense of the opposition parties. This was also the first general election in Greece in which women had the vote. The idiosyncrasies of the new electoral system encouraged virtually all the opposition parties, ranging from the Populists on the right to the United Democratic Left on the left, to contest the elections in an alliance known as the Democratic Union. Even so, the system was so heavily biased in favour of ERE that, although the Democratic Union's overall share of the vote at 48 per cent was actually higher than that of ERE at 47 per cent, it received considerably fewer seats, 132 to ERE's 165.

Two years later, in 1958, Karamanlis, following an internal split within his own party, again went to the polls. Once again a form of 'reinforced' proportional representation was adopted, a move which discriminated against coalitions. It was, however, supported by the Liberals, now led by Papandreou and Venizelos in tandem, who hoped to lure the proliferation of numerous small centre/left parties into the Liberal camp. This calculation was mistaken for the centre parties remained fragmented and the left wing United Democratic Left, with 24 per cent of the votes and 79 seats, emerged as the largest opposition party. The Liberals secured 36 seats and ERE, although its share of the vote had fallen from 47 per cent in 1956 to 41 per cent in 1958, actually increased its seats from 165 to 171. The dramatic rise in the far left vote was in part the result of the disunity of the centre parties, in part the result of growing disenchantment with the attitude of Greece's NATO allies over the Cyprus issue, which made the neutralism advocated by EDA more attractive to the Greek electorate.

The failure of a conference on Cyprus attended by representatives of Greece and Turkey and at which Harold Macmillan, the

British foreign secretary, offered a qualified degree of self-government, was followed by the appointment of Field-Marshal Sir John Harding, a former chief of the imperial general staff, as governor of Cyprus, a move which presaged a hardening of British attitudes. In March 1956 Archbishop Makarios was deported to the Seychelles, but on Cyprus the level of violence increased. EOKA's initial victims had been largely drawn from among the Greek community, but it now increasingly attacked British troops and Turkish policemen. At the end of the year Lord Radcliffe visited Cyprus and drew up a draft constitution. This was rejected out of hand by the Greek government, which continued to place its hopes for a resolution of the conflict in the United Nations. This body, however, was able to offer little in the way of concrete help to the Greeks. In April 1957 Archbishop Makarios was released from detention and, forbidden to return to Cyprus, settled in Athens. In another conciliatory gesture, Field-Marshal Harding was replaced a few months later as governor by Sir Hugh Foot, who had acquired a liberal reputation in the colonial service. But relations with Britain remained poor, and Greece rejected proposals to 'partner' Britain and Turkey in the administration of Cyprus, seeing this as a move in the direction of partition of the island between the two communities.

But towards the end of 1958 there were signs of movement. Karamanlis, alarmed at the way in which EDA had been able to exploit the disappointment felt by many Greeks at the attitude of their Western allies towards *enosis*, was anxious to obtain a settlement of the problem. So indeed was the United States, troubled by the disarray the dispute was causing to NATO's south-eastern flank. The path towards a settlement had been eased by remarks in September 1958 by Makarios to the effect that he no longer insisted on *enosis*, which was anathema to the Turks, as the only solution, but would be prepared to accept independence. The British government, moreover, in the wake of the Suez campaign, now realised that its strategic interests could equally well be safeguarded by sovereign bases as by control of the whole island.

In February 1959 Karamanlis and the Turkish prime minister,

Adnan Menderes, met in Zürich to discuss the creation of an independent Cyprus, but without representatives of either the Greek or Turkish Cypriot communities. A draft agreement was rapidly worked out and later in the month presented in London by the British, Greek and Turkish governments to the leaders of the Greek and Turkish Cypriot communities, Archbishop Makarios and Dr Fazil Kutchuk. Neither were given much say in the final agreement, which Makarios signed only with reluctance. Ominously, Grivas, who could now cast off his *nom de guerre* of Digenis Akritas, expressed disapproval at the abandoning of the sacred principle of *enosis*. Karamanlis also came under heavy fire within Greece and was denounced by the opposition for betraying the cause of Hellenism in the interests of NATO and the Americans.

The agreement provided that, in return for sovereign military and air force bases at Dekelia and Akrotiri, Britain would concede independence. In August 1960, Cyprus would become an independent republic within the Commonwealth, and the independence, territorial integrity and constitution of the new state were guaranteed by Britain, Greece and Turkey, each guarantor having the right to act unilaterally in defence of the treaty. Greece was to be permitted to station 950 troops in the island, and Turkey 650. There was to be a Greek president and a Turkish vice-president each of whom was to have veto powers in matters of foreign affairs, defence and internal security. An elaborate framework of power sharing was established in the cabinet, house of representatives, civil service and police. In all branches of government the Turkish minority was given a representation greater than warranted by its size. In the civil service, for instance, almost a third of all positions were to be reserved for Turkish Cypriots, although they only constituted less than 20 per cent of the population. In December 1959 Archbishop Makarios was elected president of the new republic and Dr Kutchuk, who was unopposed, became vice-president. But although trouble was implicit in the complex constitutional arrangements of the new state almost from the beginning, there was optimism and relief in both Cyprus and in Greece now that the violence on the island had ended.

Although the first half of the Karamanlis administration had been overshadowed by the tragic events in Cyprus, significant steps had been taken to consolidate Greece's new-found economic stability. Average per capita annual income had risen from 112 dollars in 1951, to 270 in 1956 and was to reach 500 dollars by 1964. After the traumatic inflations of the 1940s, orthodox fiscal policies had resulted in a remarkable degree of price stability. Tourism was beginning to help correct Greece's chronic imbalance of payments, as were the contributions of the Greek migrant workers who were moving in increasing numbers to the countries of western Europe, and in particular to West Germany, in search of often menial work. The numbers of Greeks engaged in the industrial and service sectors now began to match those employed in agriculture, the traditional mainstay of the Greek economy. In 1961 the urban and rural populations were balanced at 43 per cent, with 13 per cent living in a semi-urban environment. One consequence of these trends was an acceleration of the flight from the countryside to the cities, and particularly Athens. By the early 1960s, for instance, almost two million of the country's total population of eight million four hundred thousand was concentrated in the Athens region, an unhealthy development that further exacerbated the bureaucratic centralisation which had always been the bane of Greek government. The consumer boom of the 1960s was indeed largely centred on Athens and, although overall living standards were steadily rising, inequalities in the distribution of wealth continued to grow.

Under fire for his acquiescence in the Cyprus settlement, Karamanlis was also attacked by the main opposition party, EDA, for his commitment to Greece's membership of the Western alliance. It was partly fear of the neutralist tendencies of the opposition that prompted Karamanlis to open negotiations for associate status within the European Economic Community. There were cogent economic reasons underlying Greece's application, and Greece's highly protected industries were certainly in need of competition. Yet political considerations weighed equally, perhaps more heavily, in the government's calculations. Association with the EEC was seen as yet another way of binding Greece to her NATO allies. The treaty of association, the first such association agreement negotiated by the EEC, came into force in November 1962. The agreement provided for a phased reduction of tariffs and customs duties and envisaged Greece attaining full membership of the community by 1984.

Considerations of international politics, too, seem to have prompted Karamanlis to hold elections in October 1961, before the term of the 1958 parliament had ended. The building of the Berlin wall in the summer of 1961, and the international repercussions it provoked, coupled with Russian sponsorship of a plan for a Balkan zone free of either nuclear weapons or military bases, was thought likely to provoke a swing to the right among the Greek electorate. The storing of nuclear weapons at American bases in Greece had become a major issue, with the opposition highly critical and the Soviet leader Nikita Kruschev threatening to blast the Acropolis out of existence. In the aftermath of its defeat in 1958 the centre had suffered a major crisis, with two groups breaking away from the Liberals, who were now headed by Sophocles Venizelos. George Papandreou, who headed one of these splinter parties, was fully aware of the dangers posed to the centre's electoral prospects by continued fragmentation. He was particularly sensitive to the advantage this gave to the far left, and made strenuous efforts to unite the centre under his leadership. In the summer of 1961 he succeeded in forming the Centre Union by gathering together the various centre groupings. The Centre Union fought the 1961 elections in an electoral alliance with Markezinis' Progressives while EDA formed a compact with the small National Agrarian Party. Once again a somewhat modified system of 'reinforced' proportional representation was used. The distribution of seats, based as it was on the census of 1951, did not reflect the demographic realities, and in particular the rapid urbanisation, of the previous decade that were manifested in the 1961 census. Athens alone had grown by over a third during this period. With 51 per cent of the popular vote, Karamanlis' ERE won 176 seats; the Centre Union/Progressive alliance, with 34 per cent, won 100 seats; and the EDA/National Agrarian Party alliance, with 15 per cent (in striking contrast to the 24 per cent EDA vote in 1958), won 24 seats.

The results of the 1961 elections were greeted with uproar by the opposition parties, which complained that they had been the victims of an 'electoral *coup d'état*'. They alleged that the temporary 'service' government of the royalist General Dovas had failed miserably in its sole function, that of overseeing free elections. Both the Centre Union and EDA published 'Black Books', in which they made detailed charges of electoral malpractices. Papandreou claimed that in Athens alone some 100,000 bogus votes had been cast and there were many allegations of fraud and violence in the provinces. Most of these involved the behaviour of the National Security Battalions, a rural anti-communist militia created during the civil war, but charges were also made against the police and gendarmerie. Particular pressure seems to have been exercised in the border regions, which had been under virtual martial law since the time of the civil war, and within the armed forces, whose fiercely anti-communist leadership had been alarmed by EDA's successes in 1958.

It was subsequently alleged in parliament that the army's involvement in the electoral process had been the result of a contingency plan code-named 'Pericles'. Inevitably the opposition charges contained an element of rhetoric and exaggeration but there seems little doubt that intimidation and ballot rigging were employed on behalf of ERE. How far these activities were authorised by Karamanlis himself is unclear, however, and, in any case, the electoral manipulations do not appear to have been on a large enough scale to affect the overall result. But they did give George Papandreou, who was perhaps at his best in the rough and tumble of opposition politics, a useful weapon with which to belabour the government. He now launched the 'relentless struggle' for the holding of new elections which would truly reflect the popular will. The battle cry of the 'relentless struggle' also helped to unify the somewhat disparate forces that composed the Centre Union and enabled Papandreou to give the centre a cohesion that it had not enjoyed since the days of Eleftherios Venizelos.

Disquiet over the conduct of the 1961 elections helped to catalyse a growing feeling in the country that, whatever their initial rationale in the immediate aftermath of a bitterly fought civil war, the repressive mechanisms used by the right to contain the left were no longer justified. Moreover, as Papandreou pursued his campaign against both Karamanlis and King Paul for refusing to hold new elections, there were increasing signs of a loss of confidence on the part of the right. In May 1963 a sinister light was cast on the activities of the professional patriots of the extra-parliamentary right with the murder of the left wing deputy, Dr Gregory Lambrakis, who was struck down by ultra right wing thugs at a peace rally held in Salonica. Although not even his most severe critics accused Karamanlis of being personally implicated in the assassination, nonetheless considerable disquiet was aroused when investigations showed links between the assassins and highly placed state officials. Opposition claims that an unofficial, extreme right wing 'para-state' existed alongside the official state and was at times beyond its control gained new credence.

On 11 June, a month after the murder of Lambrakis, Karamanlis, harried by the opposition and beset by mounting balance of payments difficulties at a time when American aid was much diminished, tendered his resignation. Officially this was due to a difference of opinion with the Palace over the advisability of a state visit to Britain by King Paul and Queen Frederica. Karamanlis advised postponement of the visit, for Queen Frederica, during an earlier private visit, had been harassed by demonstrators protesting against the continued imprisonment of those convicted of offences during the civil war. But the king and queen insisted that the visit continue as planned and the royal visitors were duly met with large-scale demonstrations. Karamanlis' quarrel with the Palace had deeper roots than the relatively insignificant question of the timing of the state visit. It seems that he had grown increasingly resentful of the prerogatives of the monarchy and of the way in which the armed forces during the post-war period had in effect become a royal fief. He had become disillusioned, too, with the Greek political system in general, believing that the 1952 constitution unduly favoured parliament at the expense of government.

On his resignation Karamanlis called for immediate elections, and King Paul appointed as prime minister Panayiotis Pipinelis, a National Radical Union minister who was known as a staunch supporter of the monarchy. The Pipinelis government was technically a 'service' government, but the opposition, mindful of the way in which the Dovas service government had tolerated abuses during the 1961 elections, demanded a more obviously neutral caretaker administration headed by a non-political figure. Such a government, headed by Stylianos Mavromichalis, president of the Supreme Court, was formed on 28 September and the elections long sought by Papandreou were scheduled for 3 November 1963. Mavromichalis, anxious to avoid any repetition of the 1961 scandals, took measures to ensure that the elections took place in an atmosphere of freedom.

Unusually in the post-war period, there were no electoral alliances and only four parties contested the elections: the National Radical Union (ERE), Markezinis' Progressives, the Centre Union (EK) and the United Democratic Left (EDA). The elections, held under a form of proportional representation, gave a narrow victory to the Centre Union which won 138 seats (42 per cent of the vote) to ERE's 132 (39 per cent). EDA won 28 seats (14 per cent), and Markezinis' Progressives 2 (4 per cent). Karamanlis, following his resignation in June, had left for Paris. He returned to fight the November elections but, after his defeat, once again departed, expressing his disenchantment with Greek political life, for a self-imposed exile in France that was to last for eleven years. His eight-year term as prime minister between 1955 and 1963 had been the longest in Greece's independent history. The leadership of his party, ERE, was now assumed by Panayiotis Kanellopoulos.

Although Papandreou had broken the twelve-year monopoly of political power enjoyed by the right he still did not have an overall majority in parliament. His long-standing suspicion of the far left had in no way diminished, and he made it clear that he had no intention of governing with the support of EDA, preferring instead to give electoral battle on two fronts, against both right and left. After giving an earnest of his reforming zeal by releasing political prisoners, legislating for educational reform and raising wages and salaries, Papandreou tendered his resignation to King Paul on 24 December 1963, hoping that in new elections he would gain an absolute majority. The king then asked Kanellopoulos to try to form an ERE/Centre Union coalition, but Papandreou refused to have anything to do with such a scheme, and none of his parliamentary followers was prepared to defect.

The king now had no option but to call new elections, which were scheduled for 16 February 1964, and a caretaker government was formed. Papandreou's strategy paid handsome dividends, for the Centre Union, with an impressive 53 per cent share of the vote and 171 seats, won an absolute majority both in terms of popular vote and of seats. ERE, now in coalition with the Progressives, with 35 per cent of the vote won 107 seats, and EDA, with 12 per cent won 22. It was clear from the result that since the preceding November Papandreou had attracted votes both from the right and the left. Armed with a substantial majority in parliament, and seemingly enjoying the benevolence of both the Palace and the American Embassy, both of which saw in a strong centre the best guarantee against a resurgence of support for EDA, Papandreou looked set for an untroubled period of moderately reformist government. But within a mere fifteen months of the 1964 elections Greece was to be embroiled in the most serious political crisis of the post-war period.

The most immediate problem facing the new government was the Cyprus question, which had once again flared up in violence. The cumbersome constitutional machinery that had been evolved in the wake of the Zürich and London agreements of 1959 had proved unworkable in the prevailing atmosphere of mistrust between the Greek and Turkish communities. A particular stumbling block was the provision whereby Turkish Cypriots were to hold 30 per cent of jobs in the civil service. In the Greek Cypriot view, the various constitutional guarantees designed to protect the rights of the Turkish Cypriot minority had in effect enabled it to frustrate the will of the much larger Greek Cypriot majority. At the end of November 1963, Archbishop Makarios presented the Turkish vice-president, Dr Kutchuk, with thirteen proposals intended to remove some of the anomalies inherent in the 1960 constitution. These included the abolition of the presidential and vice-presidential veto and the reduction of the percentage of Turks in government service to reflect more closely their numbers in the community as a whole. The proposals were rejected, first, significantly, by the Turkish government and only then by Dr Kutchuk.

On 21 December 1963 fighting broke out between the two communities, and on Christmas day jets from the Turkish mainland flew low over the island. In January 1964, with Turkey poised for an invasion, the American President Johnson despatched General Lemnitzer to Greece and Turkey where he was able to avert the immediate danger of invasion. Meanwhile, Britain temporarily assumed the role of peace keeper, pending the despatch in March 1964 of a United Nations peace-keeping force (UNFICYP). When the threat of invasion loomed again in the summer President Johnson pointedly warned the Turkish prime minister, Ismet Inönü, that the United States would not tolerate the use of American-supplied weapons in any move against the island. Johnson's blunt *démarche* averted the very real danger of Turkish intervention. Sporadic outbreaks of violence continued, culminating in serious hostilities in August 1964 when Greek Cypriots launched an attack on the village of Kokkina, through which Turkish supplies were being infiltrated, a move that provoked retaliatory Turkish air raids. During the 1964 confrontation between the two communities many of the Turkish Cypriots on the island concentrated in enclaves from which Greek Cypriots were excluded, and an uneasy peace descended on the island. With Archbishop Makarios pursuing an increasingly independent foreign policy and seeking support from the non-aligned countries, there were indications of, at least in the short term, the abandonment of any hopes of eventual *enosis*, which in any case had been specifically excluded by the 1960 settlement. His increasingly neutralist stance occasioned some alarm in Athens, and Papandreou agreed to the return of Grivas to the island to act as a brake on the Archbishop's pretensions. At the same time Papandreou rejected a plan evolved by Dean Acheson, a former American Secretary of State, the essence of which involved the union of Cyprus with Greece, in return for the creation of Turkish military bases and Turkish Cypriot cantons on the island. It also envisaged the cession by Greece of the small island of Kastellorizo off the Turkish mainland. Thus the Cyprus issue continued to exert a considerable influence on Greek domestic politics.

On the domestic front Papandreou sought to implement the reformist programme on which he had been elected. An important education act was promulgated which raised the school-leaving age from twelve to fifteen, sought to de-emphasise the dominant role of classics in the curriculum, and made spoken demotic Greek the medium of instruction throughout the primary schools. Civil service salaries were raised, restraints on credit were lifted, income tax was cut, and peasants were guaranteed higher prices for their wheat. An important role in the formulation of Papandreou's economic policies was played by his son, Andreas, an economist who had spent many years in the United States and was now a minister in his father's government. His policies marked a significant departure from the fiscal orthodoxy of ERE, and when they resulted in a worsening of the balance of payments and a boosting of inflation to $3\frac{1}{2}$ per cent there was alarm in business circles, traditionally linked to ERE. Conservatives were also disturbed by Papandreou's release of most of those still imprisoned for offences committed during the civil war and by his policy of improved relations and increased trading contacts with the countries of the Eastern bloc.

Right wing apprehensions were further exacerbated by the uncovering in May 1965 of a purported left wing conspiracy of 'Nasserite' tendency within the army. The members of the group, which was known as *Aspida* (Shield), allegedly looked to Andreas Papandreou as their leader. While there probably was some kind of conspiratorial group, the numbers involved were small, particularly when contrasted with membership of such right wing groups in the army as IDEA, which traced their origins back to the wartime presence of Greek troops in the Middle East. In the same month the opposition press trumpeted the discovery of attempts to sabotage military vehicles on the Bulgarian/Turkish border. It was subsequently revealed that the exposer of this 'sabotage' was one Colonel George Papadopoulos, and that there was in fact no such communist plot. Papandreou now contemplated doing what his more radical supporters had long urged, namely exerting his authority over those elements in the leadership of the army and of KYP, the Greek Central Intelligence Agency, who were patently opposed to the continuance of a Centre Union government in power.

But he soon came up against the opposition of his own defence minister, Petros Garoufalias, who had close connections with the Palace. When Garoufalias refused to agree to changes in the upper echelons of the army, including the replacement of the chief of the defence staff, General Gennimatas, Papandreou tried to dismiss him. Garoufalias, however, refused to go, even after he had been removed from the Centre Union. In July the septuagenarian Papandreou asked the twenty-five-year-old King Constantine II, who had succeeded his father King Paul in March 1964, to dismiss Garoufalias, and to agree to his taking over as minister of defence. The king refused, it being argued that it would be improper for George Papandreou to head the defence ministry when his own son, Andreas, was under investigation for his alleged involvement in the Aspida conspiracy. Acting within the letter of the constitution but against its spirit the young king manoeuvred Papandreou into resigning on 15 July 1965, thus sparking off a political crisis of major proportions.

To the accompaniment of massive demonstrations by Papandreou's supporters protesting against a 'royal *coup d'état*', the king's strategy was to try to split the Centre Union by attempting to form a minority government from within its ranks. The first aspirant to succeed Papandreou, however, George Athanassiadis-Novas, the speaker of parliament, failed to attract more than a handful of defectors from the Centre Union, and was thus unable to win a vote of confidence. A second attempt by Elias Tsirimokos, a one-time leading member of EAM and a member of the left wing of the Centre Union, similarly failed. Finally, in September, Stephanos Stephanopoulos, a right wing member of the Centre Union, at the head of 45 Centre Union 'apostates', as they came to be known, was able narrowly to scrape the necessary vote of confidence, thanks to the support in parliament of ERE and Markezinis' Progressives. Some of the 'apostates' were rewarded with ministerial office, and there were rumours of bribery on the part of the Palace and the American Embassy.

The narrowness of its parliamentary majority of only two seats inhibited any decisive measures by the Stephanopoulos government. In parliament and out, Papandreou, relishing to the full this renewal of the 'relentless struggle', harried the government, against a background of continuous and large-scale demonstrations. The principal demand of Papandreou's supporters was for new elections, and a favourite slogan 'Ena ena tessara', or 114, a reference to the article of the 1952 constitution entrusting its maintenance to the patriotism of the Greek people. But although demonstrations and strikes abounded, the high rate of economic growth of the early sixties, with the economy expanding at a rate of about 6 per cent a year, was maintained, and for all the passionate emotions engendered by the crisis there was remarkably little political violence. Moreover, there were signs of a possible way out of the political impasse when in December 1966 Papandreou and Kanellopoulos, the leader of ERE, reached an agreement to hold elections on 28 May 1967. These were to be overseen by a non-political caretaker government, headed by the banker John Paraskevopoulos.

The election campaign was characterised by two major developments, both involving Andreas Papandreou. The younger Papandreou had become the focus of a group of radically inclined Centre Union deputies who suspected that George Papandreou's understanding with Kanellopoulos included a secret undertaking not to make the monarchy an election issue. It was also rumoured that Papandreou had promised not to disturb the existing command structure of the army. For a time it looked as though Andreas Papandreou's group might split from the Centre Union. Father and son, however, were reconciled, but no sooner had their quarrel been patched up than Andreas became the centre of renewed controversy. In mid-March fifteen officers charged in the Aspida affair were convicted and the public prosecutor sought to have Andreas Papandreou's parliamentary immunity lifted so that he could be charged, along with other civilians alleged to be involved.

The Centre Union was in a quandary, for under existing law,

even if the prosecutor's request were refused, Papandreou's immunity would automatically lapse with the dissolution of parliament at the start of the election campaign. Faced with the prospect of Andreas Papandreou spending the election campaign under arrest, the Centre Union tabled a law extending parliamentary immunity for the duration of the election campaign. This was too much for the hard-liners of ERE and the Paraskevopoulos caretaker government resigned early in April. Going against established convention, King Constantine did not appoint another caretaker government but asked Kanellopoulos, the leader of ERE, to form a government and oversee the forthcoming elections. Papandreou made a token protest but it was clear that he did not seriously doubt that Kanellopoulos would hold fair elections. It subsequently emerged, however, that a group of senior generals, in consultation with the king, had been secretly making contingency plans for the army to intervene if disorder were to follow the widely predicted Centre Union victory at the polls.

Moreover, unknown to their seniors, a group of relatively junior officers had been making their own plans. At 2 a.m. on the morning of 21 April 1967, they struck, catching the king, the politicians and the senior echelons of the armed forces alike off balance. Using a NATO contingency plan prepared for the event of serious internal disorders, and code-named 'Prometheus', the conspirators executed their putsch with exemplary efficiency and virtually no bloodshed, meeting with very little resistance. Later in the morning of the 21 April a decree, purportedly signed by the king and his government, was issued proclaiming martial law. Various articles in the 1952 constitution guaranteeing human rights were suspended, special courts martial were set up, political parties were dissolved and the right to strike abolished. Many thousands of people with a record of left wing political views or activity were rounded up and sent into exile in bleak camps on the islands. In the course of the day the creation of a nondescript civilian government headed by a supreme court prosecutor, Constantine Kollias, was announced. In a statement broadcast in the evening Kollias roundly attacked the politicians for failing the nation, promised social justice and declared that from now on there were no rightists, centrists or leftists, 'only Greeks who believe in Greece'.

It soon became apparent, however, that the new civilian prime minister was a mere façade and that real power lay in the hands of a triumvirate of relatively junior officers, Colonels George Papadopoulos and Nicholas Makarezos, both of whom had backgrounds in intelligence, and Brigadier Stylianos Pattakos, who were backed up by a shadowy Revolutionary Council. Papadopoulos took charge of the key ministry to the prime minister, which controlled the media. Pattakos became minister of the interior and Makarezos took over the important economic ministry of co-ordination. The 'Colonels', as the military junta came to be known, justified their coup by the need to forestall an imminent communist take-over. But no evidence was ever produced to substantiate this claim, which was in time dropped by the Colonels themselves. The real motive of the conspirators was undoubtedly the fear that a Centre Union victory in the elections scheduled for May would have been followed by a purge of officers of known ultra right wing views. Colonel Papadopoulos, as a leading functionary of KYP, the Greek CIA, and the man behind the 'communist sabotage' scare of 1965, would have been an obvious candidate for early retirement, as would have been many of his fellow conspirators.

Another likely cause of military disaffection, although one that was for obvious reasons seldom explicitly articulated, was the feeling of many officers that they had been passed by in the consumer boom of the 1960s. At the time of the coup a Greek general was paid less than a sergeant in the American army. For the most part men of peasant or lower-middle-class origin, they resented the elaborate intrigues played out by the politicians, a tightly knit and to some extent hereditary caste, in the urban affluence of Athens, while they sweated it out in the border regions or the stifling boredom of Greek provincial towns. Certainly the military, on achieving power, lost little time in securing a greater share for itself of the country's growing prosperity. Indeed, the new life-style of some of the military rulers attracted the scorn of those members of the regime, sincere if blinkered, who genuinely believed that they had a mission to preserve the traditional values of Greek society against alien Western and secular influences. The early ban, rapidly rescinded in the interests of Greece's vital tourist trade, against the entry into the country of hirsute or mini-skirted foreigners was but one example of this strain in the Colonels' thinking.

Although King Constantine had not signed the decree establishing martial law which had been issued in his name, he rejected the urgings of his last constitutional prime minister to resist the conspirators. Kanellopoulos himself, with a number of other prominent political figures, was placed under house arrest. Instead, the king grudgingly acquiesced in the establishment of the dictatorship, apparently hoping to exert a moderating influence. This decision eased the dilemma of Greece's Western allies, who had expressed varying degrees of disapproval of the new regime, over the question of diplomatic recognition, for it was argued that their ambassadors were accredited to the king rather than to any particular government. For several months the king refused to sign decrees retiring officers in all three services known for their loyalty to the crown, but in September, after a visit to the United States during which he made his distaste for the regime clear, he succumbed to the Colonels' pressure and substantial numbers of royalist officers were compulsorily retired.

There remained, however, elements in the armed forces that were loyal to the crown and these played a key part in the king's plans for a counter-coup aimed at dislodging the Colonels before they became too firmly entrenched in power. This was launched on 13 December 1967, but was organised in such a slip-shod manner that it had little chance of success. Indeed, there is some evidence that the regime knew in advance of the king's amateurish plans and was thus able to plan effective counter-measures. King Constantine launched his bid to oust the Colonels with a proclamation urging their overthrow. This, however, was little heard as it was broadcast on a short-wave transmitter in Larisa rather than on the national network. Meanwhile the king had flown to Kavalla, where he planned to link up with loyal elements of the Third Army Corps stationed in northern Greece. When it became clear, however, that his coup could only succeed if he were prepared to countenance bloodshed, the king flew to Rome with his family and prime minister Kollias, and the counter-coup rapidly collapsed. The abortive counter-coup was followed by further purges in the armed forces of those supposedly implicated or thought still to harbour royalist sympathies. It is estimated that in 1967–8 approximately one sixth of the officer corps was compulsorily retired. Besides removing those whose loyalty to the regime was in doubt, the purges also served to loosen the promotion bottle-necks within the armed forces which had been a longstanding source of professional grievance to officers. Those who owed their promotion to the regime naturally had a vested interest in its longevity.

With the collapse of the king's counter-coup, the Colonels now felt confident enough to cast off the façade of civilian government. General Zoitakis became regent and Papadopoulos, who had increasingly emerged as the strong man of the regime, became prime minister. In a process of gradually concentrating power in his own person he subsequently assumed the offices of minister of foreign affairs, minister of defence, minister to the prime minister, minister of education, minister of government policy and, from March 1972, regent, a position he combined with the premiership. With the removal of the last restraints to their absolute power the Colonels made it clear that they were settling down for a long stay in office. In this respect their regime differed significantly from Greece's pre-war military interventions. These had usually been of short duration, with their protagonists intervening on behalf of individual politicians or political parties, and stepping down from power once their immediate political objectives had been secured. The Colonels, by contrast, heaped abuse on politicians of all shades of the political spectrum, and it is not surprising that only a handful of the pre-coup politicians in turn were prepared in any way to co-operate with them.

Civil servants, school and university teachers, whose allegiance was in doubt, were dismissed, while others were required to demonstrate their loyalty to the regime or risk forfeiting their jobs. Lawyers and judges who showed too much independence were harassed and dismissed. George Papandreou's educational reforms were systematically dismantled, school textbooks were rewritten, and entry to higher education made dependent on political tests. Through press censorship and the regime's control of broadcasting the Greek people were subjected to an endless barrage of propaganda in favour of 'The Revolution of 21 April 1967', as the coup was now officially known. To justify their continued grip on power the Colonels sought to give their regime an ideological basis. Like the pre-war dictator General Metaxas, they placed much emphasis on the need to discipline the Greek character. Stressing their own humble social origins, they sought to project a populist image, claiming to have the interests of Greek workers and peasants particularly at heart. Much emphasis was laid in the regime's propaganda on the notion of 'Helleno-Christian Civilisation', that attempt to reconcile the essentially contradictory values of ancient Greece and Christian Byzantium, which had long been the ideological catchword of the far right.

In a further effort to consolidate its power, the regime, after a perfunctory attempt at public consultation, organised a referendum in September 1968 on a new constitution to replace that of 1952. Given the regime's control over the media and the fact that martial law was still in force it is not surprising that there was a 92 per cent vote in favour (4,638,543 for, 391,923 against). The constitution was a highly authoritarian document, which sought to give the military a permanent voice in the government of the country. The armed forces themselves acquired absolute control over promotions, retirements, assignments and transfers and the minister of defence was reduced to a mere figurehead. The role of the armed forces was stated as being the safeguarding of the independence and territorial integrity of the country together with the existing *political* and social order. The articles relating to individual rights were hedged about with qualifications. 'Political' strikes, for instance, were forbidden, and a number of the most important articles were in any case held in abeyance.

The fact that the plebiscite was held under martial law indicated that the regime, despite its protestations to the contrary, was uncertain as to its popularity. The Colonels had met with little opposition at the time of the coup and the initial reaction of the bulk of the Greek people was one of impotent resignation, occasioned by the inability of the politicians to reconcile their differences during the previous eighteen months. This mood of acquiescence was soon transformed into one in which resentment was combined with shame at a regime that combined brutality with incompetence. When the veteran centre politician George Papandreou died, aged eighty, in November 1968, his funeral, at which his old friend and political rival Panayiotis Kanellopoulos delivered a moving oration, became a gesture of protest against the regime on the part of the several hundred thousand mourners who attended it. Yet although the regime was undoubtedly unpopular and did not dare submit to the test of free elections, there was relatively little in the way of active opposition. A number of resistance groups came into being, among them the Patriotic Front (PAM), Democratic Defence (DA) and the Free Greeks, but the security police had little difficulty in breaking up these groups, whose leaders were sentenced to long terms of imprisonment, mostly under Law 509. This dated from 1947 and provided for severe penalties for attempts to overthrow the existing social order.

The efficiency and brutality of the security (Asphaleia) and military (ESA) police in breaking up attempts to organise active resistance served to impede the development of any mass-based opposition. Rumours soon began to leak out of the extremely harsh treatment meted out to the regime's opponents. Alexander Panagoulis, a former activist in the Centre Union youth movement, who, in August 1968, attempted to blow up the car in which Papadopoulos was travelling from his seaside retreat, was the object of particularly brutal treatment, although the death sentence imposed on him was commuted to life imprisonment after world-wide pleas for clemency. By and large it was the unknown opponents of the regime, and in particular students, who suffered most at the hands of the police. Those such as Andreas Papandreou, the composer Mikis Theodorakis, and Lady Amalia Fleming, who were well known abroad, were more leniently treated and expelled from the country. There they were active with many other émigrés, such as the newspaper publisher Helen Vlachou, in organising a highly effective propaganda campaign against the Colonels.

Partly as a result of the activities of exiled opponents of the regime, partly as a result of a continuous stream of allegations of inhuman treatment emanating from within Greece, the governments of Norway, Sweden, Denmark and Holland lodged complaints with the Council of Europe, of which Greece was a member. The European Commission of Human Rights produced in 1969 a massively documented report in which it found that in April 1967 there had been no emergency threatening the life of the nation which would have justified Greece derogating from the European Convention of Human Rights, and that there had indeed been torture and degrading treatment of the regime's opponents. This was hotly contested by the regime, but nonetheless in December 1969 the foreign minister, Panayiotis Pipinelis, withdrew Greece from the Council of Europe on the eve of a meeting of the Council of Ministers at which Greece would almost certainly have been expelled. But although many members of the Council of Europe were also Greece's partners in NATO and members of the EEC, with which Greece had an association agreement, these two bodies were far less forthright in their criticism than the Council of Europe.

The Colonels' regime was always careful to fulfil its obligations under the NATO alliance, and although from time to time certain member countries, in particular Norway, Denmark and Holland, sought to raise the question of the Greek dictatorship, American influence was always sufficiently strong to ensure that Greece came under no real pressure from her NATO allies, beyond the expression of pious hopes for an eventual return to democratic rule. The EEC also from time to time criticised the lack of democratic freedoms in Greece but its claim to have 'frozen' Greece's 1962 treaty of association did not have such serious implications for Greece as the term suggested. The removal of tariff barriers and customs duties continued on schedule and negotiations were entered into to harmonise Greek agricultural policies with those of the Community, a development scarcely compatible with a 'freeze' in relations.

The regime's main external prop was undoubtedly the United States. Although many Greeks of all political persuasions believed that the American CIA had somehow been directly involved in the 1967 coup, there was little evidence to substantiate this. But if the American administration was not involved in the actual establishment of the dictatorship it nonetheless did afford the regime a very considerable degree of aid and comfort. Although in theory shipments of heavy weapons were cut off between 1967 and 1970, America remained the major supplier of military equipment to the junta. The Pentagon was particularly anxious to maintain good relations with Greece so as to continue to enjoy base facilities in a country whose strategic importance to the Western alliance had increased following the Arab/Israeli wars of 1967 and 1973 and the rapid build-up of a Soviet naval presence in the Mediterranean. This last development prompted the negotiation in 1972 of the 'Home Port' agreement, which provided permanent port facilities for the Sixth Fleet in Greece. When the United States congress voted to cut off military aid to Greece, President Nixon was quick to take advantage of the provision that such aid could be resumed if he considered this to be essential to United States defence interests. In January 1972 he declared that the defence of Israel, a primary objective of American policy in the eastern Mediterranean, was predicated on friendly relations with Greece. As a further mark of American consideration for the regime, vice-president Spiro Agnew (born Anagnostopoulos), himself of Greek origin, visited Greece in 1971. Other influential American visitors included General Andrew Goodpaster, the commander of NATO forces in Europe, who smilingly posed alongside Papadopoulos in the summer of 1967, the secretaries of defence, Melvin Laird, and of commerce, Maurice Stans. During a visit to Athens in 1971, Stans spoke of his having been asked by President Nixon to convey his 'warm love' to the Greek government. This remark was subsequently 'clarified' by the American Embassy to 'warmth and confidence'.

In return for American support the regime was careful to avoid giving offence to its NATO allies, particularly after the regime had suffered humiliation over Cyprus at the hands of the Turks a few months after the seizure of power. Greco-Turkish talks at the border towns of Keshan and Alexandroupolis in September 1967 had ended without result due to the diplomatic inadequacies of the Greek delegation, which was led by Papadopoulos, and which had openly sought *enosis*. Greece suffered further humiliation two months later in November, after Grivas had launched a bloody attack on two Turkish Cypriot villages. Following mediation by President Johnson's representative, Cyrus Vance, agreement was reached that Greek and Turkish regular forces on the island in excess of the quotas of 950 and 650 respectively laid down in the Zürich and London agreements should be withdrawn. Some 10,000 Greek troops, who had been infiltrated into the island since the breakdown of the constitution in 1963, were withdrawn to the mainland, as was Grivas, who had been sent back to the island by George Papandreou in 1964. Relations between Athens and Nicosia were never to recover from this humiliation. In 1968 intercommunal talks between Glafkos Clerides, the speaker of the Cyprus House of Representatives, for the Greek Cypriots and Rauf Denktash, for the Turkish Cypriots, were initiated under the aegis of the United Nations Secretary General. They dragged on for several years without producing any solution to the constitutional problem on the island; meanwhile a substantial proportion of the Turkish population continued to be concentrated in enclaves.

Somewhat paradoxically, given the regime's fiercely anti-communist stance in domestic matters, Greece's relations with her communist neighbours underwent a significant improvement. President Ceauşescu of Romania was the only European head of state to plan an official visit to Greece, while in 1971 Greece and Albania exchanged ambassadors, thus ending a technical state of war that had existed between the two countries for a generation. In renewing diplomatic relations with Albania, Greece appeared to shelve indefinitely her long-standing claim to Northern Epirus. There were few official visitors of any significance from the countries of Western Europe, nor were the Colonels welcomed in

Western capitals. Instead a stream of minor African dignitaries joined the existing stream of official American visitors to Greece, and Greek leaders in turn visited some African countries, a development that was grandiosely entitled an 'opening' to Africa.

Although the Colonels' propaganda was replete with populist rhetoric their actual economic and financial policies were the antithesis of populist, and inequalities in the distribution of income grew steadily. Indeed, so grateful were Greece's shipowners for the concessions they were granted, in an effort to persuade them to register their ships under the Greek flag rather than under flags of convenience, that in March 1972 they elected Papadopoulos president for life of the Association of Greek Shipowners. In an effort to attract much-needed foreign capital measures were taken to strengthen still further the guarantees given to foreign investors in the legislation of 1953, and a number of contracts were signed conceding highly advantageous terms to foreign companies. One such, signed amidst much publicity soon after the 1967 coup, with Litton Industries, envisaged very substantial investment in Greece, but very little of this actually materialised before the contract was terminated. Some of the contracts awarded by the regime were on highly dubious terms and it subsequently emerged that, for all the public denunciations of the corruption of the old politicians, some members of the regime, at least, were unable to resist the temptation to line their own and their families' pockets with public money. However, although the long-term consequences of the Colonels' economic policies were highly damaging, nonetheless, thanks to continued expansion in the field of tourism, to the continued inflow of remittances from seamen, migrant workers and emigrants, and to an agile, if injudicious, policy of borrowing, the regime was for a number of years able to maintain the high rate of economic growth of the late fifties and early sixties. Even though there were glaring inequalities in the distribution of this growing prosperity, overall living standards continued to rise.

The fact that many Greeks were prospering in the early years of the Colonels' dictatorship was undoubtedly a factor impeding the development of any mass-based opposition. It is perhaps no accident that it was in 1973, when the Colonels were beginning to pay the price for their profligate economic policies in the form of a rate of inflation of over 30 per cent, that the first rumblings of mass discontent began to be heard. The lead in open opposition to the regime was taken by university students whose initially professional grievances increasingly took on a political colouring. The occupation of the Law Faculty of Athens University in March 1973 and its brutal suppression served to intensify student militancy, as did a law giving the regime the power to revoke the deferment from military service of those students who wilfully absented themselves from lectures.

A more serious threat to the regime's stability, however, was an abortive naval mutiny at the end of May 1973 and the defection of the destroyer *Velos* to Greece's NATO ally Italy. This was subsequently revealed to have had wide ramifications in the navy and indicated that, even after repeated purges, there was still widespread disaffection in the officer corps. Papadopoulos, now regent as well as prime minister, claimed that King Constantine had been implicated in the plot from his exile in Rome, and on 1 June declared him deposed. He proclaimed the creation of a 'presidential parliamentary republic' to be ratified by referendum, and promised to hold elections in the following year, 1974. The president was to be elected for an eight-year term and was to enjoy wide legislative and executive powers, with exclusive control over sensitive issues such as foreign affairs, defence, national security and public order. Papadopoulos' critics denounced the July referendum as a sham, pointing out that martial law remained in force in Athens and Piraeus. Although Papadopoulos was the only candidate for the presidency and there was a massive barrage of publicity urging a 'yes' vote, nonetheless some former politicians grouped in the Committee of Parliamentarians for the Restoration of Democratic Legality, and some newspapers urged a 'no' vote. Not surprisingly in the circumstances, Papadopoulos was elected president with a 78 per cent 'yes' vote, with 3,843,318 in favour, 1,048,308 against.

When he was formally sworn in on 19 August, Papadopoulos restated his intention to hold elections, overseen by a civilian government. To prepare the way for these, he lifted martial law where it remained in force and declared a sweeping amnesty for political prisoners, including his own would-be assassin, Alexander Panagoulis. Papadopoulos' choice as prime minister was Spyros Markezinis, the leader of the small pre-coup Progressive Party, who experienced difficulty in convincing other politicians and the Greek people at large of his intention to hold 'impeccable' elections. Moreover Greece's university students soon made it clear that they were not prepared to tolerate a move towards a type of 'guided' democracy, in which real power would still be held by Papadopoulos and the army. Early in November a memorial service for George Papandreou was followed by violent clashes with the police. Some days later students occupied the Athens Polytechnic and university buildings in Salonica and Patras. At first the police adopted noticeably moderate tactics in dealing with the sit-ins. But when it was clear that the students were attracting widespread sympathy, and when the Athens Polytechnic students began broadcasting appeals on a clandestine radio for a worker-student alliance to overthrow the dictatorship, Papadopoulos sent in troops and tanks to crush the students.

The eviction of the students from the Athens Polytechnic was carried out with extreme brutality, and at least 34 students and others were killed, several hundred wounded and almost a thousand arrested. This ruthless demonstration of force in the centre of Athens caused widespread revulsion. Martial law was reimposed and Papadopoulos declared his intention of proceeding with the planned elections. Within a matter of days, however, he was deposed, on 25 November 1973, in a bloodless coup mounted by the army, with the support of naval and air force units. His successors justified their counter-coup on the ground that he had deviated from the principles of the 'Revolution of 21 April 1967' and was leading the country towards an electoral adventure. Lieutenant-General Phaedon Gizikis was installed as president and a new civilian government, headed by Adamantios Androutsopoulos, was formed. It was clear from the outset that real power in the new regime lay in the hands of the prime mover of the coup, Brigadier Dimitrios Ioannidis, the commander of the military police (ESA), which had acquired a fearsome reputation for its brutality towards the regime's opponents.

The new regime showed itself quite incapable of dealing with the pressing problems confronting the country. Even harsher measures were employed against dissidents. Inflation continued unchecked, and Greece, with few indigenous sources of energy, was particularly severely affected by the oil crisis that followed the Yom Kippur war. The discovery in 1973 of oil off the island of Thasos highlighted the problem of the delineation of the continental shelves, and consequent rights to prospect for minerals, of Greece and Turkey in the Aegean. Turkey rejected Greece's claim that the Greek islands off her Aegean coast generated their own continental shelves, and granted licences to survey in waters over which Greece claimed jurisdiction. This provoked a display of sabre rattling by the Ioannidis regime in April and May 1974 and briefly raised the prospect of armed confrontation with Turkey. The Ioannidis regime also adopted an increasingly aggressive line towards President Makarios, a move that provoked the resignation of the Greek foreign minister. This open hostility was the culmination of several years of growing tension between Athens, the 'National Centre', and Nicosia. The junta had been implicated in a number of assassination attempts all of which Makarios had miraculously survived.

Relations between Cyprus and Greece reached an unprecedented level of tension when on 6 July Archbishop Makarios publicly claimed to have irrefutable evidence of a link between mainland Greek officers of the Cyprus National Guard and the EOKA-B terrorist organisation. The latter had been revived following Grivas' clandestine return to the island in 1971, and its agitation for *enosis* had continued after his death in January 1974. Makarios charged that the Athens regime was seeking to destroy the Cyprus state. His demand for the removal of almost all the Greek officers of the National Guard was followed by ten days of mounting tension between Nicosia and Athens. This culminated on 15 July in the launching of a coup against Makarios by the National Guard. The Greek army contingent on the island joined in the attack on

Makarios' supporters and it was abundantly clear that the coup had been inspired from Athens. Although his supporters were soon overwhelmed, Archbishop Makarios was able to escape from his palace and was later flown off the island in a British plane from the Akrotiri base. Nikos Sampson, a former EOKA gunman, was installed as president in his place.

Turkey began to mass troops on the mainland opposite Cyprus and the Turkish prime minister, Bülent Ecevit, flew to London to urge joint action to restore the *status quo* by the Turkish and British governments, as guarantors with Greece of the 1960 constitution. When it became clear that the British government was not prepared to fulfil its obligations, Turkey decided to exercise its right of intervention unilaterally, and in the early hours of 20 July landed troops in the Kyrenia region of northern Cyprus. Both Greece and Turkey mobilised and for a time there was a threat of outright war between the two countries. The Greek mobilisation proved to be a chaotic shambles and Greece's military commanders refused to carry out Ioannidis' orders to retaliate against Turkey. The seventy-two hours following the Turkish invasion revealed the almost total isolation of the regime in the international community. The dictatorship, which had hitherto exercised a very tight grip on the country, began to dissolve, the nominal civilian government having already faded into oblivion. General Davos, the commander of the powerful Third Army Corps stationed in northern Greece, issued, in the name of many of his officers, an ultimatum to President Gizikis demanding a return to civilian rule. Gizikis, in a rapidly deteriorating situation, called a meeting of military leaders and senior former politicians on 23 July. From this emerged a summons to the 67-year-old Constantine Karamanlis to return from his eleven-year self-exile in Paris to oversee the dismantling of the dictatorship and a return to democratic rule. Karamanlis arrived in Greece in the early hours of 24 July to a delirious welcome. Seven years of a brutal, inefficient and unpopular dictatorship had ended as abruptly as it had begun.

8

From authoritarianism to democracy, 1974–

The scenes of wild enthusiasm that greeted Karamanlis on his return to Greece on 24 July 1974 were undoubtedly a genuine expression of the relief of the overwhelming majority of the people at the downfall of the Colonels' tyranny. Nonetheless, the problems that confronted Karamanlis in his efforts to liquidate the disastrous legacy of the dictatorship and set Greece on the path to democracy were daunting in the extreme. He returned to face a situation virtually without precedent. For the Ioannidis regime had not been brought down by a popular uprising but rather had collapsed under the weight of its own manifest incompetence. Just as a section of the army had engineered the Colonels' original seizure of power in 1967, so a section of it had been responsible for the return to civilian government. Moreover, the basic command structure of an army that had achieved a tight grip on internal security and acquired a taste for political power over the previous seven years remained intact. The armed forces retained their control over the physical means of coercion, while Karamanlis was armed only with his own moral authority and tremendous popular support.

The most pressing problem that confronted Karamanlis and the impressive provisional government of conservative and centrist opponents of the regime that he rapidly drew together was to defuse the confrontation with Turkey over Cyprus. The new foreign minister, George Mavros, attended talks convened in Geneva by the three guarantor powers, Britain, Greece and Turkey. These resulted in the signing of a ceasefire, but attempts to work out a political solution broke down in mid-August. The Turkish invasion forces thereupon fanned out from their Kyrenia beachhead, halting only with the establishment of the 'Attila' line from Morphou in the west to Famagusta in the east. By the time of the second ceasefire on 16 August the Turkish army was in control of some 38 per cent of the island, including much of its productive agricultural land. Some 180,000 Greek Cypriots fled to the Greek-controlled south and, in violent demonstrations in Nicosia, the American ambassador was shot dead.

Feeling also ran high in Greece, although Karamanlis made it clear from the beginning that there could be no question of a military solution to the problems dividing Greece and Turkey. He did go some way, however, towards appeasing the wave of anti-American feeling that swept the country by withdrawing the armed forces from the military command structure of NATO and by calling into question the future of American base facilities. This anti-Americanism, which existed across the political spectrum, was occasioned by bitterness at the way in which successive American administrations had not only failed to put greater pressure on the Colonels' regime but had, indeed, appeared to acquiesce in many of its acts. There was a widespread perception too, that Dr Henry Kissinger, the American Secretary of State, had 'tilted' in favour of Turkey during the Cyprus crisis. Greeks had been outraged by Kissinger's apparent willingness to tolerate the Sampson regime and contrasted his inertia in the face of the threatened Turkish invasion with the vigour with which President Johnson had headed off a similar threat in 1964. There was also a widespread feeling that membership of NATO was of little value to Greece if the alliance was incapable of preventing two member states from coming to the brink of war.

Although Karamanlis ruled out a military solution to the conflict there was nonetheless a continuing high level of tension between the two countries and this restricted his freedom of manoeuvre in de-politicising the army. For any wide-scale purges of pro-junta officers would only have served, so it was argued, to undermine morale at a time when there was a real chance of armed conflict with Turkey. Opponents of the regime voiced their disquiet at Karamanlis' apparent lack of urgency in bringing to justice those responsible for the 1967 coup and their accomplices in the police and security services. A large number of private prosecutions were initiated by private citizens, alleging variously high treason and the torture of political prisoners, before the government was moved to launch an enquiry into the Polytechnic massacre of the previous November and to banish the original *troika* of conspirators, **Papadopoulos**, Makarezos and Pattakos to an island. There were also vociferous demands for the *apohountopoiisis*, or 'de-juntification', not only of the armed forces but also of the whole state apparatus. Martial law was lifted, all political prisoners were released, and judges, civil servants, university and school teachers dismissed by the regime were reinstated. Prefects, mayors and senior civil servants appointed by the Colonels were in their turn dismissed. Many of those who had been most active in opposition to the Colonels remained disappointed at the slow pace of 'de-juntification', but Karamanlis appears to have been anxious not to let the process of retribution go **too far**. He also believed that the punishment of those responsible for the 1967 dictatorship could only properly be undertaken through the courts and by a government that had been legitimised through democratic elections.

Retribution was but one of the pressing problems confronting the provisional government, for the profligate economic policies of the dictatorship had left a legacy of high inflation and deep suspicions of corruption. Karamanlis was to argue that the internal problems and external dangers facing the nation could best be tackled by a government armed with a popular mandate. Accordingly, in early October, he announced that elections would be held on 17 November, a bare four months after the collapse of the dictatorship. These were to be followed on 8 December by a referendum on the future of the monarchy, for the king had not returned to Greece in the aftermath of the Colonels' downfall. The elections were to be held under the system of 're-inforced' proportional representation in force for much of the post-war period, a system much criticised by the opposition parties, which were generally unhappy about the holding of elections so soon after the downfall of the dictatorship. They objected that the precipitate holding of elections did not allow enough time for the reorganisation of parties and the mounting of a proper campaign; that truly free elections could not be conducted, particularly in rural areas, before there had been a thoroughgoing purge of junta appointees from the state apparatus; and that they would be held on the basis of outdated electoral registers. Above all, however, they complained that Karamanlis, by holding elections so soon, would be able unfairly to capitalise on the immense prestige accruing to him as the man who had restored democracy to Greece.

Despite these various objections, however, a vigorous campaign was soon under way, conducted with the traditional rumbustiousness of Greek elections. Questions of timing aside, there was general agreement that the campaign was fairly conducted, with all the main political groups being accorded access to the state-controlled broadcasting media, including television, which was utilised for the first time in a Greek election campaign. The most unusual feature of the elections was that, for the first time since 1936, the communists contested power as a legal party. For Karamanlis, in a striking departure from his policy during his first premiership when he had sought to isolate the left, now sought to integrate the communists into political life by legalising the communist party, or rather parties. For in 1968, in the aftermath of the Soviet invasion of Czechoslovakia, the party, whose leadership was in exile, had split into two sections, the Communist Party [polemically called 'of the Exterior'] (KKE), which took its lead from Moscow, and the Communist Party of the Interior (KKE-es), which followed a broadly 'Eurocommunist' line. In the November 1974 elections the two parties temporarily reconciled their considerable differences and formed an electoral alliance, known as the United Left, with the pre-coup United Democratic Left (EDA).

A new element in the political spectrum was represented by Andreas Papandreou's Panhellenic Socialist Movement (PASOK) which, while drawing on the centre tradition, was significantly to the left of the Centre Union, of which Papandreou had been a leading member before the coup. In its founding declaration PASOK stated its basic objectives as being national independence, popular sovereignty, social liberation and democratic structures. Like the United Left, PASOK demanded the condign punishment of collaborators, declared its total opposition to a restoration of the monarchy and opposed any strengthening of Greece's ties with the European Economic Community. The only party contesting the election under its pre-coup colours was the Centre Union, led by George Mavros who had assumed the leadership of the party after the death of George Papandreou, Andreas Papandreou's father. The Centre Union fought the elections in alliance with a small group of intellectual opponents of the regime known as the New Forces group. The Centre Union/New Forces Alliance was strongly opposed to the return of the monarchy but shared Karamanlis' enthusiasm for closer ties with Europe.

The mainstream right was represented by Karamanlis' own New Democracy party. This was essentially the pre-coup National Radical Union, from the leadership of which Panayiotis Kanellopoulos had been unceremoniously removed. New Democracy's political platform in the 1974 elections was never very fully developed, for Karamanlis' implicit strategy was to project himself as the one person standing between the preservation of Greece's newly won democratic freedoms and a return of the tanks. But the broad outlines of New Democracy's policies were clear. The party was strongly committed to expediting Greece's accession to the EEC, and, despite the withdrawal from the military command structure of NATO, Karamanlis made clear his basic commitment to the Western alliance. In domestic affairs New Democracy was attached to the free enterprise system, with some emphasis on state intervention in key sectors of the economy. Unlike the other parties, New Democracy took no official position either for or against the restoration of the monarchy. The only party actually to espouse the king's cause was the National Democratic Union, which made a deliberate appeal for the votes of supporters of the fallen dictatorship.

Some observers believed that the experiences of the Greek people during the seven-year dictatorship had had a radicalising effect on the electorate and that the results of the elections would demonstrate a dramatic leftward swing such as had occurred under the stresses of the German occupation, a view given some credence by a marked swing to the left in student elections held just before the general election. But the electorate manifested no such leftward leanings in the elections of 17 November. These resulted in a massive victory for Karamanlis' New Democracy, whose 54 per cent of the vote constituted one of the largest majorities in Greece's electoral history. New Democracy secured an overwhelming majority of seats in the new parliament, 219 out of 300. The Centre Union/New Forces alliance, whose 21 per cent share of the vote was in striking contrast to the 53 per cent which the Centre Union had received in the previous elections of February 1964, controlled 60 seats. PASOK, with 14 per cent, won 13 seats, and the United Left coalition, which was soon to break up into its constituent parts, 10 per cent and 8 seats. The idiosyncracies of the system of 'reinforced' proportional representation were strikingly revealed by the fact that New Democracy, which received four times as many votes as PASOK, won eighteen times as many seats.

The result of the elections indicated that, for all the obloquy heaped on the old politicians and their politics by the Colonels and their propagandists, the political vacuum of the previous seven years had by no means extinguished traditional political loyalties and affiliations. The political word, as on previous occasions, had demonstrated considerable qualities of resilience, and the ranks of the new government were replete with rather elderly and un-inspiring survivors from pre-coup ERE administrations. A majority of the electorate had indicated that they prized political stability, of which they believed Karamanlis to be the surest guarantor, over the proposals for radical change espoused by militant opponents of the dictatorship. At the same time, Karamanlis had himself pro-jected a more liberal image than had been apparent during his first premiership. In the 1950s, the notion that Karamanlis might, at some future date, have withdrawn Greece from the military arm of NATO, questioned the future of the American bases, dismantled the repressive legislation of the civil war period, and, above all, legalised the communist party would have been scarcely con-ceivable.

The opposition parties, while accepting that the elections had been fairly conducted, nonetheless continued to argue that holding them so soon had given Karamanlis an unfair advantage. They were to claim that the 31 per cent vote for a restoration of the monarchy in the referendum of 8 December was a more accurate indicator of the true strength of the right than its showing in the elections. The December 1974 referendum was the sixth such referendum on the constitutional issue to have been held in the twentieth century (the others took place in 1920, 1924, 1935, 1946 and 1973) and was certainly the most fairly conducted. The 69 per cent vote against a restoration appeared to be sufficiently decisive to settle once and for all the question of monarchy versus republic that had bedevilled so much of the country's politics during the sixty years that had elapsed since the genesis of the National Schism.

Within a matter of months of his return to Greece like some *deus ex machina*, Karamanlis had both legitimised his power through an impressive electoral victory and, by legalising the communists and allowing a genuine expression of opinion on the future of the monarchy, neutralised two long-standing sources of political instability in the country. This was a remarkable achievement, but the nature of the tightrope he had been walking during these critical months became apparent when it was announced in February 1975 that the government had uncovered a conspiracy by 'a handful of foolish officers' in the army. It was clear that the threat posed by the conspiracy had been deliberately played down. The plot, which aimed at a restoration of the military dictatorship, the overthrow of Karamanlis and of President Makarios, who had returned to Cyprus early in 1975, proved to have been the fourth attempted coup by supporters of the dictatorship in the first six months after Karamanlis' return. At one stage, the prime minister was forced to spend his nights on board a yacht for three weeks for fear of assassination. The February 1975 conspiracy resulted in the purging of some sixty officers, mostly serving in the army.

The conspiracy naturally aroused fears that Karamanlis had not yet managed to re-establish civilian control over the armed forces. But that Karamanlis was indeed in control of the military was indicated by the orderly completion during 1975 of a number of trials of the protagonists in the 1967 coup, and of the torturers upon whom they had relied to maintain themselves in power, without provoking an overt backlash by serving officers. After parliament had determined that the 1967 coup had indeed been a *coup d'état* and not, as its protagonists argued, a revolution creating its own law, the way was clear for the official indictment of the leading conspirators. The most important of these trials sought to apportion responsibility for the dictatorship and resulted in the imposition of death sentences on the three ringleaders, ex-Colonels Papadopoulos and Makarezos and ex-Brigadier Pattakos. The government's immediate decision to commute the death sentences to life imprisonment, before awaiting the outcome of any appeal, infuriated the opposition. Eight others involved in the planning and execution of the coup received life sentences. These included Brigadier Ioannidis, former commander of the military police (ESA) and the regime's strong man after the overthrow of Papadopoulos in November 1973; the former regent, General Zoitakis; Lieutenant-General Spandidakis, chief of the army general staff at the time of the coup; and Major-General Roufogalis, former head of the Central Intelligence Service (KYP).

Undoubtedly the trial which aroused the most emotion was the lengthy trial of thirty-one members of the military police (ESA), which had acquired considerable notoriety for its brutal treatment of opponents of the junta. The ugly rumours which had circulated during the dictatorship about ESA's interrogation practices proved at the trial to have been well-founded. Three former commanders of one of the military regime's most notorious detention centres, EAT/ESA, received long prison sentences. Another trial which understandably aroused a great deal of feeling was that held to determine responsibility for the bloody repression of the student occupation of the Athens Polytechnic. Brigadier Ioannidis, already serving a life sentence for complicity in the 1967 coup, received a seven-fold life sentence for his part in the Polytechnic massacre, while Papadopoulos received a further 25-year sentence. Those who had served as ministers in the various civilian 'governments' of the junta were not tried as such, although a number of them were defendants in trials alleging corruption.

With his party in control of well over two-thirds of the votes in parliament necessary to ratify constitutional changes,

Karamanlis was now able to embark on plans for constitutional reform that he had harboured since the time of his first premiership. At the end of December 1974 a draft constitution was introduced for debate in parliament. Although Karamanlis took heed of some opposition protests and deleted some of the more illiberal features in the draft, its essential provisions remained intact. The 1975 constitution replaced that of 1952 which had been briefly restored when, following the fall of the junta, the Colonels' own constitution of 1968, as amended in 1973, was abrogated. The main thrust of the 1975 constitution was significantly to enhance the powers of the executive against those of the legislature, a move that Karamanlis had long believed to be essential if parliamentary government were to be protected against the kinds of abuse that had led to the breakdown of the system in the 1960s. Although considerable reserve powers were vested in the presidency, neither the new president, the 76-year-old Constantine Tsatsos, a veteran ERE stalwart, nor Karamanlis, when he succeeded to the presidency in 1980, manifested any tendency to exploit them. The opposition parties strongly contested the need for a shift in the potential centre of political gravity from parliament to government and boycotted the official promulgation of the constitution in June 1975. Andreas Papandreou, the leader of PASOK, denounced it as totalitarian.

Having successfully, and bloodlessly, engineered the transition from authoritarianism to democracy, Karamanlis was able to devote some attention to the country's depressing economic situation. The effects of the energy crisis were particularly felt in a country with few indigenous sources of energy, while incipient recession and rising unemployment in West Germany led to a significant decline in the value of migrant remittances, a key constituent, along with tourism, in the balance of payments. By employing orthodox fiscal measures, however, the government was able to bring Greece's high rate of inflation more into line with that prevailing in the countries of Western Europe. In an effort to set the economy on a sounder footing Karamanlis sought to curb some of the more flamboyant excesses of Greek capitalism. The government moved to take over three banks controlled by the financier and industrialist Stratis Andreadis and to re-negotiate some of the more blatantly disadvantageous contracts that the Colonels had made with foreign investors. Such measures were denounced by Karamanlis' right wing critics as 'socialistic', and there was a noticeable decline in interest in new investment on the part of both domestic and foreign investors. It remained true, however, that the Greek state offered generous guarantees and incentives to would-be foreign investors, although these induce-ments were frequently nullified in practice by bureaucratic obstruction and inertia.

Karamanlis' freedom of manoeuvre to undertake much needed structural reforms in such areas as education, where a flourishing private sector had developed in response to the inadequacies of the state system, was severely impeded by massive expenditures on armaments. Approximately one-fifth of the country's total budget was devoted to defence expenditure. Moreover, throughout his premiership, Karamanlis' energies were primarily engaged in the conduct of foreign affairs and the crisis over Cyprus and relations with Turkey continued to dominate the country's foreign relations.

Little progress was made in negotiating a solution to the Cyprus problem, for the Turkish side strongly insisted on a bi-zonal federation with a weak federal government, a move which the Greek side countered with the offer of a multi-cantonal federation with a strong central government. Negotiations were further impeded by the proclamation in February 1975 of a Turkish Federated State of Cyprus. Only Turkey, however, afforded recognition to the new state, and Archbishop Makarios continued to be recognised as the Cypriot head of state by the rest of the world. The Turks still living in the Greek-controlled southern part of the island were permitted to move to the north, where they were joined by immigrants from mainland Turkey, not all of whom were to prove welcome neighbours to the indigenous Turkish popu-lation. Turkish pressure resulted in almost all of the Greeks remaining in the north moving to the Greek-controlled area. Despite condemnation in the United Nations, the Turkish army remained in firm control of northern Cyprus and one of the few notes of optimism was the extraordinary economic recovery that occurred in the south of the island within a short time of the devastation and dislocation of 1974. This recovery contrasted sharply with the sluggishness of economic life north of the 'Attila' line.

From the outset, Karamanlis had maintained that any settlement of the Cyprus issue was essentially a matter for the two communities on the island and he rejected Turkish attempts to include Cyprus within the context of bilateral Greek–Turkish relations. These continued to be embittered by a whole range of disputes, the most important of which concerned the delineation of the boundaries of the two countries' respective continental shelves in the Aegean. This hitherto somewhat academic question had assumed a new significance with the discovery of oil in commercial quantities off the island of Thasos in 1973. Greece argued that the Greek islands lying close to the coast of Asia Minor generated their own continental shelves, the Turks that the islands were subsumed within the continental shelf of mainland Turkey.

Linked with the continental shelf question was the question of Greek fortification of the islands lying off the Turkish coast, such as Mytilini, Chios, Samos and Rhodes. Turkey claimed that this was in breach of the Treaties of Lausanne (1923) and Paris (1947). Greece, in return, argued that such measures were purely defensive and were justified by Turkey's establishment of an 'Army of the Aegean', which appeared to threaten the Greek islands. It was almost universally held in Greece that Turkey harboured expansionist designs on the islands, while the Turks accused Greece of seeking to turn the Aegean into a Greek lake. Greece, however, studiously refrained from extending her territorial waters from six to twelve miles, which would have left few areas of the Aegean outside her jurisdiction.

Friction between the two countries also arose out of disputes over **air-traffic** control in the Aegean region and over the treatment of the Greek minority in Istanbul and the Turkish minority in Western Thrace. Since the anti-Greek riots of 1955 the once flourishing Greek community of Istanbul had gone into a rapid decline. Its fortunes tended to be linked with the Cyprus problem, and each stage in the unfolding crisis led to further pressures on the Greeks of the city. Pressures of various kinds were also placed on the Greek populations of Imvros (Imroz) and Tenedos (Bozcaada), the two Turkish islands straddling the entrance to the Dardanelles. The Greeks of Imvros and Tenedos, together with a sizeable part of the Greek community of Istanbul, had been excluded from the 1923 exchange of populations. In the wake of the Cyprus imbroglio of the summer of 1974 still more Greeks left Istanbul, whose Greek population was now under 10,000 compared to over 100,000 in the 1920s, and which as recently as 1960 had numbered 70,000. Given that Turkish law prescribed that the Ecumenical Patriarch, the members of the Holy Synod and the clergy of the Great Church, should all be of Turkish nationality it was difficult to see how such a diminished community could long sustain the ecumenical patriarchate. It seemed only a matter of time before the centuries-old Greek presence in Istanbul was finally extinguished and the ecumenical patriarchate, the senior see of the Orthodox Church, removed, perhaps to the monastic republic of Mount Athos in northern Greece or to the island of Patmos.

To compensate for Greece's continuing poor relations with her traditional patron, the United States, Karamanlis embarked on two major foreign-policy initiatives. The first was the 'opening' to the Balkans, a process begun under the Colonels. Karamanlis made frequent visits to Balkan countries, whose leaders likewise visited Greece. While bilateral relations between Greece and her Balkan neighbours, with the exception of Turkey, continued to improve, Karamanlis' efforts to promote greater regional solidarity, particularly through the holding of a Balkan 'summit' meeting in Athens in January 1976, foundered in the wake of obstruction by Bulgaria and Turkey. The fundamentally pro-Western orientation of Karamanlis' foreign policy, however, was never in doubt and it was clear that his overriding objective was accelerated entry into the European Economic Community. Karamanlis was assiduous in his lobbying of EEC leaders and reacted vigorously to the expression of doubts by his prospective European partners. It was evident that although Greece expected to gain important economic advantages from the Community, political considerations carried as much, and perhaps more, weight in the thinking of the protagonists of Greek entry. This was seen as affording compensation for her breach with the United States and for her strained relations with NATO. Domestic advocates of membership argued that somehow it would afford a guarantee of her newly won democratic freedoms and offer protection against renewed dictatorship. It was also thought less likely that Turkey would pursue aggressive aims once Greece was within the Community. Not least, many Greeks saw in membership legitimation of Greece's status as a European country.

The signing of a defence co-operation agreement between Turkey and the United States in 1976 placed a further strain on Greek–American relations although Athens was somewhat mollified by the establishment of the broad principle that US military aid to Greece would in future constitute 70 per cent of that supplied to Turkey. Provisional agreement was also reached with the US administration over the future status of the four US bases in Greece, Suda Bay and Iraklion in Crete, Ellinikon Airport and Nea Makri near Athens. These, henceforth, were to become essentially Greek installations, each with a Greek commander, and they were not to be used for war purposes without the express consent of the government.

In late July 1976 a major crisis erupted between Greece and Turkey, when the Turkish survey ship *Sismik I* began to carry out seismological explorations in waters lying between the islands of Mytilini and Limnos which were claimed by Greece as forming part of her own continental shelf. These activities were regarded as highly provocative and Andreas Papandreou, the leader of PASOK, called for the sinking of the *Sismik*. The government protested vigorously to Turkey and, when this protest was rejected, requested an emergency meeting of the UN Security Council and appealed to the International Court of Justice at The Hague for an interim injunction restraining Turkey from conducting further explorations in disputed waters.

The Security Council unanimously urged restraint on both parties and called for the resumption of direct negotiations, while the International Court, in whose proceedings Turkey had taken no part, rejected Greece's request for an order restraining the

activities of the *Sismik*, which carried on its explorations until the
end of September. Both sides did, however, undertake to abstain
from provocative action and agreed to hold talks on their various
bilateral differences, although little progress was made.

Domestic politics continued to be very much overshadowed by
problems of external relations. A further complication was added
to the Cyprus problem by the death in August 1977 of Archbishop
Makarios, his successor as president being Spyros Kyprianou.
Characteristically, it was considerations of foreign, rather than
domestic, affairs that prompted Karamanlis to announce on
20 September 1977, following several months of speculation, that
elections would be held in November, one year before the expiry
of the term of the current parliament. The constitutional justification for this decision was the fact that during the coming year
crucial decisions would have to be taken in relation to Cyprus, to
Greco–Turkish relations in general and to Greece's application to
join the EEC, and that such decisions could only be taken by a
government armed with a fresh mandate.

In the November 1977 elections the far right was represented by
the newly established National Rally which unequivocally bid for
the support of disgruntled royalists unhappy with the result of the
1974 referendum, of supporters of the fallen dictatorship, to whose
leaders it held out the prospect of an amnesty, and of those right
wingers who considered Karamanlis' policies to be too 'socialistic'.
The traditional right continued to be represented by New Democracy. Karamanlis once again reiterated his strong commitment to
Greece's accelerated entry into the EEC, and, while reaffirming the
country's basic commitment to the Western alliance, ruled out the
possibility of the reintegration of the armed forces into the military
command structure of NATO before her differences with Turkey
had been resolved. In domestic matters New Democracy restated
its commitment to a free enterprise economy and pointed to its
educational reforms, e.g. its increased emphasis on technical education, its raising of the period of compulsory education from six to
nine years, and to its substitution of the demotic, or spoken,
language for the archaising *katharevousa* as the official language of
the state. This last move held out the prospect of an eventual

solution to the 'Language Question' which has so bedevilled the cultural and educational development of Greece since the time of the struggle for independence.

George Mavros' Centre Union, which had formally fused in 1976 with the New Forces groups to become the Union of the Democratic Centre (EDIK), while sharing Karamanlis' commitment to Europe, espoused a basically social democratic platform. Since the 1974 election Papandreou's PASOK had refined its somewhat idiosyncratic populist socialism. The three basic tenets of PASOK's 'third road' to socialism were socialisation (a somewhat vague concept to be distinguished from nationalisation), decentralisation and worker self-management. PASOK strongly opposed Greek membership of the EEC, arguing that entry would 'consolidate the peripheral role of the country as a satellite of the capitalist system'. PASOK was also implacable in its hostility towards NATO and to the granting of military facilities, on whatever basis, to the United States.

Since the 1974 election significant developments had taken place in the far left camp. The KKE now fought as a separate entity, while the Communist Party of the Interior formed an alliance with the United Democratic Left (EDA), whose *raison d'être* had largely disappeared with the legalisation of the communist party, and with three small socialist groups. This alliance accepted the principle of Greek membership of the EEC, while the Communist Party turned its back on both NATO and the Community, advocating instead the transformation of the Balkans and the Mediterranean into a 'zone of peace'.

As was widely predicted, Karamanlis' New Democracy retained a comfortable working majority in the parliament that emerged from the 20 November election, retaining control of 172 out of 300 seats. Its share of the vote, however, fell from 54 per cent in 1974 to 42 per cent. The surprise result was the dramatic rise in PASOK's vote, from 14 per cent in 1974 to 25 per cent. PASOK, with 93 seats as against 13 in the preceding parliament, became the official opposition party. By contrast, the Union of the Democratic Centre's share of the vote almost halved, falling from 21 per cent to 12 per cent, its seats from 60 to 15. EDIK's share of the vote in

1977 was less than a quarter of the Centre Union's share in the elections of February 1964. The Communist Party with 9 per cent of the vote secured 11 seats. The ultra-right wing National Rally with 7 per cent (5 seats) did significantly better than its counterpart in the 1974 elections, the National Democratic Union. The Alliance of Progressive and Left Wing Forces, with 3 per cent, won 2 seats, as did a small conservative centre grouping, the New Liberals.

The combined vote of the right wing parties (i.e. National Rally, New Democracy and New Liberals) at 50 per cent registered only a small decline since 1974, while the combined left wing vote (PASOK, Communist Party, Alliance of Progressive and Left Wing Forces) at 37 per cent was the highest in Greek electoral history. It was clear that PASOK's increased vote had been largely at the expense of the Union of the Democratic Centre, whose leader, George Mavros, stepped down from the leadership, a move that was to be followed by a crippling internal crisis in the party. One thing was clear from the result of the election. The consensus that had developed in the post-war period between government and 'official' opposition over many aspects of the country's foreign and domestic policies had ended.

If Karamanlis' strategy in going for early elections had to some extent backfired, he was proved correct in arguing that questions of foreign policy would continue to loom large in the country's affairs. A meeting in March 1978 between Karamanlis and Bülent Ecevit, the Turkish prime minister, appeared at the time to herald a new climate in Greek–Turkish relations, but little concrete progress was made towards a resolution of the two countries' bilateral differences at a series of meetings between the secretaries-general of their respective foreign ministries. Further disappointment was caused by the lifting by the US congress in August 1978 of the partial embargo placed on the supply of US weapons to Turkey in the aftermath of the invasion of Cyprus. In December of the same year, however, there was a significant breakthrough on the foreign policy front with the negotiation of the final terms of Greece's accelerated accession to the EEC. Following agreement on a post-entry transition period, the way was clear for the formal

signing in May 1979 of Greece's treaty of accession to the community. This provided for Greece to become the tenth member of
the community on 1 January 1981, somewhat later than had
originally been sought by Karamanlis but three years earlier than
envisaged in the 1962 treaty of association. When the ratification
of the treaty was under discussion in parliament in June 1979
both PASOK and the communist party boycotted the debate.
PASOK argued that an issue of such constitutional significance
required a referendum and called for a limited association agreement in place of full membership.

In an effort to counter the growing appeal of PASOK's brand
of populist socialism, Karamanlis sought to re-define New
Democracy's ideology at the party's first full congress held in
Chalkidiki in May 1979, the first such congress, outside the far left,
to have been attended by delegates elected by constituency committees at local level. Arguing that the traditional labels of right,
centre and left were irrelevant, Karamanlis decreed that New
Democracy was a party of radical liberalism, although there was
confusion in the rank and file of the party as to the precise meaning
of this concept. Significantly he also made provision for the
succession by arranging that the party's next leader should be
elected by the parliamentary party. This left the way clear for
Karamanlis to be elevated to the presidency, a move that had been
widely expected, now that he had achieved his primary objective
of securing accession to the EEC. The opportunity arose with the
expiry of Constantine Tsatsos' five-year term in 1979. The 1975
constitution provided that a successful candidate must obtain a
two-thirds majority in parliament in either of the first two ballots or a three-fifths majority in the third. Karamanlis narrowly
succeeded on the third ballot, held on 5 May, when he secured
183 votes, three more than the minimum, in the 300-seat parliament. The KKE deputies appear to have cast blank ballots,
while PASOK abstained on the ground that parliament no longer
reflected the will of the people.

Following Karamanlis' elevation to the presidency, elections
were held in the parliamentary group of the party for the new
leader of New Democracy. These, the first such leadership

elections to be held by a party outside the far left, resulted in a narrow victory for George Rallis over Evangelos Averoff, the candidate of the more traditional elements in the party, and whom Karamanlis had clearly expected to emerge as his successor. Relations between Rallis and Averoff were to remain strained and the barely concealed factionalism within New Democracy augured ill for its performance at the forthcoming elections. Rallis' short premiership was notable for his efforts to encourage greater pluralism in the mass media and for his practice of not always appointing to important public positions those whose political loyalties manifestly lay with New Democracy. Some slight improvement in relations with Turkey was signalled by the lifting of the Turkish flight control instruction and its Greek counter-instruction which had affected the routing of air traffic across the Aegean since the 1974 crisis, while in the autumn of 1980 agreement was reached on the reintegration of the country's armed forces into the NATO command structure, although negotiations over the future of the US bases in Greece were broken off. The major event of the Rallis premiership was Greece's formal entry into the EEC as the tenth member on 1 January 1981.

Less than a year later, however, on 18 October 1981, the Greeks elected the first socialist government in their country's history, headed by a prime minister, Andreas Papandreou, who had been outspokenly critical of the Community and of Karamanlis' drive for accelerated membership, even if he had significantly tempered these criticisms in the run-up to the elections. Even before the campaign got under way in the summer of 1981 PASOK had been able to seize the initiative and to force New Democracy onto the defensive. In his effort to attract the crucial 12 per cent share of the vote achieved by the Union of the Democratic Centre in 1977, Papandreou had significantly tempered the radical socialist rhetoric that had characterised the party's early years. Claiming that PASOK represented the interests of the non-privileged against the privileged, he no longer insisted that PASOK was a Marxist, class-based party and was careful to insist that his programme of radical domestic transformation, coupled with a vigorous assertion of Greek sovereignty in foreign affairs, constituted no threat to the established social order. His slogan of *Allagi*, or change, and his 'catch all' programme of domestic reform, provided a challenge which New Democracy, with its emphasis on past achievement in promoting economic development and restoring democracy rather than future promise, proved unable to match. Moreover, New Democracy was handicapped by its effort simultaneously to appeal to what remained of the traditional centre vote and to win back the allegiance of the ultra-conservatives who had given the National Rally a not negligible 7 per cent share of the vote in 1977. Rallis proved incapable of sustaining this difficult balancing act, although the National Rally did withdraw from the contest, urging its supporters to vote for New Democracy so as not to split the 'nationalist' vote.

In the event the PASOK challenge proved unstoppable and the party swept to power in the October 1981 elections. Its share of the vote, at 48 per cent, was almost double its 1977 share (25 per cent), which in turn was almost double its 1974 share (14 per cent). With 172 seats PASOK enjoyed a clear majority in the 300 seat parliament. New Democracy's share of the vote declined from 42 per cent in 1977 to 36 per cent (112 seats). The communist party was able marginally to increase its share from 9 to 11 per cent and its seats from 11 to 13. The fragmented parties of the traditional centre were virtually obliterated. All the indications were that PASOK had been able to attract virtually all the votes cast for the traditional centre in 1977 while at the same time making significant inroads among New Democracy supporters. It was plausibly argued that traditional centre supporters and disaffected New Democracy voters who had been tempted to switch to PASOK but were worried by some of Papandreou's radical rhetoric had felt able to make the switch reassured by the presence of Karamanlis in the presidency, where, armed with substantial reserve powers, he could be relied on to curb any tendency to excess. PASOK's undoubted and remarkable triumph was somewhat tempered by the results of the concurrent elections for Greece's 24 strong delegation to the European Parliament. Whereas the national elections had been held under the system of 'reinforced' proportional representation, the European elections were held under a straightforward system of proportional representation and produced some significant deviations from the pattern established in the national elections. The share of the vote of both main parties declined noticeably, PASOK's from 48 to 40 per cent and New Democracy's from 36 to 32 per cent. At the same time the votes cast for the Party of Democratic Socialism (KODISO–KAE) and the Communist Party of the Interior increased significantly enough for each to secure a single seat in the European parliament.

PASOK's electoral campaign had been characterised by promises ranging from the abolition of the highly competitive and much feared examinations for university entrance to the elimination of the *nefos*, or smog, which blankets Athens for a good part of the year. Inevitably high, and perhaps unrealistic, expectations had been aroused, but PASOK moved rapidly to sustain the image of change and to establish its credentials as a radical and reforming administration. It demanded, for instance, changes in the EEC's common agricultural policy and, unsuccessfully, sought a guarantee of Greece's eastern frontiers by its NATO allies, a move that was clearly aimed at Turkey. Papandreou moved quickly to grant diplomatic status to the PLO office in Athens, although Greece had yet to grant full diplomatic recognition to Israel. Other rapid, and low cost, innovations included the official recognition of the communist-controlled wartime resistance movement against the Axis; blanket permission for political refugees to return to their homeland; an end to official celebrations of the defeat of the communists in the 1946–9 civil war; the formal abolition of political censorship and the introduction of the *monotoniko*, a simplified system of accents in the writing of Greek.

The kinds of longer term structural reforms which Papandreou had promised, and which aimed at radical social transformation and putting an end to the perceived dependency characterising Greece's external relations, inevitably proved more elusive. Papandreou himself was quick to draw attention to the economic problems facing the country, which he blamed on the scorched-earth policies of the outgoing New Democracy government and made it clear that his ambitious programme would require two full parliamentary terms. The implementation of PASOK's ambitious plans to 'socialise' key sectors of the economy proved difficult to bring about, not least because so many Greeks worked in the service sector or on their own account. Such 'socialisation' as did take place tended to be of 'problematic' companies that had become indebted to state-owned banks. The economic situation of the country also made it difficult to carry out campaign promises such as the indexation of wages. But new legislation was introduced to 'democratise' the universities and other institutions of higher education by breaking the entrenched powers of the professoriate and a start was made on the establishment of a national health service.

If, during its first term, there was some distance between PASOK's aspirations and its achievements, nonetheless Papandreou demonstrated a remarkable capacity to articulate the aspirations, and particularly, perhaps, the frustrations, of those Greeks who had looked upon themselves as outsiders during the long reign of the right. He was able to introduce a new style into political life after an almost unbroken monopoly of power enjoyed by the right during the post-war period. PASOK also managed to create a sense among many Greeks of involvement in the political process, even if Papandreou controlled the party in an autocratic style. PASOK in a real sense was Papandreou, and dissenters within the party were given short shrift. It was characteristic that the first full party congress, in theory the supreme organ of the party, did not meet until May 1984, almost ten years after PASOK had been founded.

In matters of foreign policy also changes were more noticeable in style than substance. It soon became apparent that Greece would leave neither the EEC nor the NATO alliance, despite Papandreou's earlier hostility towards both bodies. In 1983 agreement was reached over the future of the American bases although differences remained between the Greek and American sides in the negotiations as to whether the bases would actually close down in 1988. While Greece remained in the NATO alliance and the EEC, Papandreou was frequently out of step with her partners over international matters such as the appropriate reaction to the imposition of martial law in Poland, to the shooting down by the

Soviet Union in 1983 of the Korean Airlines jumbo jet and in his outspoken support for Yasar Arafat and the Palestine Liberation Organisation.

Some indication of the extent to which PASOK in power was living up to the expectations of those who had voted for it in 1981 was afforded by the municipal elections of October 1982. The results of these were ambiguous. PASOK lost ground both to the KKE, which appeared to be the principal beneficiary of PASOK's lowering of the voting age from 20 to 18, and, to a lesser extent, New Democracy. Nonetheless PASOK, as a result of tactical alliances with the KKE, was able to secure control of a clear majority of municipalities. The first real test of PASOK's popularity, however, came with the elections to the European Parliament in June 1984. New Democracy was now led by Evangelos Averoff who, at the age of 71 had been elected to the leadership after George Rallis had stood down in the aftermath of the 1981 defeat. Averoff insisted that the New Democracy campaign should not centre on specifically European issues but rather should range 'over the whole syllabus'. Once Papandreou had taken up this challenge it was inevitable that the 1984 European elections should have assumed the character of a referendum on PASOK's performance in government. New Democracy devoted enormous resources to the campaign. The party hoped that if it were able to push PASOK into second place then President Karamanlis might authorise, as he was empowered to do under the 1975 constitution, the holding of national elections before the end of PASOK's four-year term, on the ground that the government no longer reflected the will of the people.

The campaign was conducted in an atmosphere of intense polarisation and at the cost of much incidental damage to the environment but neither party could derive much satisfaction from the results. As in the 1981 European election, a straight-forward system of proportional representation was in force. PASOK's 42 per cent share of the vote represented a marginal improvement on its performance in the 1981 European election but reflected a 6 per cent fall in its share since the 1981 national election. New Democracy's share, at 38 per cent, was 6 per cent up on its performance in the 1981 European election but only 2 per cent on the national election. A significant feature of the results was New Democracy's relative success in the major urban areas. PASOK retained 10 seats in the European parliament, while New Democracy's representation increased from 8 to 9. The KKE secured 3 seats, the KKE of the Interior one, and the ultra right wing National Political Union one.

The fact that PASOK still commanded a clear, albeit reduced, plurality of the vote put paid to hopes on the right that Karamanlis might sanction the holding of early elections, but the climate of acute polarisation in which the 1984 elections had been held helped to project the country into a pre-electoral atmosphere a full year before the next national elections were due to be held. The already charged political climate was further strained when Constantine Mitsotakis succeeded to the leadership of New Democracy in September. The 75-year-old Averoff's leadership had already been called into question even before the European election and the party's unimpressive performance increased the pressure on him to stand down. Mitsotakis, a member of a prominent Cretan political family, emerged as the clear winner in the subsequent leadership election in the parliamentary group. His earlier political career had been in the centre and, during the great crisis of July 1965, he had been one of the most prominent of the 'apostates' whose defection had brought down the Centre Union government of George Papandreou. Shortly after the 1977 election he had joined New Democracy as part of Karamanlis' 'opening' to the centre and had served as foreign minister in the Rallis government. Papandreou's reaction to Mitsotakis' election was angry. He accused Mitsotakis of having betrayed his father, George Papandreou, in 1965 and of serving as the tool of foreign and indigenous monopoly interests.

Despite the manifest personal animosity between the two leaders it appeared early in 1985 that some kind of 'gentleman's agreement' existed, whereby New Democracy would support PASOK's new electoral law, while PASOK would not oppose Karamanlis' re-election as president for a second term on the expiry of his first five-year term in the spring of 1985. Although the new electoral system was far removed from the straightforward proportional representation which PASOK was committed to introduce, its attractions for the two main parties were manifest, for it was clearly designed to ensure that a government with a small plurality of the popular vote could nonetheless form a viable government with a working majority in parliament.

The appearance of detente between Papandreou and Mitsotakis was, however, to prove deceptive for, in March 1985, the country was to be plunged into a major political crisis. This crisis, as sudden as it was unexpected, was precipitated by the imminent end of Karamanlis' term as president. Karamanlis had never publicly spoken of his aspirations for a second term, but it was common knowledge that, provided that his candidacy enjoyed the support of both main parties, he would agree to continue in office. New Democracy's support for a second term was a foregone conclusion, while Papandreou, who appeared to enjoy a good working relationship with the president, had on a number of occasions publicly praised Karamanlis' performance of his duties and had stated that he would be happy to see him continue in office. Virtually all observers looked upon the re-election of the 78-year-old Karamanlis as a formality.

After the New Democracy parliamentary group had, in early March, duly nominated Karamanlis for a second term, Papandreou, at a meeting of the 140 strong Central Committee of PASOK, announced, to the manifest surprise but vociferous enthusiasm of many of his supporters, that the party's choice was, not Karamanlis, but Christos Sartzetakis. Sartzetakis, a judge of the Supreme Court, was widely respected for his role as a young examining magistrate in bringing to justice the assassins of the EDA deputy, Gregory Lambrakis, and for his courageous opposition to the Colonels' dictatorship. At the same time Papandreou, while acknowledging that neither Karamanlis nor his predecessor Constantine Tsatsos had ever deployed the reserve powers enjoyed by the presidency under the 1975 constitution, announced proposals for constitutional reform which were aimed at considerably reducing the presidential prerogatives. He contended that the fact that these powers had not so far been deployed did not preclude their future use by a politically motivated president to thwart the will of a democratically elected government. He maintained that it would be illogical to ask Karamanlis to serve as president under a revised constitution when the 1975 constitution had been very much his own creation. In effect Papandreou was reviving his earlier demand, tacitly dropped in the run up to the 1981 election, for a 'socialist' constitution. Why he should have chosen to announce Sartzetakis' candidature in such a precipitate manner is not clear, although there were suggestions that, in doing so, he was responding to pressures exerted by the left wing of his party.

On learning of PASOK's nomination of Sartzetakis, Karamanlis promptly withdrew his own candidature, and a day later, on 10 March, announced his resignation two weeks in advance of the expiry of his term of office. Mitsotakis promptly accused Papandreou of engineering the constitutional crisis so as to remove Karamanlis from office and prepare the way for the imposition of a totalitarian constitution. He demanded elections as the only way out of the crisis, claiming that these would constitute the final confrontation between 'a liberal democratic regime and the antidemocratic pseudo-socialism of PASOK'. The presidency was temporarily assumed by Yannis Alevras, the president of parliament and a PASOK deputy, and attention was now focused on Sartzetakis' election as president. This was by no means a foregone conclusion, for PASOK's parliamentary strength fell considerably short of the minimum two-thirds of the votes (200 in a 300-seat parliament) required for the election of the president in the first two of three ballots. The party was clearly going to be hard pressed to muster even the three-fifths (180 votes) needed on the third ballot, failing which parliament would have to be dissolved.

It soon became apparent that the contest was likely to be close enough to hinge on the eligibility of the acting president to vote for his successor. PASOK contended that Alevras not only had a right but a duty to vote, while New Democracy held that he was constitutionally disbarred from doing so. Both parties enlisted the support of constitutional experts in support of their respective views. PASOK asked parliament to rule on the question of Alevras' eligibility to vote, its substantial majority ensuring a favourable decision. As expected, Sartzetakis failed to muster the requisite 200 votes in the first two ballots, in neither of which did Alevras take part. The acting president did vote in the third ballot in which Sartzetakis received precisely the minimum 180 votes required. New Democracy, which had protested vigorously against the use of coloured ballot papers and other measures to thwart the secrecy of the ballot, had abstained *en bloc* from voting and had previously declared that it would not recognise Sartzetakis as president if he were elected with Alevras' casting vote.

Mitsotakis refused to attend Sartzetakis' swearing in as president or to have any contact with him and once again, as so often before in the twentieth century, Greece was faced with the prospect of a prolonged and divisive constitutional crisis. Mitsotakis continued to demand elections as the only way out of the impasse. Once the constitutional amendments proposed by Papandreou had been approved in parliament (prior to ratification in the succeeding parliament), Sartzetakis, finding a convenient pretext in the continuing crisis over Cyprus, gave his assent to the holding of elections some four months before the expiry of PASOK's four-year term.

The tone of the election, one of the most polarised in the post-war period, was quickly set by PASOK's minister of the interior who declared, in a widely quoted phrase, that what was at issue was not 'oranges and tomatoes but a confrontation between two worlds'. Both Papandreou and Mitsotakis presented the outcome of the election in apocalyptic terms. Papandreou painted a picture of a vengeful right, determined on wreaking its revenge on the progressive forces in the country by re-introducing all the repressive measures employed by the right to contain the left in the 1950s. He contrasted the 'nationally proud' stance of PASOK in office with what he termed the subservience of the pre-1981 right wing governments. In an attempt to squeeze the far left vote he argued that every vote not cast for PASOK was in effect a vote for the return of the right. For his part, Mitsotakis proclaimed that the election represented the last chance of preserving plural political institutions and preventing the country's inexorable slide towards a one party totalitarian state on the Third World model. Emphasising his own Venizelist antecedents, Mitsotakis declared New Democracy to be a 'liberal' party and placed heavy emphasis on the encouragement of competition and the revival of the entrepreneurial *daimonio*, or genius, of the Greeks as the answer to the country's economic problems.

Given this state of polarisation and an electoral system that continued to discriminate against small parties, it is not surprising that most of the leaders of the small parties (with the notable exception of the Communist Party of the Interior) that had contested the 1981 and 1984 elections and which still retained any political appeal, actual or potential, should have scurried for the protective shelter afforded by the large parties. The KKE, which had been able to attract to its ticket some prominent defectors from the left wing of PASOK, was critical of the slow pace of change, projected itself as the champion of 'real change' and sought to stem any seepage of its traditional vote to PASOK in the hope of holding the balance in a hung parliament.

If the leaders of the main parties essentially sought to portray the contest as one between two radically differing concepts of society, which would have a critical effect on the country's future political course, the ordinary voter, as in 1981, was concerned with more humdrum matters such as inflation and unemployment. Against the background of a huge burden of foreign debt and mounting balance of payments problems, both leaders were lavish in promises of material rewards to the electorate. Despite the fact that the elections had been precipitated by the constitutional crisis, the question of the legitimacy or otherwise of the recent election of the head of state, was not explicitly raised until a late stage in the campaign. In a television interview Mitsotakis made it clear that, in the event of a New Democracy victory, he would expect Sartzetakis to resign. Sartzetakis' office made it clear that he had no intention of resigning in such an eventuality, while Papandreou declared that it was unprecedented for the leader of an opposition party to threaten a constitutional anomaly of this kind in the course of an election campaign.

The election was vigorously contested, with all the parties, as in previous campaigns, placing great store on the size of their mass rallies. There was a great deal of mud-slinging. There were, however, few of the incidents of low level violence that had disfigured the 1984 European election campaign and agreement was reached on measures to limit the indiscriminate fly-posting and slogan painting that had characterised the previous year's election. PASOK's 46 per cent of the vote, was only 2.3 per cent down on the 1981 national election and was 4.2 per cent up on the 1984 European election and was easily large enough to secure an effective working majority of 161 seats in the 300-seat parliament. New Democracy, which, as in 1984, performed noticeably better in urban than in rural areas, improved its share of the vote, at 41 per cent (126 seats), by 5 per cent in comparison with the 1981 national election and by 3 per cent in comparison with 1984. The KKE's vote, at 10 per cent (12 seats), was 1 per cent down on its 1981 national vote and almost 2 per cent down on its 1984 vote, some of its supporters fearful of a return of the right clearly having switched their votes to PASOK. Whereas only three parties had been represented in the 1981 parliament, there were now four, for the 'Eurocommunist' Communist Party of the Interior secured one seat. The extent to which the election had been transformed into a duel between Papandreou and Mitsotakis is illustrated by the fact that the percentage of the vote cast for the two main parties, at 87 per cent, was significantly higher than in any election since the restoration of democracy in 1974. In the wake of PASOK's convincing victory, Mitsotakis moved quickly to say that New Democracy was now prepared to recognise Sartzetakis as president.

Some observers had predicted that the abrupt departure of President Karamanlis from the political scene in March 1985 would damage PASOK's chances of re-election. There was little sign of this, however, and PASOK had been returned for a second term with a substantial majority, only marginally reduced from that secured in its great triumph of 1981. PASOK's attempts during its first term to implement the promises which it held out of radical social transformation on the domestic front, coupled with a determined effort to break free from the dependency that had characterised the country's foreign relations for much of her independent existence, had proved somewhat faltering. Andreas Papandreou, however, had long argued that the implementation of PASOK's ambitious programme would require two full four-year parliamentary terms. Whether, during his second term, Papandreou, particularly in the light of a deteriorating economic situation, would be able to satisfy the high expectations aroused by the re-election of the first socialist government in Greece's history remained to be seen. In the years since the downfall of the military regime in 1974 Greece had experienced four elections, all of which had been accepted as the authentic expression of the people's will. The spectre of military dictatorship that had blighted Greece between 1967 and 1974 appeared to have been firmly exorcised and the country's erstwhile dictators continued to languish in jail. But if Greece's democratic institutions appeared to be firmly established ten years and more after the downfall of the military regime in 1974, nonetheless the events of March 1985 continued to cast something of a shadow over the country's political life.

Bibliography

Recent years have witnessed a remarkable transformation in the historiography of Modern Greece in languages other than Greek. There is now available a substantial and growing number of serious studies of Greek history and society in English. The most convenient way of keeping abreast of these publications, and of developments in the field of Modern Greek studies generally, is through two newsletters: *Modern Greek Society: A Social Science Newsletter* (eds. Nikiforos Diamandouros and Peter Allen, PO Box 9411, Providence, RI 02940, USA) and *Mandatophoros: A Bulletin of Modern Greek Studies* (c/o Byzentijns-Nieuwgrieks Seminarium, Nieuwe Doelenstraat 16–18, 1012 CP Amsterdam, Holland). For a much fuller listing of works, mainly in English, on Modern Greece than is possible here see the volume on Greece, compiled by Mary Jo and Richard Clogg, in the World Bibliographical Series published by Clio Press, Oxford (1980).

GENERAL

John Campbell and Philip Sherrard, *Modern Greece* (London 1968) is a valuable introductory study which gives full weight to cultural matters and to the nature of Greek society. Its predecessor in the Nations of the Modern World series, William Miller, *Greece* (London 1928), paints a fascinating picture of Greece during the turbulent decade of the 1920s. C. M. Woodhouse, *The Story of Modern Greece* (London 1968, 2nd edn 1977) is a concise history of the Greek people from the foundation of Constantinople until the present day. Douglas Dakin, *The Unification of Greece 1770–1923* (London 1972) is a detailed study, particularly valuable for its emphasis on the struggle for a 'Greater Greece'. M. S. Anderson, *The Eastern Question, 1774–1923: A Study in International Relations* (London 1966) is an indispensable guide to the international context in which this struggle took place. Nicholas Kaltchas,

Bibliography

Introduction to the Constitutional History of Modern Greece (New York 1940, reprinted 1970) is a brilliant treatment of a complex aspect of Greek history. Theodore A. Couloumbis, John A. Petropulos and Harry J. Psomiades, *Foreign Interference in Greek Politics: An Historical Perspective* (New York 1976) treats of the 'external factor' which has had such a profound influence on the foreign relations and domestic politics of the independent state. John T. A. Koumoulides, ed., *Greece in Transition: Essays in the History of Modern Greece 1821–1974* (London 1977) is a collection of essays dealing with various aspects of Greece's post-independence history. Robert Browning, *Medieval and Modern Greek* (London 1969) is a concise survey of the development of the Greek language and includes a useful discussion of the 'Language Question', which is such a baffling phenomenon to outsiders. Linos Politis, *A History of Modern Greek Literature* (Oxford 1973) and Constantine Dimaras, *A History of Modern Greek Literature* (London 1974) are scholarly surveys of the history of Greek literature. The four-volume handbook on Greece published between 1943 and 1945 by the Naval Intelligence Division of the British Admiralty is a mine of geographical and historical information. The *Area Handbook for Greece* (Government Printing Office, Washington 1977) is more up to date but less comprehensive.

THE DECLINE OF THE BYZANTINE EMPIRE

George Ostrogorsky, *History of the Byzantine State* (Oxford 1968, 2nd edn) is a magisterial survey of Byzantine history, which may be supplemented by Dimitri Obolensky, *The Byzantine Commonwealth: Eastern Europe, 500–1453* (London 1971). The last centuries of the empire are surveyed in the scholarly studies of D. M. Nicol, *The Last Centuries of Byzantium 1261–1453* (London 1972) and Apostolos Vacalopoulos, *Origins of the Greek Nation: The Byzantine Period, 1204–1461* (New Brunswick 1971). Speros Vryonis, *The Decline of Medieval Hellenism in Asia Minor and the Process of Islamization from the Eleventh through the Fifteenth Century* (Berkeley, Los Angeles 1971) is a detailed study of the transition from Orthodoxy to Islam in Asia Minor and William Miller, *The Latins in the Levant* (London 1908) and *Essays on the Latin Orient* (Cambridge 1921) deal with the history of the various Frankish colonies in the Greek lands between 1204 and 1566. Steven Runciman, *The Fall of Constantinople 1453* (Cambridge 1965) is a moving account of the end of the Byzantine Empire.

OTTOMAN GREECE

Apostolos Vacalopoulos, *The Greek Nation, 1453–1669: The Cultural and Economic Background of Modern Greek Society* (New Brunswick 1976) covers the early centuries after 1453 while D. A. Zakythinos, *The Making of Modern Greece: From Byzantium to Independence* (Oxford 1976) treats the period between the conquest and the establishment of an independent state. During the period of Ottoman rule the role of the Orthodox Church in Greek society was of paramount importance. This role is studied in Steven Runciman, *The Great Church in Captivity: A Study of the Patriarchate of Constantinople from the Eve of the Turkish Conquest to the Greek War of Independence* (Cambridge 1968), T. H. Papadopoullos, *Studies and Documents relating to the History of the Greek Church and People under Turkish Domination* (Brussels 1952, reprinted 1973) and Timothy Ware, *Eustratios Argenti: A Study of the Greek Church under Turkish Rule* (Oxford 1964). William Martin Leake affords an invaluable contemporary insight into conditions in Greece in the crucial first decade of the nineteenth century in *Travels in Northern Greece,* 4 vols. (London 1835) and *Travels in the Morea,* 3 vols. (London 1830). G. P. Henderson, *The Revival of Greek Thought 1620–1830* (Edinburgh and London 1971) describes the intellectual revival that preceded the struggle for independence, while Stephen Chaconas, *Adamantios Korais: A Study in Greek Nationalism* (New York 1942) focusses on the leading protagonist of the 'Neo-Hellenic Enlightenment'. Richard Clogg, *The Movement for Greek Independence 1770–1821: A Collection of Documents* (London 1976) consists of documents, mostly translated from the Greek, illustrating various aspects of the national movement.

THE STRUGGLE FOR INDEPENDENCE

Mrs E. M. Edmonds, transl., *Kolokotrones: The Klepht and the Warrior: Sixty Years of Peril and Daring: An Autobiography* (London 1892) and H. A. Lidderdale, transl., *Makriyannis: The Memoirs of General Makriyannis 1797–1864* (London 1966) are translations of the memoirs of two leading protagonists in the War of Independence. The philhellene George Finlay was an acute observer of Greece during the war and the early decades of independence and the relevant volumes (V, VI and VII) of his *History of Greece* (Oxford 1877), ed. H. F. Tozer, remain invaluable. C. M. Woodhouse, *The Greek War of Independence: Its Historical Setting* (London 1952) is a concise study of a subject treated at greater length in Douglas Dakin, *The Greek Struggle for Independence 1821–1833* (London 1973). C. W. Crawley, *The Question of Greek Independence: A Study of British Policy in the Near East, 1821–1833* (Cambridge 1930) is a thorough treatment of the international ramifications of the war. Richard Clogg, ed., *The Struggle for Greek Independence: Essays to mark the 150th anniversary of the Greek War of Independence* (London 1973) consists of the papers delivered at a commemorative seminar at the University of London in 1971 and is complemented by the proceedings of a similar symposium in the United States, Nikiforos P. Diamandouros, John P. Anton, John A. Petropulos and Peter Topping, eds., *Hellenism and the First Greek War of Liberation (1821–1830): Continuity and Change* (Salonica 1976). The somewhat overrated story of the philhellene volunteers is told by C. M. Woodhouse, *The Philhellenes* (London 1969) and William St Clair, *That Greece might still be free: The Philhellenes in the War of Independence* (London 1972). C. M. Woodhouse, *The Battle of Navarino* (London 1965) is an exciting account of the great naval battle of 1827 that ensured that Greece would obtain some kind of independence and the same author's *Capodistria: The Founder of Greek Independence* (London 1973) is a scholarly study of the life of the man who oversaw the last stages of Greece's progress towards independence.

INDEPENDENCE

John Anthony Petropulos, *Politics and Statecraft in the Kingdom of Greece 1833–1843* (Princeton 1968) is a masterly study of the politics of the early years of the reign of King Otto, who is the subject of Leonard Bower and Gordon Bolitho, *Otho I: King of Greece: A Biography* (London 1939). The church settlement of the early years of Otto's reign is studied in Charles A. Frazee, *The Orthodox Church and Independent Greece 1821–1852* (Cambridge 1969). Charles Tuckerman, *The Greeks of Today* (New York 1878) is a lively account of later nineteenth-century Greece by the American minister to Greece. Romilly Jenkins, *The Dilessi Murders* (London 1961) is a skilful reconstruction of the murder of a group of English travellers in Greece in 1870 which throws much incidental light on the nature of Greek society in the second half of the nineteenth century, the period also covered by R. A. H. Bickford-Smith, *Greece under King George* (London 1893). The vexed question of Greece's foreign debts in the nineteenth century is treated in John A. Levandis, *The Greek Foreign Debt and the Great Powers 1821–1898* (New

Bibliography

York 1944). Aspects of Greece's foreign relations in the later nineteenth century are covered by Domna Dontas, *Greece and the Great Powers 1863–1875* (Salonica 1966) and Evangelos Kofos, *Greece and the Eastern Crisis 1875–1878* (Salonica 1975).

TWENTIETH-CENTURY GREECE

William Miller, *Greek Life in Town and Country* (London 1905) is one of the most interesting books ever written about Greece. Douglas Dakin, *The Greek Struggle in Macedonia 1897–1913* (Salonica 1966) is a detailed study of the Macedonian conflict during its most critical stage. Victor Papacosma, *The Military in Greek Politics: The 1909 Coup d'État* (Kent, Ohio 1977) examines a major turning point in Greek history, the Goudi coup, which marks the beginning of a persistent pattern of military intervention in politics in the twentieth century. George Leon, *Greece and the Great Powers 1914–1917* (Salonica 1973) examines the controversial role of the Powers in Greece's internal affairs during the First World War and the same author's *The Greek Socialist Movement and the First World War: The Road to Unity* (New York 1976) treats of the attitudes of Greece's small socialist movement to the war. Michael Llewellyn Smith, *Ionian Vision: Greece in Asia Minor 1919–1922* (London 1973) is a scholarly study of Greece's disastrous venture in Asia Minor, which is also treated from a contemporary perspective by Arnold Toynbee, *The Western Question in Greece and Turkey* (London 1922). The catastrophic end to this chapter in Greek history is examined in Marjorie Housepian, *Smyrna 1922: The Destruction of a City* (London 1972). The ensuing Exchange of Populations between Greece and Turkey is the subject of Dimitri Pentzopoulos, *The Balkan Exchange of Minorities and its Impact on Greece* (The Hague 1962). The massive influx of refugees from Asia Minor gave a significant boost to the development of the Greek communist party which is the subject of D. George Kousoulas, *Revolution and Defeat: The Story of the Greek Communist Party* (London 1965). George Th. Mavrogordatos, *Stillborn Republic. Social Coalitions and Party Strategies in Greece, 1922–1936* (Berkeley 1983) is an indispensable guide to the politics of the inter-war period. A useful collective survey of Greece in the late 1920s is provided in Eliot Grinnell Mears, *Greece Today: The Aftermath of the Refugee Impact* (Stanford 1929). John Koliopoulos, *Greece and the British Connection 1935–1941* (Oxford 1977) offers a thorough analysis of Britain's relations with Greece on the eve of the Second World War. Mario Cervi, *The Hollow Legions. Mussolini's Blunder in Greece, 1940–1941* (London 1971) is a good account of Mussolini's ill-fated attempt to invade Greece. The tripartite German, Italian and Bulgarian occupation of Greece that followed the German invasion of April 1941 is the subject of John Hondros, *Occupation and Resistance: The Greek Agony, 1941–1944* (New York 1983). Stefanos Sarafis, *ELAS: Greek Resistance Army* (London 1980) is an account of the role of the left wing resistance army by its military commander, while Dominique Eudes, *The Kapetanios: Partisans and Civil War in Greece 1943–1949* (London 1972) chronicles the fortunes of the left during the occupation and ensuing civil war. Britain's wartime role in Greece is the subject of much controversy. Useful for this aspect of the occupation are E. C. W. Myers, *Greek Entanglement* (London 1955), an account by the first commander of the British Military Mission to the Greek Resistance, Reginald Leeper, *When Greek Meets Greek* (London 1950), the memoirs of the British ambassador to the Greek government-in-exile, and Phyllis Auty and Richard Clogg, eds., *British Policy towards Wartime Resistance in Yugoslavia and Greece* (London 1975). John Iatrides, *Revolt in Athens: The Greek Communist 'Second Round', 1944–1945* (Princeton 1972) is a balanced account of the communist insurgency in Athens in December 1944. George Alexander, *The Prelude to the Truman Doctrine. British policy in Greece 1944–1947* (Oxford 1982) is a careful analysis of Britain's involvement during the critical period after liberation. The pivotal role of Greece in international relations at the end of the war is treated fully by Stephen Xydis, *Greece and the Great Powers 1941–1949: Prelude to the Truman Doctrine* (Salonica 1963). Indispensable for the study of the wartime resistance and ensuing civil war are two books by Colonel C. M. Woodhouse, Brigadier Myers' successor as commander of the British (Allied) Military Mission in Greece, *Apple of Discord: A Survey of Recent Greek Politics in their International Setting* (London 1948) and *The Struggle for Greece 1941–1949* (London 1976). The civil war is also the subject of Edgar O'Ballance, *The Greek Civil War 1944–1949* (London 1966) and Lawrence S. Wittner, *American Intervention in Greece, 1943–1949* (New York 1982). Bickham Sweet-Escott, *Greece: A Political and Economic Survey, 1939–1953* (London 1954) provides a useful overview of the war and immediate post-war periods.

Bibliography

CONTEMPORARY GREECE

W. H. McNeill, *The Metamorphosis of Greece since World War II* (Chicago 1978) is a highly perceptive analysis of the dramatic changes that have taken place in Greek society in the post-war period. Keith R. Legg, *Politics in Modern Greece* (Stanford 1969) includes a description of the Greek political system in the 1950s and 1960s. The author also covers the early years of the Colonels' regime, whose brutal and inefficient dictatorship is the subject of a considerable and frequently propagandistic literature. Andreas Papandreou, *Democracy at Gunpoint: The Greek Front* (London 1971) is an account of the background to the 1967 coup by one of the most interesting figures on the Greek political scene. 'Athenian' [Rodis Rouphos] *Inside the Colonels' Greece* (London 1972) and Richard Clogg and George Yannopoulos eds., *Greece under Military Rule* (London 1972) cover the early years of the Colonels' regime. More sympathetic to the junta is David Holden, *Greece without Columns* (London 1972). A comprehensive analysis of the period is given in C. M. Woodhouse, *The Rise and Fall of the Greek Colonels* (London 1985). Laurence Stern, *The Wrong Horse: The Politics of Intervention and the Failure of American Diplomacy* (New York 1977) is a well-informed and highly critical account of American policy towards Greece and Cyprus in the post-war period. Nicos Mouzelis, *Modern Greece: Facets of Underdevelopment* (London 1978) is a sophisticated and perceptive collection of essays on modern Greek society and politics written from a neo-Marxist standpoint. Richard Clogg, ed., *Greece in the 1980s* (London 1983) is an 'anatomy' of Greece at the beginning of the decade. For an introduction to the contemporary political scene see Richard Clogg, *Parties and Elections in Greece: the Search for Legitimacy* (London 1987).

SOCIETY

Irwin T. Sanders, *Rainbow in the Rock: The People of Rural Greece* (Cambridge, Mass. 1962) is a sociological analysis of rural Greece in the 1950s, while Ernestine Friedl, *Vasilika: A Village in Modern Greece* (New York 1963) focusses on one village in Boeotia. J. K. Campbell, *Honour, Family and Patronage: A Study of Institutions and Morals in a Greek Mountain Community* (Oxford 1964) is an anthropological study of the Sarakatsani community of transhumant shepherds. Juliet du Boulay, *Portrait of a Greek Mountain Village* (Oxford 1974) records the final stages of the transition of a small mountain village in Euboea from

Bibliography

'social solidarity to fragmentation'. Muriel Dimen and Ernestine Friedl, eds., *Regional Variation in Modern Greece and Cyprus: Toward a Perspective of the Ethnography of Greece* (New York 1976) brings together some thirty-five papers on the anthropology, ethnology and sociology of Greece and Cyprus. The Greeks as a people have been much given to *xeniteia*, or emigration. A favoured destination has been the United States, whose very large population of Greek origin is the subject of Theodore A. Saloutos, *The Greeks in the United States* (Cambridge, Mass. 1964). S. A. Papadopoulos, ed., *The Greek Merchant Marine (1453–1850)* (Athens 1972) and *Greek Handicraft* (Athens 1969) are two handsomely produced and illustrated volumes published by the National Bank of Greece.

CYPRUS

George Hill, *A History of Cyprus*, vol. III, *The Frankish Period 1432–1571* and vol. IV, *The Ottoman Province, The British Colony, 1571–1928* (Cambridge 1952, reprinted 1972) is a well-documented study. On a smaller scale is H. D. Purcell, *Cyprus* (London 1969). Charles Foley, *Island in Revolt* (London 1962) is a lively account of Cyprus during the 1950s campaign for *enosis* with Greece. The same author has edited *The Memoirs of General Grivas* (London 1964), the leader of the EOKA campaign to overthrow British rule. The movement for *enosis* is thoroughly analysed by Nancy Crawshaw, *The Cyprus Revolt: An Account of the Struggle for Union with Greece* (London 1978). The genesis of the independent republic of Cyprus is the subject of Stephen Xydis, *Cyprus: Conflict and Conciliation 1954–1958* (Columbus 1967) and *Cyprus: Reluctant Republic* (The Hague 1973). The troubled history of the republic since 1960 is treated by Stanley Kyriakides, *Cyprus: Constitutionalism and Crisis Government* (Philadelphia 1968). The implications of the 1974 Turkish invasion for the island are considered by Polyvios G. Polyviou, *Cyprus: The Tragedy and the Challenge* (London 1975). Peter Loizos, *The Greek Gift: Politics in a Cypriot Village* (Oxford 1975) is a fascinating study of politics at the local level and T. W. Adams, *Akel: The Communist Party of Cyprus* (Stanford 1971) focusses on a party that constitutes a powerful political force in the island.

Index

Index

Index

conference: on Cyprus (1956) 173; in Lebanon (1944) 148, 151; of London (1827–32) 66; in London (1921) 116
conferences, for Balkan Entente 127; of the Great Powers (1912) 102–3
Constantinople 70, 78: capture of (1261) 6; Church in 13–14; coup in (1913) 103; and Entente 107; Greek traders in 34; Greeks expelled from 80; political development in 101; sack of (1204) 1, 5; siege of (1396) 11, (1453) 1, 6, 14–15; *see also* Istanbul
constitution: idea of 44–5; development of (1822) 58; (1827) 64, 65, 73–4, 75; (1844) 75, 81; (1864) 83, 92; (1911) 99, 100; (1927) (republican) 124; (1952) 168, 185; (1968) 190, 210; (1975) 210
convention: Russo-Turkish commercial (1783) 34; in May (1832) 68; Greek-Turkish (1923) 120–1; Greek-Turkish (Ankara, 1930) 126, Geneva (1958) 214
Corfu 16: occupation of (1797) 46, (1923) 126; seizure of (1916) 109
Crete 16, 17, 21, 22, 26, 62, 88, 89, 93, 109, 134: crisis in (1866–9) 87, (1895) 93; and *enosis* 79, 87, 97; Greek government in (1941) 138; status of 94; uprising in (1938) 134
Cyprus 22, 170: agreement on 174–5, 181, 212–13; British administration of, 89; British annexation of (1914) 106, 170ff; capture of (1191) 4; and Colonels' government 194, 198–9; constitution for (1960) 175; Convention (1878) 89, 106, 170; demonstrations in (1955) 172; and *enosis* 171–2; and EOKA 174, 198; fall of, to Turks (1571) 16; Geneva talks on (1974) 200–1; independence of 175; and Karamanlis 200, 224; National Guard 198; partition of 213; population of 170; Turkish invasion of 199, 201; unrest in (1963) 181ff

Damaskinos, Archbishop of Athens, as regent (1944–6) 155–6, 157
Deliyannis, Theodore, 19th cent. prime minister and foreign minister 90, 92, 93

Demertzis, Constantine, acting prime minister (1935–6) 129–30
Don Pacifico incident (1847) 79
Dragatsani, battle of (1821) 52

EAM *see* National Liberation Front
Eden, Anthony, British foreign secretary 137, 149, 155, 171
EDES *see* National Republican Greek League
education: Greek attitudes to 36–7, 39–40; in the Ottoman Empire 36; reform of 91, 100, 183; re-hellenising 77
Egypt: crusades and 4; emigration to 97; invasion of (1798) 40, 46; as Turkish allies 62, 64, 65
ELAS *see* National Popular Liberation Army
elections: (1859) 81; (1870–5) 84; (1875) 86; (1882) 90; (1895) 93; (1910) 99; (1912) 101; (June 1915) 108; (December 1915) 109; (1920) 115; (1923) 123; (1926, 1928) 124; (1932) 127; (1933) 127–8; (1935) 129; (1936) 130; (1946) 156–8; (1950) 166; (1951) 167; (1952) 168–9; (1956) 173; (1958) 173, 177; (1961) 177–8; (1963) 180; (1964) 181, 206; (1967 proposed) 185–6; (1974) 203–7; (1977) 220–4
electoral system 124, 130, 166, 167–8, 173, 177, 203, 206, 221
enosis 79, 87, 97: and Cyprus 170, 171, 182; British attitude to 171, 172; *see also* Cyprus; Crete
Entente, Balkan 127, 170
Entente (Britain, France, Russia): attitude of, to Greek government 110; and Bulgaria 106; vs. Central Powers 105
Enver Pasha, leader of Young Turks 103
EOKA *see* National Organisation of Cypriot Fighters
Ephimeris (1790–7) first Greek news sheet 44
ESA *see* police, military
Ethniki Amyna (National Defence 1915–16) 109, 110
European Economic Community (EEC) 176, 192, 204, 211, 216, 224

France 39, 44, 46, 79, 80, 113; attitude of, to Greek independence 62, 63;

239

Index